LAUREL & HARDY

LAUREL & HARDY

From the Forties Forward

Scott MacGillivray

Foreword by Steve Allen

Vestal Press

Lanham • New York • Oxford

VESTAL PRESS, Inc.

Published in the United States of America
by Vestal Press, Inc.
4720 Boston Way
Lanham, Maryland 20706

Copyright 1998 © by Vestal Press
Foreword 1998 © by Steve Allen

Library of Congress Cataloging-in-Publication Data

MacGillivray, Scott, 1957–
    Laurel & Hardy : from the forties forward / Scott MacGillivray ;
foreword by Steve Allen.
        p.   cm.
    Includes bibliographical references and index.
    ISBN 1-879511-35-5 (cloth : alk. paper). — ISBN 1-879511-41-X
(pbk. : alk. paper)
        1. Laurel, Stan.   2. Hardy, Oliver, 1892–1957.   3. Comedians—
United States—Biography.   4. Motion picture actors and actresses—
United States—Biography.   I. Title.
PN2287.L285M24   1998
791.43′028′092273—dc21
    [B]   98-16059
                                                              CIP

ISBN 1-879511-35-5 (cloth : alk. paper)

∞ ™ The paper used in this publication meets the minimum requirements of American
National Standard for Information Sciences—Permanence of Paper for Printed Library
Materials, ANSI Z39.48-1984. Manufactured in the United States of America.

———◦———

For Jan and Ted,

and in fond memory of Tony Hawes

———◦———

.

Contents

Foreword

BY STEVE ALLEN

As anyone with more than a casual interest in comedy quickly learns, surprisingly heated arguments can arise regarding personal preferences. Strictly speaking, the old saying "there's no accounting for taste" isn't literally true, but it's evident enough that it is difficult and probably impossible to get unanimity, even about judgmental criteria, as regards any of the arts. I have no doubt that there are on earth individuals who would actually prefer a picture of Elvis Presley painted on black velvet to the Mona Lisa, which of course points to one of the dangers of democracy.

Nevertheless, there is often widespread agreement as to who are the most able practitioners of a given art and who, on the other hand, are third-rate, if that. In the field of comedy, it is generally accepted that few if any comedy performers rank higher than Stan Laurel and Oliver Hardy in the esteem of both professional critics and the general public. Any one of their delightful performances would have been sufficient to secure their reputations, but the fact is they produced a remarkable volume of work.

So much that is adulatory and analytical has been written about Stan and Ollie that there is probably no one on earth who has read all of it. All the more surprising, therefore, given the pair's deservedly elevated status as practitioners of the comic arts, that historians have largely neglected the later works of the two comic geniuses. The dividing line is the year 1940. So we are presented with a true mystery: libraries full of commentary about the early decades, after which even many of their most fervent admirers seem to lose interest in "the boys." Fortunately

Scott MacGillivray, in this engaging study, fills in the blanks and provides a good deal of record-straightening.

One of the fondest recollections of my life was that in 1959, at a time I was doing a weekly prime-time comedy show for NBC-TV, some of my writers and I visited Stan in his modest apartment near the beach in Santa Monica. It is a particular and all-too-rare sort of pleasure to be able to meet and spend social time with those public figures to whom we first became attached in our childhood. And even today, almost forty years later, the recollection that for a few hours I was actually in Stan Laurel's presence is something like the recollection of a pleasant dream. All of us that day were thunderstruck when it became clear that Laurel was more interested in talking to us about our shows and sketches than in recalling his own films.

I have, in keeping with the rest of the world, enormous respect for the work of Charlie Chaplin. The word *genius* is applied to him accurately, but as regards the simple factor of *funniness* I confess that I laugh more at Laurel & Hardy.

All the world's admirers of Laurel & Hardy will now forever be indebted to Scott MacGillivray for providing so much new information about two of the world's most beloved figures.

Preface

Laurel & Hardy fans—and there are legions of them—haven't had much to say about the comedy team's later movies, produced after 1940. This is partly due to historians and biographers discussing this body of work as little as possible. Virtually every published study of Laurel & Hardy dwells lovingly on the team's prime years of the silent era and the early talkies—and then screeches to a halt after 1940. The authors have often dismissed this period as being unsuccessful and unrewarding, and have always glossed over it in a few brief pages or even paragraphs.

The films in question have not seen general release in recent years. With so little published material available, and so little opportunity to evaluate the films, audiences have been compelled to accept these low critical opinions as gospel. Many Laurel & Hardy enthusiasts are so negatively conditioned that they recoil in horror at the mere mention of Stan and Ollie's wartime pictures.

This volume attempts to give these films, and those that followed, a closer look. Although they may invite comparisons with the team's acclaimed comedies of the twenties and thirties, it's an apples-vs.-oranges exercise since the "forties films" were produced, marketed, and consumed under different conditions.

Laurel & Hardy *can* be compared to other famous funnymen who enjoyed long careers. In later years Abbott & Costello, Jerry Lewis, and Mel Brooks kept making movies, though their new releases were not in the same league as their efforts of fifteen to twenty years before. Although the material wasn't up to the old standard, newer generations of moviegoers didn't mind—they just wanted to laugh.

Laurel & Hardy's wartime films were extremely popular in first-run release, and they hold up well today. Contrary to legend, some of these neglected films are surprisingly good, and have much to offer comedy fans. While it is true that some of these later movies are inferior, few have considered *why* the films turned out as they did.

Disregarding Laurel & Hardy's later films would be like closing one's eyes to any feature Charlie Chaplin made after **Modern Times,** or any Marx Brothers effort after **A Day At The Races,** or any of Buster Keaton's numerous sound comedies. These later pictures may not be the most celebrated titles in filmdom, but they are legitimate additions to the comedians' film libraries and deserve more attention from fans.

The actors and technicians who worked with Stan Laurel and Oliver Hardy called them comic geniuses. Stan and Ollie could do more with less than any other comedians, and nowhere is this more evident than in their later pictures. One admires how much the comedians brought to their films when lackluster scripts disappointed them.

Watching Laurel & Hardy work in a 1940s movie is like watching a magician escape from a strait-jacket. Granted, it's a confining, challenging situation, but the observer is interested in what bit of theatrical expertise will make the act succeed. The ways the performers work can indeed be magical.

The wartime films were not the final chapter of the Laurel & Hardy canon. Dozens of Laurel & Hardy movies followed: numerous reissues, compilation features, TV revivals, home-movie and video offerings. The entire spectrum is detailed in these pages.

The "forgotten" Laurel & Hardy pictures have been in the dark for too long. This book is intended to put them back in the spotlight.

Acknowledgments

The idea for this volume came from two people. Several years ago Ted Okuda, then managing editor of *Filmfax* magazine and author of several valuable film histories, asked me if I thought Laurel & Hardy's later films would merit a book-length study. I said no—there might be enough material for a magazine article, but not a book. To invoke a Laurel & Hardy movie title, "Wrong Again!"

Around the same time Jan Carey, a perceptive film columnist who shared my affection for Laurel & Hardy, also urged me to pursue a book project. (We embarked on another ambitious project when we got married a couple of years later.)

Compiling the story of Laurel & Hardy's post-1940 works was like putting together a complicated puzzle. Each isolated fact or statistic was part of some bigger picture. Most Laurel & Hardy authors, reluctant to discuss the later films at all, toyed with the "forties puzzle" briefly and abandoned it, leaving most of its elements untouched and uncollected. Even less attention was paid to the Laurel & Hardy revivals of the 1950s and '60s. The random pieces of the puzzle have now been assembled, and the gap in most Laurel & Hardy chronologies can be filled. The majority of the material in this book is chronicled for the first time.

Many of the events occurred a half-century ago, but I was fortunate to obtain firsthand accounts. Stan Laurel's daughter, Lois Laurel Hawes, offered insights into her father's life and career. Lois's husband, writer-producer Tony Hawes, recounted his memories of Laurel & Hardy during their European-tour period. Lois and Tony patiently endured hours of interviews, and furnished dozens of never-before-published photographs from Stan Laurel's personal collection. Tony Hawes passed away in 1997, much to the regret of the many Laurel & Hardy admirers who knew him. I cannot thank Lois and Tony enough for their co-operation.

The late William K. Everson was an authority on motion pictures; he wrote the first book-length study of Laurel & Hardy's films in 1967. His final months were beset by illness, but I am very proud and grateful that his last interviews were granted for this book. He spoke with color, humor, and enthusiasm about his friend, producer Robert Youngson. I thank Karen Latham Everson for allowing me to include her husband's remarks in this book. Robert Youngson's wife, Jeanne Keyes Youngson, volunteered her own perspective of her husband's work. I thank Mrs. Youngson for her generous contributions to this text.

Show-business veterans Trudy Marshall, Diosa Costello, Tony Caruso, and Felix Knight graciously spoke about their careers, and their recollections of working with Laurel & Hardy are included in this book.

The interviews were supplemented by very helpful information from Jack Roth, Steve Randisi, Alex Bartosh, Jim Neibaur, Charles Vesce, and the late Lucille Hardy Price. The late Norman Kay, Richard Finegan, Alan Levine, and The Boston Public Library Music Department gave me access to rare trade periodicals, and Brigitte J. Kueppers of the UCLA Special Collections Library made research materials available. Molly King, George Seban, Kim McTighe, Keith Arnowitz, Brian Dow, and Ted Wadsworth prepared the many rare photographs for publication.

For over twenty years I have been involved in Sons Of The Desert, the international Laurel & Hardy society founded by the team's biographer, John McCabe. My interest in the team's later films struck a responsive chord with several Sons members, who forwarded a "puzzle piece" or two over the years: Rick Greene, Leo Brooks, Sharry Han, Carl Mattison, Brad Farrell, Kay Lhota, Bruce Church, Kevin Mulligan, Larry Byrd, Lee Blackburn, Lori Jones McCaffery, Tracy Tolzmann, Del Kempster, Jeff Missinne, Chris Seguin, Bob Spiller, Walt Mitchell, Alison Grimmer, Roger Colson, and Randy Skretvedt. Additional facts were furnished by Eleanor Keaton, Bob Burns, Robert Nott, Gordon Berkow, George Feltenstein, Stuart Linder, Michael Agee, Kit Parker, Larry Urbanski, Edward Watz, Jerry Haendiges, John Gassman, George Gimarc, Hannes Kleim, and Jerry Miller.

Filmmaker Brian Anthony offered invaluable assistance, and I appreciate his diligence. It was Brian who discovered a "lost" Laurel &

Hardy story property among fifty-year-old documents at 20th Century-Fox. I also thank Alan Adler of 20th Century-Fox and Richard May of Turner Entertainment.

I owe special thanks to Ted Okuda, for his assistance and encouragement, and to my wife, Jan, for reviewing the text and offering valuable editorial suggestions.

I am deeply indebted to Steve Allen, who took time out from a busy schedule of personal appearances and broadcasting projects to prepare the foreword for this book. The versatile Mr. Allen is a noted author, composer, comedian, and Laurel & Hardy buff. Janice Silver, representing his office, was of great assistance.

I thank the publishers and editors of this volume for their involvement and commitment: James Lyons, Nancy Ulrich, Lynn Gemmell, and Elaine Stuart.

I also thank my parents, Allan and Jane MacGillivray, for their interest in the author's progress. I must confess that this whole thing started over three decades ago, when my mother suggested that a movie starring an unknown quantity named Laurel & Hardy would help pass an eight-year-old's boring afternoon. That movie was one of the "forties films." The rest—or at least, the rest of this book—is history.

Stan and Ollie

Stan Laurel and Oliver Hardy were the greatest comedy team in motion-picture history. Their humor is physical, but the accident-prone buffoonery is distinguished by the stars' friendly, kindly personalities and their great devotion to each other. The "Stan and Ollie" characters are grown-up children, a skinny-and-fat pair of life's innocent bystanders who always run afoul of irate landlords, pompous citizens, angry policemen, domineering women, antagonistic customers, and apoplectic bosses. Their well-meaning solutions to the simplest problems are hilariously disastrous. When they set out for a pleasant Sunday drive, they don't get any farther than the front door. When they cook dinner, they nearly burn the house down. When they sell something, they ruin the merchandise. And so it goes throughout a hundred movies, as Stan's dimwitted attempts to help his friend end with Ollie muttering, "Well, here's *another* nice mess you've gotten me into!"

Stan Laurel, the thin half of the team, was born Arthur Stanley Jefferson in Ulverston, Lancashire, England on June 16, 1890. The son of a prominent theatrical producer, Stan grew up in show business, and at the age of twenty he joined a theatrical troupe which featured another young comic, Charlie Chaplin. Stan entered the film industry in 1917, and alternately played brash go-getters and worried simps for the next ten years.

Oliver Norvell Hardy was born in Harlem, Georgia on January 18, 1892. His mother operated a hotel, and the young Hardy was fascinated by the "show folk" that passed through the community. A stint as a boy singer led him into theatrical enterprises, and by 1910 he was a movie-house projectionist. Three years later he joined a local comedy-film company, and in a few short years Babe Hardy (as he was known informally) became well established as a comic villain with expressive panto-mime skills.

In 1927 both Laurel and Hardy were working at the Hal Roach stu-dio in Culver City, California. Roach had become a leading producer of comedy short subjects, and his stars included Harold Lloyd, the "Our Gang" kids, and Charley Chase. Stan was on the payroll as a writer and director, while Babe was playing prominent character roles. They began performing together, and their chemistry was immediately noticeable. Gradually their movies were written with a team in mind. Their charac-ters became "Stan and Ollie," dumb-bells in derby hats. The new duo became Hal Roach's biggest stars.

Off-screen, Laurel & Hardy were the opposite of their movie charac-ters. The energetic Stan Laurel carefully supervised his own pictures. When he wasn't in front of the camera, he was behind it, collaborating on the scripts, the direction, and the editing. This was fine with the easygoing Babe Hardy, who spent his free time on hobbies: cooking, playing golf, and watching sporting events.

Laurel & Hardy were among the few stars of silent movies to enjoy greater fame in sound films. Their two-reel, twenty-minute shorts be-came a staple of movie programs everywhere. A three-reel special, **The Music Box**, won the first short-subject Academy Award. Hal Roach soon added feature films to his production schedule, and Laurel & Har-dy's features were often expensive, carefully crafted spectaculars. Their full-length hits included **The Devil's Brother** (1933), **Sons Of The Desert** (1933), **Babes In Toyland** (1934), **Our Relations** (1936), and their own favorite, **Way Out West** (1937).

Hal Roach radically changed his policy in 1937. He stopped making two-reel comedies entirely, changed distributors from M-G-M to United Artists, and mounted more ambitious features like **Topper, Of Mice And Men**, and **One Million B. C.** Stan Laurel and Oliver Hardy were under separate contracts, and Roach did not renew them.

In 1939, although he had abandoned the short subject, Roach felt there was a market for comedy featurettes, which would fit nicely in double-feature theaters. He nicknamed his forty-minute format "the streamliner," and rehired Laurel & Hardy to test his theory.

The experiment, filmed in mid-1939, was **A Chump At Oxford**, a parody of M-G-M's prestigious feature **A Yank At Oxford**. Street sweepers Laurel & Hardy inadvertently foil a bank robbery and are rewarded with a scholarship to London's Oxford University. The students are delighted by the arrival of these awkward freshmen, and stage several bewildering pranks. Stan and Ollie are shown to their quarters, which the students fail to identify as the dean's bedroom.

A helpful valet recognizes Mr. Laurel as "Lord Paddington," a long-lost scholastic and athletic champion who suffered amnesia and wandered away from the campus. Stan and Ollie are skeptical, until a bump on the head restores Stan to his "Lord Paddington" identity. Hare-brained Stanley instantly turns into an autocratic, upper-crust genius, to Ollie's irritation. Lord Paddington vanquishes both the prank-playing students and Ollie, until another head-bump brings "Stanley" back for good.

The 42-minute "streamliner" was edited in a hurry. Some of the scenes that were left in offer surprises for the Laurel & Hardy fan. Hardy is unusually harsh toward his chum; after a humiliating college hazing, he vows that he'll never trust anybody again. "That's a good idea," says Stan. "Not even *you*," Ollie snaps angrily. There are also gaps in continuity: when Stan first appears before the valet, the editor cuts out the introductory dialogue and rushes to the servant's startled reaction.

After finishing **A Chump At Oxford**, Laurel & Hardy made a Foreign Legion comedy feature for producer Boris Morros. **The Flying Deuces** was released by a major studio, RKO Radio Pictures, and was a success. Hal Roach realized that his first streamliner was more valuable as a full-length feature, and he called Laurel & Hardy in to shoot two more reels of footage. The added material was an employment-agency sequence, which preceded the street-sweeping scene. The amplified print now ran 63 minutes, and was intended for the European market.

Most Laurel & Hardy fans have assumed that the European version of **A Chump At Oxford**, apart from the new opening, is identical to the streamliner. Not so—it's an entirely different cut. Editor Bert Jordan ignored the four reels already assembled and started from scratch, drawing upon unused takes, alternate set-ups, and scenes of different length to flesh out the narrative. The feature-length **Oxford** makes a bit more sense: Hardy's sharp remarks toward his pal were removed, and the boys' introduction to their valet was restored.

Most theaters rejected the featurette in favor of the feature. The "European" version became the standard release print for all markets. Hal

Roach learned his lesson: he kept making streamliners but reserved Laurel & Hardy for another feature.

The title, **Saps At Sea** (1940), was again a burlesque of an "A" picture, Gary Cooper's **Souls At Sea**. Hardy goes on a rest cure for his nerves, and runs afoul of an escaped killer. That is literally all the plot to be found in this 57-minute quickie. The balance of the film consists of sight gags and blackouts, "Laurel & Hardy themselves being 90% of the action," as *Variety* put it. The boys never needed stories to be funny, and the film *is* funny, but it is a casual, disjointed pastiche. It was obvious that Hal Roach, having achieved new heights with his elaborate, sophisticated feature films, no longer had time for Laurel & Hardy's humble slapstick comedies.

The actual production had been turned over to Hal Roach, Jr., so that the boss's son could learn the business. Stan Laurel was accustomed to staging his own comedy sequences, and didn't care for the new producer's interference. According to Stan Laurel's daughter, Lois Laurel Hawes, Stan resented the young Roach's smug, authoritarian attitude. "Here was this kid out of military school on vacations, that would come in, clap his hands at 9:00 and say 'Okay, boys—let's get funny.'"

After **Saps At Sea,** the team's "streamliner" contract with the Roach studio was allowed to lapse. While waiting for offers from other studios, Laurel & Hardy were invited to perform a comedy sketch for a benefit show. The sketch was so popular that the comedians took it on the road. They hired one of their second bananas from the Hal Roach days, James C. Morton, to appear in their featured spot as a baffled policeman. Critics and fans agreed that the troupe of comedians and musicians in *The Laurel & Hardy Revue* offered high-grade vaudeville during the fall of 1940.

"I joined my dad in Pittsburgh, around Thanksgiving vacation of '40," recalls Stan's daughter, then twelve years old. Stan Laurel was bitten by the show-biz bug as a teenager; did Lois Laurel have any theatrical ambitions? "No way!" she laughs. "I hung out with the [chorus] girls, for hamburgers after the show. Several of the girls came down with very bad colds and laryngitis, and one of the dancers, Maxine Conrad, thought I would fit one of the costumes, so they could have me fill in. I fit the costume—with a lot of Kleenex in the upper half! So one night they drilled me in all of their songs and music. I went on, but I wasn't up to the tap-dancing part, so I just shuffled off the stage at that point.

"I opened in Steubenville, Ohio in this musty, dusty old theater. Babe and [his wife] Lucille knew about it. They asked my father to come down to see the new girl, and there I was. And I thought, 'Uh-oh, what's gonna happen when I shuffle off?' " The scene echoed a 1906 incident, when Stan Laurel's formidable father had witnessed his nervous son's stage debut. Now it was Stan's turn to face his own offspring. Lois smiles gently when she finishes the story: "He had tears in his eyes, so I knew I was safe."

At the tour's end, Laurel & Hardy were all set to take their *Revue* to England. "We were packed, the trunks were ready to be picked up," says Lois, "and overnight the whole thing was cancelled," due to the war in Europe.

Stan Laurel and Oliver Hardy returned to Hollywood. On June 8, 1941 they participated in an all-star revue for the U. S. Army's Field Artillery troops at Camp Roberts, California. Laurel & Hardy shared the stage with emcee Red Skelton, Chico Marx, Ella Logan, Jane Withers, Margaret Whiting, Sidney Miller, Joan Leslie, and Larry Adler. According-ing to the camp newsletter, Stan and Babe, doing their *Revue* act, "pan-icked the assembly with a properly mixed-up exposition on what apparently was how *not* to get a driver's license . . . The thousands who attended this mammoth entertainment event Sunday afternoon at the Camp Roberts Bowl all agreed that it was the best, and funniest show ever seen or heard. If you were one of the unlucky ones who were away and did not see it, believe us, brother, you were gypped!"

The Camp Roberts show was a personal success for Laurel & Hardy, and demonstrates that in mid-1941 they were still very much in com-mand of their performing skills. Having conquered the stage, and now free from their Hal Roach contracts, they were anxious to resume work-ing in pictures. Laurel especially looked forward to more creative free-dom and the chance to experiment with new ideas and projects. The comedians, together with their attorney, Ben Shipman, formed their own corporation, Laurel and Hardy Feature Productions. They would enjoy tax benefits, make their own executive decisions, and circumvent any clashes with stubborn bosses.

On July 11, 1941 they started making movies again—for 20th Cen-tury-Fox.

Their New Job

Twentieth Century-Fox was one of the largest and most successful film factories in the industry. Each year the studio offered a balanced slate of musicals, dramas, adventures and mysteries. There weren't too many comedies, however. Fox's major comedy contributors were The Ritz Brothers and Jane Withers (who in fact were teamed for the Ritzes' final opus at Fox). The rest of Fox's lighter fare was forgettable fluff for neighborhood theaters, with minor stars and modest production values. The results were pleasant enough, but unspectacular.

In 1936 the studio inaugurated a very successful program of economically made "B" pictures, made specifically for double-feature moviehouses. Most of the major companies had clearly defined "A" and "B" units: the "A" team made the important epics while the "B" crew churned out the low-budget fillers. The 20th Century-Fox "B" department was headed by Sol M. Wurtzel (1881–1958), who had been with the company since 1914, before it was even incorporated.

Wurtzel was a tough, efficient producer who never wasted time, money, or resources on his work. He keyed his efforts to series films and star vehicles: Charlie Chan, The Jones Family, Jane Withers, Mr. Moto, The Ritz Brothers, The Cisco Kid. The public always bought the product, regardless of quality, so these popular personalities and characters appeared in film after film.

When Laurel & Hardy joined the 20th Century-Fox staff, they were immediately handed to Sol Wurtzel. This didn't mean Laurel & Hardy were no longer major stars. The studio simply wanted to cash in on the popularity of Universal's smash comedy team of Abbott & Costello as quickly as possible. A & C's first starring feature, the military comedy **Buck Privates**, was a runaway sensation in 1941. Every studio in town was frantically signing other teams to compete in the marketplace. (If Fox hadn't offered Laurel & Hardy a contract, a rival studio certainly would have.) Since time was of the essence, Laurel & Hardy had to report to Wurtzel, who was geared to making pictures on abbreviated schedules.

Laurel's dreams of creative liberty were immediately dashed. He found, to his shock, that he and his partner were hired only as actors, and were neither expected nor allowed to contribute to the technical preparation of their pictures.

Stan Laurel's daughter Lois noticed her father's distress. "He sort of looked unhappy when I visited him on the set. Generally he was unhappy at Fox because of the lack of control. The writers wrote, the directors directed, and they didn't consult him. He was unhappy with the writers that Fox had on staff, because they weren't brought in for a particular picture, they were just *there*, and were given assignments whether they were good at comedy or whether they weren't."

Laurel's assignment to Fox's "B" squad was a blow to the actor's pride. The Fox studio was too busy to bother with the grievances of individual performers, and the company didn't particularly care about a pair of comedians in the Wurtzel unit. After all, Laurel & Hardy were hired not because they were Laurel & Hardy, but because they might be another Abbott & Costello. The people didn't matter as much as the product.

"It was just too big a studio from what they had worked before, and it was too hard to battle," confirms Lois Laurel, who recalls the new working conditions as being far more regimented. "For one thing, I could hardly get in the gate, where I'd walk right through at Roach. I would wait maybe fifteen, twenty minutes, especially if my dad didn't know ahead of time that I was coming. They'd give me a temporary badge, which you'd turn in when you left, and I was escorted to the soundstage. I was told that I wouldn't be wandering around—'you stay where your dad is, in the soundstage'—where at Roach I'd be in the barbershop and down to see the 'Our Gang,' I could go where I wanted to or fall in the lake.

"I heard my father say [the Fox films] 'weren't the caliber that we made at Roach,' so that's where I first heard the comparison—that there *was* a comparison. I think I noticed that they were bigger productions. I can remember a girlfriend of mine [was impressed,] saying, '*Ohhh*, your dad's at *Fox* now!' If she hadn't said that, I probably wouldn't have thought anything about it."

Great Guns

Released October 10, 1941 by 20th Century-Fox. Produced by Sol M. Wurtzel. Directed by Montague Banks. Screenplay by Lou Breslow. Photographed by Glen MacWilliams. Edited by Al DeGaetano. Running time: 74 minutes.

Cast: Stan Laurel and Oliver Hardy (themselves); Dick Nelson (Daniel Forrester IV); Sheila Ryan (Ginger Hammond); Edmund MacDonald (Sgt. Hippo); Ludwig Stossel (Dr. Schickel); Paul Harvey (Gen. Taylor); Charles Trowbridge (Col. Ridley); Ethel Griffies (Aunt Agatha); Mae Marsh (Aunt Martha); Kane Richmond (medical officer); Charles Arnt (doctor); Alan Ladd (customer at photo shop); Irving Bacon (postman); Russell Hicks (Gen. Burns); Pierre Watkin (Blue Army colonel); James Flavin (White Army adjutant); Harold Goodwin (target instructor); Max Wagner and Jimmy Dundee (mess-hall louts); Billy Benedict (hillbilly soldier at corral); Dick Rich (chef); Cyril Ring (PX clerk); Bud Geary (soldier at bridge); Dave Willock (soldier beside target).

The first of Fox's Laurel & Hardy features, to no one's surprise, was a military comedy on the order of **Buck Privates**. The Fox version was entitled **Great Guns**.

Their director was Monty Banks, Italian-born star of acrobatic silent comedies, billed jokingly as "Montague Banks" for his dignified screen credit. Banks's days as a screen attraction were over; he had spent the previous decade in Great Britain, where he married the popular English comedienne Gracie Fields. When Fields was signed by 20th Century-

Fox to make films in Hollywood, her husband was also added to the payroll. Lois Laurel explains, "My dad had been very close to Gracie Fields and felt sorry for Monty. He was having trouble getting a job." The volatile Banks earned his keep directing **Great Guns**, but he had little patience with his crew, and little aptitude for the production end of the business. He hung up his megaphone after the film's completion.

A whimsical musical rendition of "You're In The Army Now" accompanies the **Great Guns** credits. We first see Mr. Laurel as the gardener at an imposing estate, manicuring the lawn with a small pair of scissors. A gabby postman arrives with a draft notice for Daniel Forrester IV, the young master of the manor (Dick Nelson). Mr. Hardy, the chauffeur, considers it junk mail, since Daniel is so frail and allergy-prone that he is certain to be rejected by the Army. The boys are debating whether to deliver the notice when Stan's pet crow Penelope snatches the envelope and flies off with it.

A deleted scene had Stan and Ollie trying to reclaim the letter from the crow, which is now up a tree. Traces of this futile enterprise may be glimpsed in the existing print; Ollie's coat has dust and debris on it, indicating dirty work, while Stan is holding a large feather, the only trophy of the chase.

According to legend, the "crow" scenes weren't worth the effort, since the bird repeatedly clawed at Stan Laurel's shoulder during filming. The professional Mr. Laurel is said to have taken the abuse without complaint. Stan's daughter, who saw a great deal of her father on the set, dismisses the story as publicity fiction. The crow was really a trained raven named Jimmy, who knew how to behave for the cameras. Jimmy appeared as a mascot in Frank Capra's comedies, and was regularly hired out to various studios.

The bird delivers Daniel's draft notice. The bedridden millionaire is delighted by the call to arms, but his overprotective maiden aunts are horrified. Faithful retainers Stan and Ollie, and the fussy family doctor, escort Daniel to the induction center. The doctor fails to impress the Army medics with X-rays of his "pitiful" patient, so Stan and Ollie try to influence Daniel's examiner themselves.

Laurel & Hardy's forte was pantomime, but screenwriter Lou Breslow emphasized dialogue humor. This seems to be an effort to modernize Laurel & Hardy's act, and speed up the proceedings in the manner of Abbott & Costello and Hope & Crosby, the cutting-edge comedy teams of the day. The new emphasis on fast patter is most apparent in the medical-examination scene. During Daniel's physical, Stan and Ollie have to pop in and out of view from behind a curtain and heckle the doctor.

> *Doctor:* Your blood pressure is perfectly normal, son.
> *Daniel:* I can't believe it.
> *Ollie:* If you'll tap him you'll find that his blood is pure sugar!
> *Stan:* Dr. Schickel says he's a walking maple tree!

The scene continues along these lines, with the boys constantly interrupting. Hardy's timing is especially good—he tears open the curtain, fires out his dialogue, and whisks the curtain shut, like the "joke wall" of the *Laugh-In* TV show where comedians suddenly came out of nowhere with one-liners. Daniel passes the exam easily, since there is actually nothing wrong with him, but Stan and Ollie collapse in a faint.

The boys decide to enlist, to see that Daniel gets proper care. The new recruits are met at the troop train by hard-as-nails Sergeant Hippo (Edmund MacDonald), who makes them run to the mess hall. Stan and Ollie finish the run and collapse *again*.

The sergeant has allowed only a short time for breakfast, and the mess hall is crowded with men waiting to be served. Daniel's servants expect first priority, but the line isn't budging. Laurel takes charge and cuts through the line, gathering generous servings of food from under the chefs' noses. Single-minded Stan is totally oblivious to the kitchen staff going about its business, and the staff doesn't notice Stan—until he absently hands the messy end of a ladle to a dumbfounded cook. In the Hal Roach days, many of the team's memorable pantomime set pieces were performed by Laurel alone, and this is one of the rare Laurel solo turns in the Fox series. Unfortunately the scene reverts to dialogue with an obvious "joke" punchline: Stan, holding a cup of coffee, inquires "Sanka?" and a server replies "You're welcome." There is more uncharacteristic verbal humor when two brawny toughs help themselves to the boys' breakfast. Stan claims that the eggs are theirs. "Yeah?" asks one of the mugs, "When did you lay them?" "I laid them on the tray just a minute ago!" protests Stan. "An army travels on its stomach, you know," says Ollie righteously. "What're you beefing about?" snaps the other mug, pointing to Hardy's ample midsection. "You got enough there to make China and back."

Some of Lou Breslow's dialogue in **Great Guns** is very brash, and is better suited to wisecracking Lou Costello than timid Stan Laurel:

> *Sergeant:* What did I ever do to deserve a couple of yaps like you?
> *Stan:* Maybe you were good to your mother.

Oliver Hardy doesn't fare much better:

> *Sergeant:* Now at 10:00 you're all going over for an IQ test . . .
> *Ollie:* Maybe they'll put me in the intelligence corpse.
> *Sergeant (indicating Laurel):* Brother, you're with him right now.

This is a key fault of Breslow's work: he often reinvented the established characters of popular screen personalities. His Jane Withers, Ritz Brothers, and Laurel & Hardy scripts for Sol Wurtzel hampered the stars with ill-fitting, unconvincing material.

Stan Laurel has to struggle with malaprops and dated slang, making "Stanley" more stupid than childlike. When he refers to a face-blackened explosion victim as "Old Black Joe," the humor is too cruel for his innocent screen character. Oliver Hardy, long associated with the courtly Southern manner, has several awkwardly florid expressions. He does the unimaginable in **Great Guns**: not only does he look straight into the camera, but he actually *talks* straight into the camera for the only time in history. This then-fresh device was popularized in the Hope & Crosby "Road" pictures. The dialogue wasn't really necessary: Hardy plays a trick on Laurel, and when it backfires Hardy tells us, "Something went wrong."

Apparently, according to the script, Laurel & Hardy are to be regarded as bungling buffoons and are not supposed to resemble "normal" human beings. Looking at a photo of Ollie and Stan, a cast member incredulously asks, "What's that, a balloon? What's that next to him?" and then, "Has Ripley seen them?", a reference to Robert Ripley's "Believe It or Not" newspaper features about oddball phenomena.

The boys' makeup jobs in **Great Guns** are another form of oddball phenomena. Not only aren't the "Stan and Ollie" characters permitted to act as they usually do, they can't *look* as they usually do. After only seventeen months away from the screen, Stan and Ollie appear to have aged badly. This was because Fox insisted on a lighter, more transparent type of facial makeup, instead of the clown-white greasepaint favored by Laurel & Hardy. The greasepaint method was losing its effectiveness, anyway; in their previous picture, **Saps At Sea**, one can plainly see unnatural expanses of chalky pallor in the boys' faces. "My father was used to doing his own makeup at Roach, and he wasn't allowed to at Fox," says Lois Laurel. "So he was very critical of his makeup—but it was union," she shrugs. The inadvertent result was that lines and wrinkles were being played up, instead of washed out.

The new style of makeup was supposed to make Laurel & Hardy look more like "regular people," yet the **Great Guns** script implies that the boys mustn't be mistaken for regular soldiers. Every other soldier is neatly and efficiently attired, but Stan and Ollie wear baggy "doughboy" uniforms or denim work clothes (Ollie even has a denim *derby*). The comedians hadn't worn denim outfits since their first feature film, **Pardon Us** (1931), and Laurel acknowledges the earlier appearance by wearing his hat the same way.

Laurel & Hardy spoil their first dress parade just by showing up. They saunter into the regimental lineup, greet the senior officer informally, and ask him to take their picture, as Sgt. Hippo glowers.

The army camp is a cavalry installation, and Sgt. Hippo arranges a rodeo exhibition to introduce the company to hard riding and bronco-busting. Hippo offers Daniel a chance to ride one of the wild stallions, and Daniel accepts the challenge, to Stan and Ollie's hysterical dismay. Daniel comes through with flying colors, but the jealous sergeant tries to top him with even fancier riding. He fails, and Stan and Ollie fail to hide their amusement.

The sergeant is so fed up with Laurel & Hardy that he orders them to exercise a pair of horses—uphill for five miles. The horses escape, leaving the boys stranded in the country. A tent-shaped military vehicle rolls past, and the boys climb aboard for a free ride back to camp. Unfortunately they are reclining inside a mobile target during gunnery practice. The boys react to the unusual noises with scholarly detachment. "Sounds like an Oregon woodpecker," comments Stanley. "No, an Oregon woodpecker makes a much softer sound," corrects Oliver. "That's more like the *Tennessee* woodpecker that thrives on hickory." This erudite dialogue is totally out of character for the comedians, as Laurel & Hardy suddenly become "bird-brains."

Once the bullets hit their mark, the scene shifts to good, predictable thrill comedy, as holes puncture the canvas, perilously close to the boys. Their terror heightens when Hardy's shirt buttons are shot off one by one, but the vehicle mercifully comes to a stop before further damage can be done. This scene is well staged but is *too* well photographed: in the close shot of Hardy one can see the perforations on the canvas where the "bullet holes" will appear.

Cameraman Glen MacWilliams frames his shots to benefit the stars. Whenever the troops are lined up in formation, MacWilliams allows Laurel & Hardy to make an entrance. Other ensemble scenes have Mac-Williams zooming in on the two principals whenever possible. Glen MacWilliams was favorably disposed toward Laurel & Hardy: Babe Hardy had remembered MacWilliams from a silent-film crew of almost twenty years before, and asked the studio to engage him as the team's cameraman. Stan Laurel was very pleased with his partner's choice. "Glen MacWilliams was an Englishman, very talented, and my dad adored him," says Lois Laurel. "With all the problems they were having with Twentieth, that was one happy time to go to work, because they had Glen." MacWilliams did two pictures under this arrangement.

The inspection scene in **Great Guns** is surefire, hokey comedy. For sheer belly laughs this is one of the all-time great Laurel & Hardy clips. The situation has a gloriously predictable set-up: Laurel's pet crow shows up during an important inspection, and Laurel has to stash it down the back of Hardy's uniform pants. Of course, Ollie can't stop fidgeting. His delicate hip-swinging and leg-crossing soon become a frenzied fit, as he rushes into the arms of a superior officer. Any comedian could have gotten laughs by registering uneasiness, but Oliver Hardy's extreme discomfort borders on incontinence. His coy facial gestures, assuring the officers that nothing is wrong, alternate hilariously with his panic-stricken groans and grimaces. Finally the commanding officer sees something protruding from the rear flank. "Was that a blackbird?" asks the general in amazement. "No, sir," replies Private Hardy calmly, "they don't come this far south." (This mild double-meaning joke refers to *Hardy's* southern quarter.)

In the barracks, the team has some opportunities for visual nonsense. When Laurel tries to make his bed, he lifts the pillowcase by its closed end and the cushion falls out. Hardy doesn't get *that* far—the sergeant slams a pillow into his face! When Laurel prepares to shave, he tries to sharpen his safety razor on a strop, and the light bulb won't work when he needs it. He unscrews the bulb—which glows in his hand—and continues to shave as Ollie looks on in disbelief. This gag is similar to the "mixed-up plumbing and electricity" in Laurel & Hardy's previous feature **Saps At Sea**.

Two additional pantomime gags were filmed on the barracks set. One had Stan diligently drawing a tic-tac-toe game in the air, and "erasing" it with his sleeve after he loses. The other had Stan hitting the keys of an invisible typewriter, accompanied by appropriate sound effects, as he composes a transparent letter to himself—which Ollie mustn't read because it's personal! Both of these scenes made it into the working print but were removed just before release, which is a shame because they have the hallmarks of genuine Laurel & Hardy humor.

Daniel has become acquainted with Ginger Hammond (Sheila Ryan), the attractive proprietor of the photographic shop at the post exchange. (One of her customers is Alan Ladd, then on the threshold of stardom.) Ginger has resisted the crude attentions of Sgt. Hippo, and seems surprised that Daniel fails to make any flirtatious advances toward her. But the bashful soldier is scrupulously trustworthy, and the two quickly warm up to each other. The photo-shop set is liberally decorated with posters and literature for Kodak cameras and films, which lends period charm to these scenes. Fox's publicity department must have forgotten about this when they launched an advertising tie-in campaign on behalf of Bell & Howell, Kodak's leading rival!

Stan and Ollie disapprove of Daniel's budding romance, fearing that it will be too much for his delicate system, so they decide to pay Ginger off. They appear at her apartment in rented formal wear, masquerading as business tycoons. Ginger recognizes her visitors as Daniel's army buddies and indulges in theatrics herself. The script is unkind to Laurel & Hardy in this scene, forcing them to recite insipid dialogue. Laurel is called "Sylvester Sneer" ("Silly for short") and Hardy "Mr. Murgatroyd" (which Stan mangles as "Purgatory"). Oliver Hardy seems to recognize just how stilted the dialogue is, because he makes fun of it; his hammy delivery saves the scene. Sheila Ryan earns her own laughs with exaggerated, dramatic-school inflections and poses. The quiet Stan Laurel confines his participation to a few tried-and-true reactions: catching his nose in his pince-nez glasses, or applauding after his friend's impassioned speech.

The boys resort to drastic measures to break up Daniel's affair. They hit the sergeant with a wet washcloth and allow Daniel to be blamed. He is imprisoned for insubordination as Laurel & Hardy weep uncontrollably (another scene that strikes a false note).

The troops are split into two teams for a practice mission. During their field maneuvers, they will risk being captured by "enemy" patrols and attacked from the air by sacks of flour (representing bombs). The White Army's objective is to destroy a bridge that is being constructed on the river's edge by the Blue Army.

Comedy fans will recognize this premise as a direct theft from Abbott & Costello's **Buck Privates**. In truth, Stan Laurel conceived the sequence first, in 1940. Lois Laurel was there when it happened: "Before Abbott & Costello made **Buck Privates**, they would come to our house for dinner. My dad wasn't working at the time. They were having real trouble getting things right, and they came to Dad and said 'What do you think?'" Stan advised novice film actors Bud and Lou about suitable material for a military comedy, and they incorporated his suggestions into **Buck Privates**. When Laurel & Hardy found themselves making their own Army picture, Stan remembered the routine. "I can see why there was a similarity when Dad and Babe did the picture at Twentieth, because they had worked it out," says Lois. "And chances are they never even *saw* **Buck Privates**. Dad never went to the movies."

In **Great Guns** Laurel & Hardy are assigned to the White Army and are issued a jeep, which runs riot over hill, over dale, and over a minefield. (The camerawork by Glen MacWilliams is effective, including good process shots of the boys driving the wildly jouncing vehicle.) The script reaches low for a sight gag: the jeep's front end tips upward under Hardy's weight on the back end. (The script fails to explain why the jeep behaved normally when Hardy *first* got into it.) A playful bombardier drops several flour sacks, one of which hits Hardy. Laurel reacts by *insulting* his friend: "You look like a biscuit! Ha-ha-ha!" This is way out of line for the sympathetic "Stanley" character, and forsakes characterization for the sake of a cheap laugh.

Stan and Ollie locate the river by driving into it. They are immediately captured by the Blue Army troops and put to work building the enemy's bridge. This introduces one of the oldest gags in the Laurel & Hardy book: Stan enters from the left of the screen, carrying a *very* long plank. Passing Hardy, he walks out of frame but the plank continues to pass Hardy for an interminable period. The longer the plank, the greater Ollie's mystification. This gag is repeated with a couple of variations, and is true to the "traditional" Laurel & Hardy style except for Stan having to whistle aimlessly while the plank is passing.

Back at camp, Sgt. Hippo gloats that Daniel's pals have been captured. Daniel escapes from the guardhouse and turns Stan's pet crow loose. He then prevails upon the colonel to have the troops follow the bird, who is sure to lead them to the Blue forces. They do and she does. Daniel gets Ginger, and Stan and Ollie get "promoted" to the sanitary unit.

Great Guns moves like lightning—unusual for the methodically paced Laurel & Hardy comedies. The excellent editing job was by Al DeGaetano, a staff cutter who had efficiently assembled many of Fox's "B" comedies and mysteries. DeGaetano was forced to cut a number of promising comedy scenes out of the picture. Laurel & Hardy enthusiasts might unfairly blame the Fox filmmakers for not knowing good material when they saw it. The real reason these scenes were scrapped involved running time. Sol Wurtzel's "B" films were designed for double features, and theater owners could not support lengthy programs. Fox's "B" unit rarely allowed a film to exceed an hour and a quarter, and editor DeGaetano tested the upper limit by cramming as much as he could into 74 minutes. A good deal of the footage is devoted to army maneuvers, at the expense of the deleted comedy scenes, but audiences of the period were fascinated by the new military equipment and vehicles, and they found the war games just as entertaining as the fun-and-games.

Dick Nelson, who plays the juvenile lead, was a radio performer who had leading-man possibilities. Trade reviewers applauded his screen debut in **Great Guns** and looked forward to seeing more of him, but his career was interrupted by the war. **Great Guns** turned out to be Nelson's only screen credit, and three decades later he was genially bemused by Laurel & Hardy fans seeking his autograph.

Sheila Ryan also received kudos for her performance, although she confessed that she would have preferred a more prestigious showcase. "Sheila was under a stock contract," notes Lois Laurel, "and if you weren't busy at the time you still got the same salary. Sheila said it was sort of a disgrace if you weren't doing anything and they just put you into a Laurel & Hardy comedy. It was a comedown. They were low men on the totem pole, there's no doubt about that."

Laurel & Hardy had been off the screen for almost a year and a half, so **Great Guns** was greeted as a "comeback" feature. It had few of the traditional ingredients of a Laurel & Hardy picture, but it had all of the requirements for a topical, lightweight entertainment and the moviegoers of 1941 thoroughly enjoyed it. *The Motion Picture Herald* covered an advance screening and "the preview showed that [Laurel & Hardy] are just as funny as they ever were; that their antics provoke hilarious outbursts from audiences, and that their appeal has not diminished . . . [The audience,] having just viewed [Abbott & Costello in] **Hold That Ghost**, laughed itself into near-hysterics at this." "Grand business, good comedy," raved a Midwestern exhibitor. "It gives one a great deal of pleasure to hear such carefree laughter, as you will hear if you play this. We loved it." The film did equally well in other countries; a Newfoundland reviewer found it "a great comedy that went over big here. They laughed long and loud at these two famous comedians."

Great Guns was not, as has been reported, the first in a new series of 20th Century-Fox features. It was actually a one-shot proposition, true to the Sol Wurtzel way of working. Wurtzel often introduced a new screen personality or character in a single picture; if it was accepted by audiences, the producer turned it into a series.

Sol Wurtzel didn't wait for the preview to assess his entry in the Army-comedy sweepstakes: he knew he had a hit. **Great Guns** turned out so well that it moved the head of the "B" unit to actually thank his two stars formally. This was unprecedented for the crusty Wurtzel, who was notoriously stingy with money and compliments. In a letter dated August 13, 1941, Wurtzel wrote, "I wish to take this opportunity to tell you how very happy I was in making this picture with you. Your sincerity and cooperation were deeply appreciated . . . It is my sincere hope that we can continue to make many more pictures together."

Great Guns became one of the biggest commercial successes of the team's career, which must have been a mixed blessing to the stars. They were enjoying a spectacular comeback at a major studio, but their creative input was limited by company policy. (Buster Keaton experienced the same frustration in the 1930s: his big-studio features were no longer "his" productions, and he had no control over them, but they made more money than ever before.)

Great Guns was actually released twice. It was rushed out in 1941 to cash in on a rival comedy team's military lampoon, and it served the same purpose in 1950. This time the competition was Dean Martin and Jerry Lewis, whose **At War With The Army** was bringing service comedies back into vogue. A two-page press sheet was hastily assembled for exhibitors (as opposed to a twelve- to twenty-page pressbook) with new advertising copy for publication. A squib about the **Great Guns** supporting cast mentioned Ludwig Stossel, "seen in the Jolson pictures"; the diminutive Stossel was being confused with distinguished Ludwig Donath, who portrayed Al Jolson's father in Columbia's popular musical biographies. Sadly, while Laurel & Hardy's brand of humor was hailed as timeless, the team itself was referred to in the past tense: "Laurel and Hardy's near-legendary history in the picture business will mean more to the old folks than the young . . . Just tell them that Laurel & Hardy came way before Abbott & Costello."

The "bottom line" determined a film's status, so 20th Century-Fox had every reason to consider **Great Guns** a success. The fact that it was not an *artistic* success was of little consequence to Fox—it made money and the people liked it. The studio, taking up its option for more Laurel & Hardy movies, agreed to pay the team's corporation the sum of $50,000 per picture, and Sol Wurtzel ordered another script from his writers.

While the new film was being prepared, Stan and Babe were approached by theatrical producer Eddie Dowling. Dowling's touring company, "The Flying Showboat," was going to perform variety shows at American military installations. The troupe consisted of comedians Stan Laurel and Oliver Hardy, pianist-comic Chico Marx, dancers Ray Bolger and Mitzi Mayfair, vocalist Jane Pickens, and master of ceremonies John Garfield. They were the first entertainers to volunteer their services to the 1940s war effort.

"The Flying Showboat" left New York in November, 1941, and made its way down the east coast to Florida. From there the company visited army camps in Puerto Rico, Antigua, Santa Lucia, Trinidad, and British Guiana.

The entertainers found the conditions primitive and uncomfortable. Tropical heat and swarming insects followed them everywhere. Theatrical equipment was virtually nonexistent, according to Robert Nott, John Garfield's biographer: "The troupe performed where there was room—in hangars, open fields, even under (or on) the wings of planes. More often than not, the troupers performed without a piano, so Chico and the dancers would have to improvise, utilizing any tool that could be considered an instrument. The lack of technical support did not matter to the Showboaters. What mattered most, [Garfield] said, was the actor's connection with his audience. The material here was weak . . . but [Garfield] claimed you couldn't tell by the response of the audiences . . . [which] helped keep up morale when local conditions threatened to dampen spirits."

Laurel & Hardy returned to Hollywood in March of 1942, their star status reinforced by a hit picture, a noteworthy Armed Forces tour, and now a long-term movie contract. They had no idea that their next achievement would become one of their biggest professional disappointments. While making **Great Guns** they were "guests" at 20th Century-Fox; upon their return, they were full-fledged employees on the Sol Wurtzel assembly line.

—◄▦▯◆▭▦►—

A-Haunting We Will Go

—◄▦▯◆▭▦►—

*Released August 7, 1942 by 20th Century-Fox. Produced by Sol M.
Wurtzel. Directed by Alfred Werker. Screenplay by Lou Breslow; story by
Lou Breslow and Stanley Rauh. Photographed by Glen MacWilliams.
Edited by Alfred Day. Running time: 67 minutes.*

Cast: Stan Laurel and Oliver Hardy (themselves); Dante the Magi-
cian/Harry A. Jansen (himself); Sheila Ryan (Margo); John Shelton
(Tommy White); Elisha Cook, Jr. (Frank Lucas); George Lynn
(Darby Mason); Don Costello (Doc Lake); Lou Lubin (Dixie
Draper—listed as "Beeler" in the credits); James Bush (Joe Mor-
gan); Addison Richards (Malcolm Kilgore); Edward Gargan (De-
tective Foster); Richard Lane and Robert Emmett Keane (con men
Phillips and Parker); Frank Faylen (railroad bouncer); Tom Dugan
(motorist); Mantan Moreland (Stan and Ollie's waiter); Willie Best
(Dante's waiter); Ralph Dunn and Edgar Dearing (policemen); Bud
Geary (stagehand).

"This doesn't rate with **Great Guns**," grunted the movie trade paper
The Exhibitor in a masterpiece of understatement. **A-Haunting We Will
Go** is a typical 20th Century-Fox "B" picture of the period. Unfortunately for Laurel & Hardy, however, the Fox "B" unit of 1942 specialized in crime dramas and murder mysteries. This picture has all of their
usual trappings: a gang of crooks, a complicated "swindle" scheme, an
imposing coffin which contains an unexpected victim, an exotic and
eerie exhibition of magic, and a young couple whose romance is threatened by a dark secret from the gentleman's past. The film plays exactly

like one of Fox's "Charlie Chan" mysteries, with a stellar cast of B-movie perennials in their familiar roles (including Richard Lane, Mantan Moreland, Sheila Ryan, and Elisha Cook, Jr.).

Where do Laurel & Hardy fit into this web of murder and intrigue? Quite simply, they don't. The "Stan and Ollie" characters just do not belong in this picture. Fox was trying to imitate Abbott & Costello's **Hold That Ghost**, released the previous season. When viewed as a "Charlie-Chan-picture-but-with-Laurel-and-Hardy," **A-Haunting We Will Go** has its moments for the fan of "B" movies. As a Laurel & Hardy comedy, however, it fails in almost every respect and is the weakest of all the team's features. Despite the film's lack of merit, it has received revival bookings and TV playdates as a spooky Halloween offering for kids, solely on the strength of its title.

The stars recognized the problem at the time, as shown by their unenthusiastic performances. Contrary to previously published reports, **A-Haunting We Will Go** was not the happiest experience that Laurel & Hardy enjoyed at Fox. In fact, it was probably the low point in their career as a team.

Laurel & Hardy hated making this picture, according to Richard Lane, who shared one scene with the boys. In 1978 Lane told interviewer Jim Neibaur how enthused he was to be hired for a Laurel & Hardy comedy, since their sets were noted for being a lot of fun, and how disappointed he was to find that there was no humor or merriment on the set at all.

It was obvious to Lane that Laurel & Hardy did not get along with their director. The dour Alfred Werker had just finished a Milton Berle film for Fox called **Whispering Ghosts**, hence his assignment to **A-Haunting We Will Go**. Laurel & Hardy soon discovered that Werker filmed his scenes strictly according to the printed page. Stan Laurel was totally detached from the material, and after each take he would wander off the set. Oliver Hardy was also unhappy with the script, but he would at least joke around on the set and attempt to socialize.

Dick Lane found Laurel & Hardy to be polite and pleasant, but noticeably lifeless, doing things by rote for the camera. They paid so little attention to their work that two years later, when they saw Lane again, they had no recollection of having worked with him before.

Lane stressed that at no time did Laurel & Hardy bemoan their fate to co-workers. There were no displays of anger or tension, and the team's conduct was professional. But Lane was surprised by latter-day accounts of Laurel being a creative dynamo, because on this job he was quiet and withdrawn.

The symptoms of an unfunny, unhappy comedy are evident from the very beginning of the film. Stan and Ollie are being escorted out of a police station by two courteous cops, who hope the vagrants enjoyed their stay. "Well, to be truthful, my oatmeal was a little lumpy," cracks Stan without a hint of humor. "And I would have been a lot more comfortable with another mattress on my bed," murmurs wiseacre Ollie. As in **Great Guns,** Lou Breslow's dialogue might have suited a bolder, wilder team like The Three Stooges or The East Side Kids, but it doesn't ring true coming from Laurel & Hardy. The boys aren't even allowed to employ their own trademark catch-phrases; Ollie has to say, "Here's another nice *predicament* you've gotten us into." The script should read *mess*, and rightly so.

Breslow presents Laurel & Hardy's characters in his script as being incredibly stupid. Instead of being dumb but likable innocents, they appear as oblivious idiots who always wind up as the fall guys for the "smarter" characters. Breslow's "legitimate" approach was too realistic for Laurel & Hardy's screen characters; Stan and Ollie's behavior wasn't so unusual in the Hal Roach farces, which had broad, exaggerated characters living in a slightly cockeyed world.

Laurel & Hardy traded upon their characters' lack of intelligence; four consecutive L & H movie titles (**Block-Heads, The Flying Deuces, A Chump At Oxford** and **Saps At Sea**) specifically referred to Stan and Ollie's dumbness. Any moviegoer could feel superior to Laurel & Hardy. However, this feeling of superiority was intended for the audience, not the cast of characters in their films. In **A-Haunting We Will Go** *everyone* is superior to Laurel & Hardy, and the supporting cast's almost contemptuous attitudes toward the leaden leads make it difficult to warm up to the film at times.

Stan and Ollie get off on the wrong foot by trying to hitch-hike to Florida. ("I'm dying for an orange," says Laurel for no good reason.) An affable motorist picks them up, but his battery fails immediately and Stan and Ollie have to push his car all the way to his driveway—where he thanks the boys cordially and leaves them flat. (The driver is Tom Dugan, familiar as a Hitler impersonator in Ernst Lubitsch's wartime comedy **To Be Or Not To Be**. Dugan had been a featured player and occasional gagman at the Hal Roach studio, where he had worked briefly with Laurel & Hardy.)

Meanwhile, a quartet of hardened criminals (including the boyish Elisha Cook, Jr.) is hatching a plan to sneak one of its members out of town. A sizable inheritance waits to be claimed in Dayton, Ohio, so the crooks hide the heir, Darby Mason, in a coffin and ship him to Dayton by train. Stan and Ollie ("a stupider pair of jerks I've never seen," snarls Mason) are hired as unsuspecting "fronts" to escort the casket to Mason's confederates. Mason is dryly portrayed by George Lynn, who was also featured in **To Be Or Not To Be**.

At the railroad station, the coffin entrusted to Stan and Ollie is mixed up with a theatrical casket used by Dante the Magician in his stage act. Incidentally, the depot is based in Georgia, which was Hardy's home state. Nobody speaks with Southern drawls or inflections except Hardy and two servants aboard the train. Even the mobster named "Dixie Draper" is played not by a Southern gentleman but by Lou Lubin, a birdlike, Runyonesque actor specializing in seamy comic roles.

Aboard the train, Stan and Ollie make the acquaintance of two sharpsters (beautifully characterized by Richard Lane and Robert Emmett Keane) who show off their miraculous money-printing device "Inflato." This amazing machine turns a dollar bill into a ten-dollar note, and escalates that to a hundred-dollar bill. It's plainly a primitive toy novelty but the boys are too naive to know that. The con men magnanimously allow Stan and Ollie to use their "Inflato," in exchange for all of their ready cash. (As he and his partner hastily depart, Lane calls Stan and Ollie "a couple of jerks.")

The boys order a huge meal in the dining car and pay the check using their machine. Of course, it now fails to produce genuine currency, much to the boys' agitation and the waiter's amusement.

Willie Best appears as a waiter in the dining-car scene. Best, a black actor sometimes known as "Sleep 'n' Eat," specialized in playing frightened servants, and his role in this film was evidently to react nervously to Laurel & Hardy's phony money. However, Best was replaced by a broader black comedian, Mantan Moreland, whose bulging eyes and infectious giggle enhanced the scene. Willie Best wound up with only one line of dialogue, but he did receive billing. Moreland, a last-minute inspiration, did not.

"I was working on another picture out there at Fox at the time," recalled Moreland in 1968 for interviewers Larry Byrd and Lee Black-burn. Moreland was on the Laurel & Hardy set only briefly, "because at that time I was bicycling it! I was on *that* set, and what I had to do was race from that set and back." (Moreland's other job was the Betty Grable musical **Footlight Serenade**.)

Either Werker's back was turned during the shooting of this scene, or Mantan Moreland's presence tempted Stan Laurel to try some horseplay. Laurel comes to life with a couple of improvisations. Helping his friend, Stan gets Ollie's necktie caught in the rollers of the "Inflato" machine. A few moments later, arising from the dinner table, he negligently drags his umbrella across the tabletop, which upsets all of the dishware. (The cameraman wasn't ready for the ad-lib and just barely kept it within frame, so a matching shot was taken, repeating the gag from a distance.)

"We were ad-libbing on that train," confirmed Mantan Moreland. "The three of us started ad-libbing. I think Stan started it, and then Hardy, and we kept on . . . We were just kidding and they kept it in, and it was very funny."

After Moreland exits, Dante examines the boys' money-making ma-chine and muses, "Those are a lot of fun." "Not for *us,* they're not," remarks Stan—the only time a Laurel wisecrack works, because he isn't delivering it as a joke, but as a simple statement of fact. When a snide railroad official threatens to throw Stan and Ollie off the train, Dante offers to pay the boys' check. Harry Jansen, who used "Dante" as a stage name, was a magician first and an actor second; he recites his lines pleasantly if not always convincingly.

The next day, in Dayton, Laurel & Hardy appear backstage at Dante's theater to repay him. Stan fiddles with a sandbag, only to be interrupted by Ollie—who gets the sandbag on his own head.

Dante is demonstrating his latest illusion: two booths which magically transport their occupants from place to place. Stan keeps entering one cabinet and emerging from the other, to Ollie's mystification, until a duplicate of *Ollie* pops up in the booth! Visions of *both* Stan and Ollie exchange positions as the real Ollie watches in amazement. This scene, one of the best in the movie, is very well shot by Glen MacWilliams, using jump-cuts and process photography to accomplish the trick. Oli-ver Hardy's very expressive face enhances the "surprise" element of the humor in this scene.

The coffin, which has been neglected of late, returns to the forefront of the plot. The stage crew elevates the casket (which actually contains a mobster) to the theater ceiling. And there it hangs, ominously casting a pall over the proceedings, much like the complicated plotline itself.

Stan and Ollie, hired as comic assistants for the magician's act, are fitted with beautifully resplendent Turkish costumes with turbans, embroidered vests and balloon trousers. "You look like a page out of the Arabian Nights," observes Dante. "Ollie looks like the whole *book*," agrees Stanley. "I sure *do!*" confirms Ollie genially until he realizes what he's saying.

The other three members of Mason's mob confront Stan and Ollie and demand to know where their confederate is. The three crooks start squabbling in underworld slang, which may add flavor to a gangster movie but doesn't do much for a comedy. When they order Stan and Ollie to "start singing," our heroes mechanically begin to harmonize. The two "stupes" are dispatched to find the man in the coffin, whom they know as "Charlie."

Dante the Magician takes the stage for an extended performance of his levitation trick. The scene is presented as a straight specialty act, with no cutaways or intrusions. While it is certainly atmospheric, it isn't entirely convincing; one assumes that the illusions are achieved not by the magician but by some sort of technical fakery by the film crew. It isn't even Dante's own trick, having been engineered in 1939 for Sol Wurtzel's production of **Charlie Chan At Treasure Island**. The same set decorator and art directors worked on both films, which employ the same equipment and at least one of the stage props. (And the Chan film actually reveals how the magician does the trick!) So it appears that Dante, like Laurel & Hardy, was not allowed to do his traditional act, for the sake of expediency.

Backstage, Laurel & Hardy are scouring the theater looking for "Charlie." The Abbott & Costello feature **Hold That Ghost**, which was the inspiration for this picture, had the team being confounded by an elusive cadaver named Charlie (the film's working title had in fact been **Oh Charlie**). Scriptwriter Lou Breslow apparently thought that, in order to guarantee the same kind of laughs, it was sufficient to have Laurel & Hardy repeatedly calling for "Charlie." Obviously he was mistaken, because the scene falls utterly flat.

Breslow made another mistake in his next scene. Stan sees something interesting on a stage backdrop and beckons Ollie. "I can't see through the window," Stan explains. "Why, it's a *painted* window, you dope!" snaps Ollie. Mr. Hardy usually dismisses Mr. Laurel's remarks with an annoyed groan, but Breslow's script compels Hardy to actually insult his partner.

Lou Breslow wasn't the only one who made mistakes. Alfred Werker, a workmanlike director but a reportedly humorless man, did not know how to properly stage a gag sequence. An old L & H routine involving the improper reassembly of a broken statue fails completely because a) Werker doesn't set it up, and b) Werker doesn't give it a punchline. In the original 1929 rendition of the piece, Hardy breaks the statue and registers embarrassment at its being a nude figure. Covering the indecent section with his coat, he hastily repairs the damage and leaves without examining the statue—which now has its middle section reversed. Laurel happens by sometime later, and reacts in a variety of ways to the figurine's striking physique.

As originally conceived, the bit is good for a number of laughs, but in the 1942 version we don't see the "embarrassment" part of the gag, nor do we see the puzzled reactions. The boys merely break the statue, put it together again, and walk away. Thanks to Werker's ignorant handling, there is no punctuation and no embellishment, thereby smothering a proven laugh-getter.

The crooks confront Laurel & Hardy (again), and the boys escape to the stage (where Dante is idly amusing the audience with very simple playing-card flourishes!). Dante enlists the boys for his rope trick. As Ollie plays furiously on a reed instrument, Laurel apprehensively climbs a rope which rises from a basket. Whenever Hardy stops for breath or is otherwise distracted, the rope goes limp and Stan sways perilously above the theater audience. That's all there is to this one-joke sequence, which is supposed to be a key comic episode.

Fortunately this is followed by a more promising example of Laurel & Hardy gumming up a magic trick. Hardy, fleeing from his pursuers, hides in a cabinet just before two stagehands prepare the next act by plunging swords through the box. This tried-and-true routine relies on the frightened reactions of the cabinet's occupant as the sabers narrowly miss him, and once again Oliver Hardy's facial gestures carry the comedy. Stan Laurel just stands to one side and cries throughout the sketch.

When the crooks confront Laurel & Hardy (*again*), the boys direct them to a convenient exit, which leads to a trap door and a lion's cage. This keeps the crooks occupied for awhile.

Stan holds a gong for Ollie to herald Dante's grand finale. Ollie is surprised when the sound and accompanying vibrations issue from *Stan* — while the gong remains still! Dante places a hypnotized Stan in a cabinet on stage, then fires a pistol at the coffin suspended above the audience. When the coffin is set upright on the stage, a body falls out. (This sort of thing, while suitable for a mystery, is too gruesome for a Laurel & Hardy comedy.) Hardy panics and tries to find his pal, who has vanished into thin air.

A detective (Edward Gargan) takes charge of the murder scene. The various motives, suspects and culprits are sorted out for the next several minutes. One almost expects Sidney Toler as Charlie Chan or Lloyd Nolan as Michael Shayne to step in from an adjacent 20th Century-Fox set and solve the crime. The resolution of the gangster plot is deadly serious—or just plain deadly if the viewer is waiting for more of Laurel & Hardy, because they do not appear in the climax at all. The story comes to its conclusion without the participation of the stars.

Laurel & Hardy finally show up for the fade-out gag. Hardy is still looking for Laurel, and hears his friend's familiar tearful voice in the distance. Suddenly an egg rolls toward Ollie, growing bigger and bigger as Stan's cries become more distinct. Hardy cracks the eggshell and a miniature Laurel pops out, weeping. Hardy laughs cruelly as the film mercifully ends, and the orchestra plays "Happy Endings."

The Laurel & Hardy names insured the picture's financial success. Trade reviewer William R. Weaver predicted, "When a showman has announced to his customers that this [picture] brings Stanley Laurel and Oliver Hardy around again, he will have done about all there is to do." However, once the moviegoer had been lured to the theater and had bought his ticket, it was too late. Weaver reported that the film was previewed "on a Thursday evening to a mainly adult audience which manifested only minor symptoms of amusement and some of disappointment."

"Lacking in laugh content on a sustained basis, this latest Laurel & Hardy feature gets boresome during its unfolding," panned *Variety*. "More than half of the footage is consumed in the preliminaries, and by the time L & H are inducted into the Dante spectacle it's too late to retain audience interest . . . Director Alfred Werker was apparently in a daze trying to direct the pair with the inadequate material provided."

Fox intended **A-Haunting We Will Go** to be the companion feature to **The Pied Piper**, a sophisticated Monty Woolley comedy, but the Laurel & Hardy film stood on its own. Even though it ran short of seven full reels, it got by as an "A" picture in many situations, and stayed in circulation for the better part of a year. Some theaters used the film as a kiddie-matinee special. A California exhibitor reported that "business [was] only fair, but the children are still very fond of these two old favorites." "Played [this picture] single with the final chapter of **Batman**," boasted an Indiana showman. "Glad to see these two stars are producing regularly again. Our patrons like Laurel and Hardy very much." An Arkansas theater manager warned his peers against the picture: "Audience was disappointed as it is not as good a picture as they have made in the past. My advice—don't play [it] in small towns."

The actors involved in **A-Haunting We Will Go** were aware that the quality didn't matter. Mantan Moreland observed that Laurel & Hardy "made some bad pictures and still got 'A' bookings. When they were working for Roach, he gave them everything they wanted. Fox gave you something to do comedy with, but they didn't want to give you sets. If you asked for a mansion, they'd give you a five-room house. If you had any ideas for comedy you'd have to cut it down to this five-room house. That's what made this picture bad."

Alfred Werker's reputation for efficiency was intact; he finished this "B" job a few days ahead of schedule, to the stars' relief. Laurel & Hardy couldn't wait to get out of this unfortunate project. In fact, they left town after filming their final scenes! They signed on with "The Hollywood Victory Caravan," a fundraising show-business troupe bound for Washington, D. C. There they met First Lady Eleanor Roosevelt at the White House.

The Caravan featured such top talents as Bob Hope, Bing Crosby, Cary Grant, James Cagney, Claudette Colbert, Charles Boyer, Joan Bennett, Pat O'Brien, Joan Blondell, Frank McHugh, Merle Oberon, Bert Lahr, Groucho Marx, and Desi Arnaz. Laurel & Hardy's contribution to the Caravan was the vaudeville sketch from *The Laurel & Hardy Revue*. They were the hit of the show.

The Caravan toured a dozen American cities in six weeks, and returned to California in May. Laurel & Hardy steeled themselves for another go-round with 20th Century-Fox, but another studio gave them a breather.

The Lion Roars

In 1942, with two hit pictures to their credit, Stan Laurel and Oliver Hardy were the valuable property of 20th Century-Fox—but Metro-Goldwyn-Mayer, the giant of the movie industry, didn't see it that way.

Fifteen years earlier, Laurel & Hardy first became partners under M-G-M's sponsorship. M-G-M enjoyed great success with the new team, releasing dozens of Hal Roach's Laurel & Hardy films under the familiar "Leo the Lion" trademark. The team was among M-G-M's most popular and bankable star attractions.

M-G-M lost its ace comedians in 1938, when Hal Roach took his business elsewhere. Theater owners who bought M-G-M product felt the loss when Laurel & Hardy continued to be a potent box-office draw.

Now, rival studio 20th Century-Fox was making money with stars that M-G-M had cultivated and promoted. M-G-M fought back by re-releasing some of the team's choice two-reelers (**Going Bye Bye**, **Their First Mistake**, etc.) as program fillers in the winter of 1941–42. "Although these are somewhat old," remarked a Canadian showman, "they still pack a lot of entertainment."

M-G-M listened to its customers. In March of 1942 Guy G. Black, operator of a moviehouse in Lyons, Nebraska, addressed an open letter to the studio: "We believe Metro would be much better off to stop their high-class pictures and give us more good comedies like 'The Thin Man,' 'Kildares,' '[Andy] Hardys' and re-engage Stan Laurel and Oliver Hardy for a few comedies. Everyone wants comedy and music to help them forget the hardships and heartaches brought them by the war. All studios should go all-out on national defense and do their part to help America laugh. Keep our boys in uniform in good spirits as well as the folks at home and they will whip the Axis to their knees."

Black's sentiments made sense to superpatriotic studio chief Louis B. Mayer. Mayer prized his company's high standing in the industry, and enjoyed leading the other studios by example. By following Black's suggestion, Mayer could make a patriotic gesture, earn some goodwill among exhibitors, and produce a couple of profitable "B" quickies in one fell swoop.

Laurel & Hardy were hired in late July. Perhaps the proper word is not "hired" but rather, "invited." M-G-M was the best equipped, most respected studio in the world, and the company chose its personnel carefully. To be invited to work at M-G-M added immeasurably to one's prestige in the film community.

As a commercial commodity, Laurel & Hardy were hotter than ever. The coming year would be their most productive in a decade, with three full-length comedies in release. Most of the team's feature-film contemporaries from the thirties were inactive by the forties (The Marx Brothers, Wheeler & Woolsey, Buster Keaton), so Laurel & Hardy were among the very few "current" stars with long-standing name value. Now they were heading for bigger and better things at M-G-M. The resulting pictures were certainly bigger, and if not in the same league as their 1930s work, they were indeed better than their immediate predecessor.

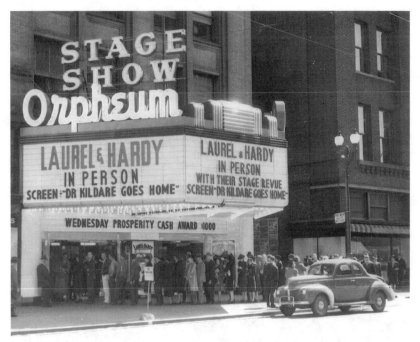

Business was brisk when *The Laurel & Hardy Revue* played America's theaters in 1940. This crowd consists almost entirely of adults, demonstrating that Laurel & Hardy weren't strictly a "family" or "kiddie" act.

On stage with *The Laurel & Hardy Revue,* Chicago, 1940: Stan Laurel, Oliver Hardy, and James C. Morton.

During their first day at 20th Century-Fox, Laurel & Hardy reported for a series of wardrobe stills for *Great Guns.* A mathematical breakdown of scenes is indicated on the slates. The comedians had never experienced such formal, rigid procedures.

A poster for 20th Century-Fox's first Laurel & Hardy picture, *Great Guns* (1941).

Sol M. Wurtzel, head of Fox's "B" division, who produced most of the 1940s Laurel & Hardy pictures.

In *Great Guns,* the chauffeur and the gardener have unsuccessfully pursued Penelope the crow.

Edmund MacDonald in *Great Guns*, giving good-housekeeping tips to Ollie, Stan, and Dick Nelson.

Sheila Ryan plays hard-to-get in this posed shot from *Great Guns.*

```
                    TWENTIETH CENTURY-FOX FILM CORPORATION

                                   STUDIOS

                           Beverly Hills, California
   Office of
   SOL M. WURTZEL                   August 13, 1941.


           Mr. Stan Laurel & Mr. Oliver Hardy,
           Laurel & Hardy Feature Productions,
           511 Pacific Mutual Building,
           Los Angeles, Calif.

           Dear Stan and Oliver:

           Your letter of August 11th made me very happy.

           I wish to take this opportunity to tell you how very happy
           I was in making this picture with you.  Your sincerity
           and cooperation were deeply appreciated.

           I am sure we are going to have a picture that will do credit
           to both the corporation and to you, and will also be popular
           with the motion picture audiences.

           It is my sincere hope that we can continue to make many
           more pictures together.

           I am working now on the cutting of the picture and it looks
           as tho we may be able to have it ready to ship to New York
           by the end of this month.  As soon as the picture is recorded
           with music and sound effects, I will get in touch with you
           so that you will be able to come over and look at it.

           My kindest personal regards to you both.


                                   Sincerely,

                                   Sol Wurtzel
```

One for the history books: a complimentary, personal letter from the tough, businesslike Sol Wurtzel—proof positive that 20th Century-Fox *liked* Laurel & Hardy.

USO entertainers Ray Bolger, Babe Hardy, and Stan Laurel chat informally with troops at Borinquen Field, Puerto Rico, November 1941.

The boys are just going through the motions in the uninspired *A-Haunting We Will Go.*

The affable Dante the Magician poses with his assistants in *A-Haunting We Will Go*.

"Heyyyyy, Abbott!" *A-Haunting We Will Go* was Fox's second and final attempt to turn Laurel & Hardy into Abbott & Costello.

One of the few bright moments of the filming of *A-Haunting We Will Go* was this visit from Stan's fourteen-year-old daughter, Lois.

They're back: Laurel & Hardy return to M-G-M in December 1942.

"Outside — both of you!"

Edgar Kennedy, master of the comedy of frustration, tangles with Stan and Ollie in *Air Raid Wardens*.

Air Raid Wardens introduced two new faces: Horace (later Stephen) McNally and Jacqueline White.

During the filming of the "garage" sequence in *Air Raid Wardens*, Laurel & Hardy's first-aid methods were scrutinized by graduate nurse Florence Maher from the studio infirmary.

The M-G-M "low point"—when the fortunes of the comedy stars hit bottom. Stan and Ollie have just been discharged from the air raid wardens' patrol.

The last of the Laurel & Hardy shorts: a scene from *The Tree In A Test Tube*.

Stan Laurel is not interested in the plans being hatched by Vivian Blaine, Bob Bailey, and Oliver Hardy in *Jitterbugs*.

In this scene from *Jitterbugs* Col. Watterson Bixby and his valet arrive, as (from left) Hal K. Dawson, Robert Emmett Keane, and Bob Bailey watch with interest.

Stan and Ollie with Vivian Blaine, the studio's new discovery, in *Jitterbugs*.

Ready for the dance floor in *Jitterbugs*.

Graphic arts directors Louis Shanfield and Theodore Jaedicker rated a bow for this beautiful *Jitterbugs* one-sheet.

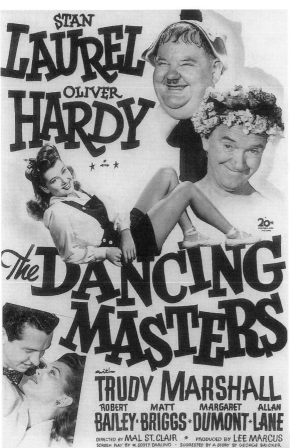

The one-sheet poster for *The Dancing Masters.*

George Lloyd and Robert Mitchum present the business card of the Last Mile Insurance Company in *The Dancing Masters.*

Bob Bailey was too mature for juvenile roles, but he made a convincing romantic lead in *The Dancing Masters.*

One of the scenes cut from *The Dancing Masters.* Ollie, having a private conversation with truck driver William Haade, indicates who was responsible for the mishap with the grandfather clock ...

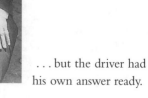

... but the driver had his own answer ready.

"Action" stills from the boys' wartime films are very rare. Here's one nice mess after another, from reel five of *The Dancing Masters*.

Professor Fendash Gorp and his American representative prepare for their ray-gun demonstration in *The Dancing Masters*.

A dignified family photo: The Professor poses with Lois Laurel, September 1943.

Air Raid Wardens

Released April, 1943 by Metro-Goldwyn-Mayer. Produced by B. F. (Bennie) Zeidman. Directed by Edward Sedgwick. Screenplay by Martin Rackin, Jack Jevne, Charles Rogers, and Harry Crane. Photographed by Walter Lundin. Edited by Irvine Warburton. Running time: 67 minutes.

Cast: Stan Laurel and Oliver Hardy (themselves); Edgar Kennedy (moving man, unidentified in the film but listed as "Joe Bledsoe" in the credits); Horace [Stephen] McNally (Dan Madison); Jacqueline White (Peggy Parker); Howard Freeman (J. P. Norton); Nella Walker (Millicent Norton); Donald Meek (Middling); Henry O'Neill (Rittenhause); Don Costello (Heydrich); Russell Hicks (Major Scanlon); Paul Stanton (Captain Biddle); Robert Emmett O'Connor (Charlie Beaugart); Philip Van Zandt (Herman); Joe Yule (Ryan); Frederic Worlock (Otto); William Tannen (Joseph); Charles Coleman (Norton's butler); Forrest Taylor and Edward Hearn (plant watchmen); Betty Jaynes (waitress); Bobby Burns (citizen at town meeting); Daisy (dog).

Considering the miserable experience Stan Laurel and Oliver Hardy endured while making **A-Haunting We Will Go**, the opportunity to work somewhere else must have come as an absolute blessing. Here was a chance to make a new film with a crew of their old cronies from the Hal Roach studio, and "those Fox people," as Stan Laurel ruefully called them, would have nothing to do with it.

The producer was Bennie Zeidman, who had ambitiously packaged some small-scale features for the Grand National company in the mid-

1930s, and was doing as much for M-G-M a few years later. After making this picture, Zeidman worked in M-G-M's shorts department for several months until he was released due to staff reductions. He later returned to the studio and made a second Laurel & Hardy feature.

The story, already in preparation when Laurel & Hardy were contracted, was outlined by writers Martin Rackin, Howard Dimsdale, and Jack Jevne. After Rackin and Jevne carried it to the scripting stage, two more collaborators were brought in. Harry Crane was a Metro staff writer who went on to work with many top comedy stars in movies, radio, and television. Charlie Rogers, one of Stan Laurel's closest associates from the Hal Roach days, was hired at Oliver Hardy's suggestion. Laurel's morale was at a new low after the **A-Haunting We Will Go** debacle, and Hardy thought that Rogers's presence on the staff would bolster Laurel's enthusiasm.

The cast and crew were assembled at the end of the year. For a few weeks during the holiday season of 1942, it was almost like the old Hal Roach days. Edward "Junior" Sedgwick had directed Laurel & Hardy in **Pick A Star** in 1937; cameraman Walter Lundin had worked on many Roach features and shorts; gagmen Charlie Rogers and Jack Jevne were veterans of the Roach writers' room; comedian Edgar Kennedy was featured opposite the team for years; Bobby Burns, an elderly character comic who played small roles in two-reelers, had starred in Oliver Hardy's earliest movies.

With all of these "old-timer" filmmakers, the new Laurel & Hardy unit was regarded as a charity ward by studio management. It was a handy place to put actors and crew members who needed work. A case in point is director Edward Sedgwick, who in the early 1940s was still employed by M-G-M but not doing much of anything. He had worked closely with Buster Keaton since the late 1920s, but as the years passed he was entrusted with fewer assignments, as there was little demand for his brand of mainly visual comedies. In 1942, the "old-fashioned" Sedgwick passed the time with the equally obsolescent Keaton, building Rube Goldberg-styled machines in their office. **Air Raid Wardens** was Sedgwick's first chance to direct in over two years. (He had been replaced on another production earlier in 1942.) Perhaps he was chosen because he was an anachronism. Sedgwick, like Laurel & Hardy, appeared to cling stubbornly to familiar, almost outmoded formulas. After completing the film, he returned to his office when no further offers materialized. He made two more lower-eschelon comedies several years later.

"Ed was a lovely man, everybody loved him. I don't think he had an enemy in the world," recalls Eleanor Keaton, Buster's wife, then working as a dancer at M-G-M. "His directing days were pretty well over. I never quite figured out why he was on the payroll all the time."

The Sedgwick-Keaton office, located near the company commissary, stayed open throughout the 1940s. "Anybody who was hiding from work would be there," says Mrs. Keaton. Buster was the studio's resident technical wizard, so "if they had a problem they wanted solved, they'd come and get him. But the purge came around 1950–51, when we all got fired. They were losing money like crazy because of television." On the **Air Raid Wardens** set, the easygoing Edward Sedgwick was much more agreeable to Laurel & Hardy than their difficult Fox directors had been, and it shows in the finished product.

"B" movies gave young contract players a modest showcase and valuable training in screen techniques. Two freshmen on M-G-M's 1942 campus were given a chance to advance. Horace McNally, age 29, was a former lawyer who became a Broadway star with his first stage appearance, in "The Man Who Killed Lincoln." Two more stage credits led to an M-G-M contract in 1942. The handsome McNally lent sincerity and authority to his **Air Raid Wardens** role. He later changed his screen name to Stephen McNally and went on to bigger pictures, but a sensitive actor with dramatic experience would hesitate to include a Laurel & Hardy "B" comedy among his illustrious screen credits. In the interest of his dramatic career, McNally left **Air Raid Wardens** out of his resumé.

Jacqueline White, age 20, had won national high-school honors in theater, and one of her college roles attracted the attention of M-G-M talent scouts. **Air Raid Wardens** was her fourth picture and her first movie lead. She wasn't given much to do in the film, except for a confrontation scene where she offers a heartfelt speech on Laurel & Hardy's behalf, but she kept **Air Raid Wardens** in *her* resumé.

Air Raid Wardens superficially looks like vintage Laurel & Hardy. Suddenly they appear to be several years younger, thanks to M-G-M's careful and flattering makeup jobs. The "Stan and Ollie" characters are more resourceful and less imbecilic than they were at Fox, and Laurel & Hardy's performances are more relaxed and spontaneous. Although they didn't find the new conditions ideal, since there was little room for "working loose" at such a big studio, Laurel & Hardy got a better deal in **Air Raid Wardens**. The script situations are appetizing, the direction is pantomime-friendly, and the patented M-G-M production gloss is well in evidence, even for this "little" picture.

The stars' timing and teamwork are as sharp as ever, but **Air Raid Wardens** is constantly sabotaged by M-G-M's traditionally stately pacing. Try as they might, the M-G-M people couldn't make comedies that moved. The once-charming "Our Gang" series, another perennial of the Hal Roach studios, was now plodding and heavy-handed under M-G-M's supervision. In **Air Raid Wardens** the cast and crew are racing hard for laughs, but the leisurely editing slows the film to a mild canter. The film suffers from a complete absence of background music, which magnifies the dead spots. There are long, arid stretches of silence as the gags are being set up; even some of the crowd scenes are eerily still, which does not bode well for a raucous slapstick comedy. Curiously, Nat Shilkret receives credit for contributing the "musical score," but apart from the main and end titles there is no music at all. (The cutting continuity, a written transcript of the film's contents, actually counts the occasional "whistle improvisation" as a musical selection.)

Nobody at M-G-M seemed to know how a Laurel & Hardy movie should be cut, so the film editor, Irvine "Cotton" Warburton, went to the Hal Roach studio to confer with the Roach editing staff. Warburton tried to get the most out of his footage, but didn't always succeed.

While there is a surprising number of good, solid laughs, especially when seen with an audience to smooth over the awkward silences, **Air Raid Wardens** looks slower than it actually is. It resembles a "rough cut," a first-draft version of a film which could have been greatly improved by faster cutting and adroit scoring. One can judge the damage by viewing the **Wardens** coming-attractions trailer, which is cut and scored at a whirlwind tempo and shows all the gag payoffs to good effect.

The feature begins very promisingly, as the fortunes of Stan and Ollie are encapsulated in a montage of their failed small-town businesses. When they are the first to enlist in the armed forces, the recruiting posters vehemently shout "No!" (The film's opening narration sets the film in December of 1941, immediately after the Pearl Harbor attack, but the rest of the picture looks and sounds like late '42.)

Stan and Ollie return to their place of business, currently a bicycle shop, where a taciturn moving man (Edgar Kennedy) is hauling their property out. This leads to a fine pantomime skirmish between the boys and the easily exasperated Kennedy, which is cut short by the arrival of the store's mild-mannered new tenant, Mr. Middling (Donald Meek). Middling offers to share the store with Laurel & Hardy.

Spurned by the service, the boys greet the local banker, Mr. Norton (Howard Freeman), who sarcastically suggests that they pay their outstanding debts. "You two blundering failures," he accuses. This may be an attempt to induce audience sympathy for the heroes, but the script lays it on a bit thick.

Newspaper editor Dan Madison (Horace McNally) gives Stan and Ollie a pep talk. "Uncle Sam wants everybody," he urges, noting that there's plenty of war work to be done on the home front.

Reinvigorated, the boys set out with paste and paper to hang signs around town. As Laurel & Hardy have never been noticeably adept in this department, one may expect a well-meaning but slapdash job. They do manage to smear paste on a few posters, but mostly they slather each other as well as Mr. Norton's snooty wife.

At that night's town meeting, volunteers apply for air raid warden duty. Dan addresses the gathering about how vital a small town's war effort can be. (M-G-M liked to include lessons about good citizenship in its films whenever possible.) Stan and Ollie, late for the meeting, try to sneak in unnoticed, but this is impossible thanks to a frisky dog (the remarkably intelligent "Daisy" from Columbia's "Blondie" series). Stan's tiptoeing makes a loud, squeaky sound. When he removes his shoes, the squeaky sound still comes from Stan's legs! "My rheumatism," the script forces him to explain, yet after the punchline when Stan keeps walking, the squeak suddenly stops.

This funny sequence has the boys getting comfortably seated, a difficult process which involves mixing up their derbies and trying to shush Daisy. Daisy emphatically dislikes banker Norton and snarls at him when he speaks. Stan and Ollie can't contain the dog, and Stan's stealthy attempt to collect the canine interrupts Norton's speech and causes a riot in the auditorium.

As part of their training, the novice air raid wardens are dispatched to administer first aid to "victims" in simulated disaster areas. Naturally, anywhere Laurel & Hardy go will become a disaster area. Their instructions are confused with those of two other wardens (one of whom is Mickey Rooney's father, Joe Yule). Stan and Ollie were supposed to remove a splinter from a policeman's finger, but they wind up with a high-risk scenario, "rescuing" Mr. Norton. Thanks to Laurel & Hardy's innovative medical techniques, the banker is successively knocked out, bandaged up, jolted around, and flung out into the street! The sketch could have been accelerated, but part of the fun here is watching Laurel & Hardy telegraph the jokes (the audience knows that a ludicrously large gob of axle grease has to be destined for Norton's face).

The "garage" sequence has visual gags involving machinery, which was a Buster Keaton specialty. Eleanor Keaton remembers how closely her husband worked with Edward Sedgwick, and thinks it's "more than likely" that Buster contributed ideas to **Air Raid Wardens**.

The wardens' command center issues a blackout alert, and homes and businesses dutifully dim their lights. The all-clear sounds, and lights are restored, but apparently Stan and Ollie did not hear the siren. They call on a local resident to turn off his lights or pull down his shades. The householder is the truculent Edgar Kennedy, who purrs, "Would you like to pull them down *for* me?" The boys precede Kennedy into the house, and Kennedy gives the camera a juicy, malevolent look as he closes the door, assuring the audience that there will be some roughhouse tonight.

Mr. Kennedy obstinately refuses to co-operate, but it is the boys' solemn duty to enforce the law at any cost. When Kennedy blocks their access to his light switch, the boys use Kennedy's head to short-circuit it. When Kennedy smacks them with heaping spoonfuls of cake batter, they soak his face with a sink-sprayer. When Kennedy hurls a rolling pin at Stan's head, Stan throws it back and it breaks a window. The comics' give-and-take pantomime is good, but the scene doesn't deliver as much as the viewer expects. What should be a comic highlight fails to achieve its maximum effect, owing to awkward pacing.

The boys are drummed out of the volunteer service for their bungling. This scene is played absolutely straight, thanks to a technical advisor who insisted that civil-defense proceedings must not be taken lightly. Decorum was not to be laughed at in an M-G-M picture, and the stern, staid atmosphere emphasizes the boys' shabbiness, making the characters pathetic misfits instead of charming underdogs. In the Hal Roach days, Laurel & Hardy would upset a dignified setting with their buffoonery, making fun of the ponderous types around them. At M-G-M, Stan and Ollie are inferior to everybody else—and sadly, they know it themselves.

Stan even has to make a self-pitying speech. "Well . . . you know best," he stammers to the defense officials, his voice choking with emotion. "Mr. Madison told us that we could do this kind of work and it made us happy. We tried hard. I guess we're not smart like other people. But if we can do something for our country by not doing this work, we'll do that too." The final blow comes as the boys have to hand in their equipment, and when Stan has to give up his beloved whistle he looks like he's about to cry. Not the comic "Stanley" cry, but an expression of anguish and despair.

This scene has more heart than usual for a Laurel & Hardy picture, and also more sustained dramatic acting, but it either impresses or depresses the Laurel & Hardy fan. Actually, this kind of scene wasn't so unusual for M-G-M. The company had an inflexible formula for comedies, going back to Buster Keaton's **The Cameraman** (1928) and later used repeatedly for The Marx Brothers. It called for the leading comics to reach a "low point," a sequence when things couldn't possibly get worse, and once they had the audience's sympathy they would bounce back to triumph and vindication. **Air Raid Wardens** adheres to formula, low point and all.

Stan and Ollie, utterly crushed, witness two suspicious characters taking charge of their shop. They are Nazi spies, bent on destroying the town's new magnesium plant. Because no one in town will believe them anymore, Stan and Ollie have to capture the saboteurs themselves.

They trail the spies to their lair, an abandoned hotel several miles away. "This is a job for the detectives," whispers Ollie. "Maybe we'd better turn it over to the FHA," suggests Stan. "This must be their hidein." Apart from the dramatic monologue, this feeble dialogue is the first really jarring thing Stan has had to say. Most of the boys' dialogue in **Air Raid Wardens** is true to their characters.

Stan and Ollie have less than 45 minutes to stop the Nazi sabotage. They climb a ladder (badly) and enter by an upstairs window (ineptly) to escape the notice of the enemy (unsuccessfully). One of the more sadistic Nazis is played by dialect specialist Don Costello, who had appeared in **A-Haunting We Will Go** as a quack doctor. In a scene reminiscent of Laurel & Hardy's **Bonnie Scotland** (1935), Stan is forced to execute Ollie, but misses. They escape in the resulting confusion.

Commandeering a derelict tin lizzie from a junkyard, the boys head for town. The car crashes into a tree, and Laurel & Hardy try a salvage operation. This scene is shot in long takes with some funny ad-libs by both Laurel and Hardy, and the 52-year-old Laurel gamely takes a pair of sprawling pratfalls.

The Nazis have occupied the plant and are preparing to destroy it. Meanwhile, Stan and Ollie have towed their car to a lunchroom. (The nondescript waitress behind the counter is Betty Jaynes, once groomed for stardom in the 1939 musical **Babes In Arms**.) The boys phone for help, and their call is mistaken for an official directive. Stan, who is exceptionally bright for a change, cues Ollie to give an appropriate response and warns him that one of the spies, their landlord Mr. Middling, is among the air raid wardens.

Thanks to the boys' call, the wardens descend upon the Nazis. When the villains shoot at Dan and threaten more mayhem, a firefighter unleashes a torrent of water on the saboteurs. (No one took any film of Laurel & Hardy at the water controls, which would have made a better finish.) The town is saved, and Stan and Ollie deliver the sneaky Mr. Middling to the authorities for the fade-out.

Two prints of **Air Raid Wardens** were submitted to The Library of Congress for copyright registration on March 24, 1943. The Library was then screening and evaluating every war-related film, in the interest of national security. The movie characters were closely scrutinized, and classified in terms of national origin, social and economic status, and deportment. This well-intentioned but ultimately futile policy was imposed upon various Hollywood movies for about a year.

The Library's screening committee looked most favorably upon serious stories with inspiring wartime themes. Even the juvenile adventure serials were applauded for their patriotic content. The civic-minded librarians had no use for silly comedies, and one staffer, Elisabeth Z. James, didn't mind saying so. She screened **Air Raid Wardens** in April, and summarized it a week later as "a stupid vehicle for the tedious, slow-motion slapstick comedy of the actors starred. Tiresome throughout. Directing [is] adequate to the above. Script tedious and often meaningless. Music routine." (*What* music?)

The Library's "official" review didn't hurt the film at all. Laurel & Hardy's first feature of 1943 was very well received, especially by servicemen. They had enjoyed the team as children, and were now embracing Laurel & Hardy as a nostalgic reminder of home. "The boys are drawing better than they did for awhile," observed an Idaho exhibitor, "as the folks like relief from war pictures." "Timely title, enjoyed by all," wrote a Connecticut showman. "One of their best in a long time."

An Indiana theater manager commented on his higher-than-usual receipts: "People who would not give Laurel and Hardy a look in on their former pictures came, in what may have been an escapist mood, to relax and get a laugh." A New Yorker agreed: "If your people like these fellows, Laurel and Hardy, they'll thoroughly enjoy this picture. It's real slapstick all the way through, loaded with laugh-provoking situations, and ought to make most people forget their troubles."

First-run trade ads contained photographs of ticket lines at New York's Rialto Theatre extending around the block. "**Air Raid Wardens** Rialto Premiere Smash!" blared Metro-Goldwyn-Mayer's ad copy. "Tops all M-G-M records here. Do the folks pay for howls? Oh boy!"

The studio publicists weren't exaggerating. As Theodore Strauss of the *New York Times* observed, "Laurel and Hardy are again gamboling across the Rialto screen to a house densely packed with soldiers, sailors, family parties, and small fry aged 3 to 13 . . . When Laurel's feet become entangled with the rungs of a ladder, the audience squirms with delight; when the pair solemnly open and close a window without a pane in it, chuckles break out like a rash all over the house; when Laurel puts on his best cry-baby face for the Nazi saboteur who is about to shoot him, the guffaws ring out loud and clear. Obviously the Rialto is not suffering from box-office anemia this week. But to at least one lone courier **Air Raid Wardens** seems little more than a mild two-reel comedy thinned out to feature length . . . the simplest acts such as pulling a rope or climbing a ladder become operations hardly less complicated than the invasion of Europe . . . Meanwhile the folks in the Rialto pews are laughing their heads off."

Air Raid Wardens made money for exhibitors, so there was little cause for complaint, although an Ohio showman with a long memory assessed the product in a single sentence: "I don't think this picture was quite as entertaining as their former pictures were."

Despite the film's success, M-G-M had no intentions of elevating Laurel & Hardy to higher endeavors or bigger budgets. With its feature output sold in blocks, M-G-M couldn't be bothered to promote a minor product which was thrown in with the better features (even the M-G-M short subjects got more publicity). The Laurel & Hardy movies were left to sell themselves, and to some degree, they did.

A footnote to Laurel & Hardy's reunion with Edgar Kennedy: on November 25, 1943, the three comics performed in a radio playlet with comedienne Patsy Moran (another veteran of L & H movies). The sketch was first recorded in 1941, with the same principals, as a pilot for a projected Laurel & Hardy network series; the 1943 version, recorded on broadcast-transcription discs by RCA Victor, was aired on program #66 of Armed Forces Radio's *Mail Call* series. In "The Wedding Night," Stan elopes with Patsy as Ollie rouses justice of the peace Kennedy at three in the morning. It goes without saying that Kennedy is constantly frustrated by his callers' indecisive bumbling, and the marriage ceremony never takes place.

It is interesting to hear Laurel & Hardy adapt their screen characters to the spoken-word medium. Hardy handles the script with assurance; unable to enhance his performance visually, he shades his dialogue with an expressive, blustery tone. Laurel, however, delivers each line and then trails off, mumbling a few extra words after each gag speech. Perhaps this random improvisation was deliberate—Laurel's way of making the "Stanley" character *sound* as vague as he looked. Edgar Kennedy is delightfully grouchy, and Patsy Moran makes a fine fourth.

In a time when many radio comedians wanted to become movie stars as well (Jack Benny, Lum and Abner, Fibber McGee and Molly, etc.), Laurel & Hardy were movie stars who wanted to establish themselves on radio. Three months later Stan and Babe returned to the microphones for another tryout. *The Laurel & Hardy Show,* performed before an NBC studio audience on March 6, 1944, was intended to be a half-hour situation comedy. Long presumed lost, the disc is part of the Jerry Haendiges collection of old radio shows. The episode, titled "Mr. Slater's Poultry Market," emphasized obvious verbal humor at the expense of Laurel & Hardy's movie characterizations. The audition record did not find a sponsor, and was never broadcast.

The boys' radio experiments failed to give their career a new outlet—"Stan and Ollie" had to be seen to be fully enjoyed. The surviving recordings do have great novelty value, although not as much as the team's first short subject in eight years.

The Tree In A Test Tube

(16MM KODACHROME COLOR)

Distributed by the United States Government in 1943. Produced by the United States Department of Agriculture Forest Service. Directed by Charles McDonald. Photographed by A. H. C. Sintzenich. Edited by Boris Vermont. Running time: 10 minutes.

Cast: Stan Laurel and Oliver Hardy (themselves); Pete Smith (off-screen narrator for Laurel & Hardy sequence); Lee Vickers (off-screen narrator for second half of film).

This very obscure reel of film presents a rare glimpse of Laurel & Hardy in color. It is a quick and informal affair—their footage was filmed outdoors during a lunch break. It has always been assumed that the sketch was staged at 20th Century-Fox, but it might have been filmed on the M-G-M lot during the production of **Air Raid Wardens**. This would explain the small-town settings, the cool-weather wardrobe, and the participation of Pete Smith, the wiseacre commentator of M-G-M's one-reel novelty shorts.

When the camera crew caught up with Laurel & Hardy, the comedians were wearing street clothes instead of their costumes: Laurel sported a cream-colored sportcoat (very unusual for his screen character), while Hardy had a casual, tan-plaid jacket. Transforming into their "Stan and Ollie" identities, the boys put on their trademark derbies, and Ollie combed his hair into bangs and hung his necktie outside of his vest, as the camera started to roll.

That camera was loaded with 16mm Kodachrome film, an amateur product used for home movies and nontheatrical applications. Kodachrome films shot decades ago still look crisp and fresh today, and **The Tree In A Test Tube** is no exception. Original-release prints, which are now almost impossible to find, reveal that the color values are still vividly gorgeous. (Most circulating versions of this film are taken from bootlegged copies; the colors have faded badly and a great deal of detail is no longer visible. The film should not be judged by these inferior reprints.)

The Tree In A Test Tube was printed in 16mm because it was not intended to be shown in movie theaters. (Contemporary trade papers have no record of the film being released through theatrical channels.) It was actually made available for institutional screenings at town meetings, schools, libraries, churches, and other assemblies.

This Forest Service film has a message for wartime audiences, and it gets down to business immediately. Laurel & Hardy are detained by the off-screen voice of Pete Smith, who asks the boys if they have any wood on their persons. The boys look blank (which for them isn't too difficult), so Smith explains that the average person uses any number of things derived from wood sources. Stan and Ollie open their suitcase for Smith. As Smith itemizes the contents, Laurel shows the various objects to the camera and hands them to his partner. Most of these wood-based products are of a personal nature, like eyeglass frames or a toothbrush, giving Ollie a chance to sample the merchandise. There is quite a lot of merchandise, so the boys rest their stuff on the rear bumper of a parked car.

The topic affords the team little opportunity to be funny, but there are a few spontaneous bits. When Smith asks Ollie for more wood, Ollie indicates Stanley's head! As Laurel's derby bounces off the top of his head, punster Smith comments, "A new spring hat, eh? Ouch." When Mr. Laurel is reluctant to display certain things for the camera, Mr. Hardy's insistent intervention reveals a pair of imitation-silk stockings hidden in a billfold, and a gaudy pair of shorts! After the boys have placed practically all their possessions on the car bumper, the car drives off and the boys chase it down the street.

Pete Smith's nasal New York patter segues into Lee Vickers's dignified Southern-accented narration for the second half of the film. The scene shifts to the Forest Service's research laboratory in Madison, Wisconsin, where "they figuratively put the tree in a test tube." Most latter-day prints of the film end here, but the complete film continues with five more minutes of instructional footage, showing the miraculous properties of wood.

Among the lab's accomplishments are an all-wood aircraft, a new variety of wooden skis, and a manufactured slab of laminated wood whose strength is tested by a circus elephant. "These are some of the little things that help to win a war," comments Vickers. The reel has a literally flag-waving conclusion, with propagandistic narration condemning "pirate nations" and praising America's fighting forces.

The technical limitations of the portable 16mm format are obvious. Laurel & Hardy were good choices to star in this film, as their pantomime skills overcame the absence of sound equipment. The editing was done hurriedly, home-movie style, with splices very plainly visible. The helpful post-production enhancements include optical transitions, and a good synchronized soundtrack by Reuben Ford. Edward Craig's effective score provides reedy, whimsical accompaniment for Laurel & Hardy, and brassy, martial music for the serious patriotic footage.

It may be a minor footnote to Laurel & Hardy's comedy legacy, but thanks to Kodachrome **The Tree In A Test Tube** is a major highlight of the team's film career.

Writers' Block

In late 1942, during Laurel & Hardy's absence from the 20th Century-Fox studios, Sol Wurtzel tried to think of another premise for the comedians. His first Laurel & Hardy film was suggested by a current hit, **Buck Privates**. His second was sparked by **Hold That Ghost**, another popular comedy. For his third, Wurtzel needed an inspiration, and he surveyed the movie marketplace for ideas.

One of the better-received "B" movie series was Columbia's "Boston Blackie," which often had as many laughs as thrills. Chester Morris had the title role, a sharp, breezy ex-convict. Blackie had all the answers, especially regarding fine jewels, and was an expert on the underworld. His comical sidekick, "The Runt," played by George E. Stone, was slight, eternally worried, and inseparable from Blackie.

Apparently Sol Wurtzel enjoyed the chemistry of Morris and Stone, and thought a similar vehicle could be written for Laurel & Hardy. Wurtzel engaged the man who wrote most of the Blackies, Paul Yawitz. (Yawitz was not hired, as one author claims, as a fledgling screenwriter breaking into the industry. He was simply the logical person to write a "Boston Blackie"-type script.)

Yawitz submitted a story called **Me And My Shadow** (which has the same amusement-park setting as 1941's **Meet Boston Blackie**). Laurel & Hardy are cast as proprietors of a wax museum on the midway, and like most of the boys' businesses, this one is struggling. The cashier, Joan, is smitten with their neighbor Eric, a refugee from Nazi Germany. A pair of enemy spies, posing as a married couple, smuggles microfilm in "their" baby's clothing. When the baby gets mixed up with one of Stan and Ollie's miniature wax dummies, the spies are duped, and Stan and Ollie now have a foundling on their hands.

The boys' landlord, a local gangster, threatens Stan and Ollie with eviction—until he sees the baby. Now the tender-hearted goon threatens them with dire consequences if any harm comes to the infant. The spies try to snatch the baby, while Stan and Ollie try to protect it. Observing all of this suspicious activity is a wily detective (who might as well be "Inspector Farraday" from the "Boston Blackie" series).

The spies are through playing. A Nazi collaborator takes over the shooting gallery—directly across from Laurel & Hardy's base of operations. Now Stan and Ollie are menaced on three fronts, and a chase through the amusement park finds Stan hiding with the baby aboard a daredevil airplane ride. At the end of the story, the Nazis are foiled, Eric and his sweetheart find happiness, and Stan and Ollie try to find their way out of a hall of mirrors.

Sol Wurtzel did not accept **Me And My Shadow**. Paul Yawitz captured the gangster milieu, but didn't pick up on the "Stan and Ollie" characters. The stars' only function is to be menaced at every turn, and any two actors with comedy experience could have played the parts. In Yawitz's favor, the story moves quickly and the various criminal doings have a comic undercurrent, unlike the stony stoicism of **A-Haunting We Will Go**. This was a step in the right direction, so Wurtzel tried again.

On December 8, 1942 Charles Roberts and Eugene Ling submitted a story for Laurel & Hardy. Again, there are Nazis skulking around endlessly. It seems that Mr. Hardy has inherited a sanitarium for nervous disorders, and he and Mr. Laurel go to Switzerland to run it. The world is at war, but Laurel & Hardy are oblivious to the international intrigue surrounding them. Two of their guests, Mr. and Mrs. Schweiz, are really British intelligence agents.

Two women, Greta and her maid Anna, are fleeing from Greta's Nazi husband. (The outline makes it clear that Greta is an American.) A St. Bernard dog—named Bernadine, obviously enough—finds the distressed travelers and escorts them to Laurel & Hardy's resort. When Captain Reinhard of the Gestapo arrives with his assistant Heinrich, Stan has to pose as a girl to divert them. Reinhard knows that Greta is in hiding, and he alerts the storm troopers.

Mr. and Mrs. Schweiz try to get a radio message through to the Allies. A monk arrives at the resort, but Heinrich recognizes him as a member of British intelligence and kills him. Mrs. Schweiz evens the score by killing Heinrich, but the Nazis retaliate by killing Anna.

Laurel & Hardy suddenly reappear to transport Mr. and Mrs. Schweiz by car through the mountain roads, with the storm troopers in hot pursuit. We never find out what happens to Greta, but the others "escape to Spain and safety."

There are about two-and-a-half comic situations in this outline: Laurel pretending to be a girl, the car chase through the mountains, and (this one counts as one-half) Stan and Ollie not knowing there's a war on. Otherwise there is nothing amusing about this story. There are three cold-blooded killings in this tastelessly grim "comedy." Writers Roberts and Ling couldn't think of a title appropriate to this little frivolity, so they submitted it as **Untitled Laurel & Hardy**.

The outline went to the development stage, and the narrative was fleshed out with badly needed comedy sequences. The masquerade scene was given sharper focus, with Stan posing as "Katrinka," the maid, rebuffing the lecherous Heinrich. The climax was also expanded, with the automobile chase giving way to a cable-car fracas high above the ground. The revisions didn't help in the end; **Untitled Laurel & Hardy** went unfilmed.

What the writers failed to understand is that Laurel & Hardy's plotlines had to be tailored for them. In the 1930s the comedians usually relied on a loose framework *instead* of a story (a prison comedy, a western comedy, a military comedy, etc.). When they did use a story, it was often adapted from operatic literature, which furnished a colorful, flamboyant "make-believe" backdrop for the team's antics. The characters or situations had to have enough possibilities as comedy devices, with Laurel & Hardy always the center of attention. At 20th Century-Fox, however, the writers apparently devoted themselves to a "straight" plotline, and assumed that Laurel & Hardy would somehow fend for themselves.

Laurel & Hardy's association with M-G-M was prestigious and profitable. Twentieth Century-Fox tried to assemble an equally suitable vehicle and crew for the comedy team. Sol Wurtzel, having rejected two original stories, badly needed a scenario in time for Laurel & Hardy's return. Evidently still clinging to the "Boston Blackie" idea, he went through a pile of old scripts, found one he liked—and called in a rewrite man.

Jitterbugs

Released June 11, 1943 by 20th Century-Fox. Produced by Sol M. Wurtzel. Directed by Mal St. Clair. Screenplay by Scott Darling; story (uncredited) by Scott Darling and Mal St. Clair, from a screen story (uncredited) by William Conselman and Henry Johnson. Photographed by Lucien Andriot. Edited by Norman Colbert. Original songs by Charles Newman and Lew Pollack. Running time: 74 minutes.

Cast: Stan Laurel and Oliver Hardy (themselves); Vivian Blaine (Susan Cowan); Bob Bailey (Chester Wright); Douglas Fowley (Malcolm Bennett); Noel Madison (Tony Queen); Lee Patrick (Dorcas); Robert Emmett Keane (Henry Corcoran); Charles Halton (attorney Samuel J. Cass); Hal K. Dawson (desk clerk); Francis Ford (old-timer at carnival); Chick Collins (mobster guard Joe Taylor); Tony Caruso (henchman Mike); James Bush (henchman Jimmy O'Grady); Syd Saylor (carnival barker); Jimmy Conlin (announcer for bearded lady); Gladys Blake (dice-game operator); Harrison Greene (angry carnival patron); Cy Slocum (dance-floor bouncer; also stunt double for Oliver Hardy); Virginia deLuce (dancer at carnival).

Now that Sol Wurtzel had a screen story for Laurel & Hardy, he needed someone to film it. Neither Monty Banks nor Alfred Werker had been appropriate directors for the comedians. The studio was faced with a wartime manpower shortage (809 Fox employees were serving in the armed forces at the time), so Laurel & Hardy's new director had to be someone who was already on the payroll.

Mal St. Clair (1897–1952) broke into directing in 1919, working for Mack Sennett and then Buster Keaton. St. Clair soon gained a reputation for sophisticated comedy (thanks to such features as **Are Parents People?** and **The Grand Duchess and the Waiter**), but his roots were in slapstick shorts. By the late 1930s he was a staff director at Fox, in charge of the "Jones Family" series of domestic comedies. He remained friendly with Buster Keaton, and hired him to contribute gags and cameo appearances for two of the "Jones" episodes.

In 1939 Fox produced **Hollywood Cavalcade**, an elaborate Technicolor feature starring Alice Faye and Don Ameche in a fictionalized biography of Mabel Normand and Mack Sennett. The script called for re-creations of silent-comedy vignettes, so Fox tapped Mal St. Clair to direct the slapstick sequences. (St. Clair in turn arranged for Buster Keaton to star in the film-within-the-film.)

St. Clair remained with Fox into the forties, but he shared the same plight as M-G-M's Edward Sedgwick: he was an "old-time comedy" specialist with fewer current assignments. The inactivity and insecurity bothered St. Clair. In 1942 the director, working on the all-star film **Tales Of Manhattan**, asked for Buster Keaton's technical assistance—anonymously. St. Clair didn't want his bosses to think that he required help. It doubtless did little for St. Clair's peace of mind when his contribution was cut from **Tales Of Manhattan**, and he was unable to take part in the film's critical prestige. At least the studio kept St. Clair occupied; he directed **Over My Dead Body** (1942), Fox's third and final attempt to star Milton Berle in movie comedies.

Fox executives then selected Mal St. Clair for the Laurel & Hardy unit, which revived his career and solidified his position at the studio. He was enough of a "company man" to respect the studio's production policies, so he was bound to a script to some degree, but he was also an enthusiastic comedy craftsman, which endeared him to Laurel & Hardy.

Laurel & Hardy became extremely friendly with their new director, who gave them far more freedom to perform than they had been allowed at Fox. The film was made at Fox's old studio on Western Avenue in Hollywood, which housed ten soundstages and a theater. Here the comedians could work with less interference, far from the management's new headquarters in Beverly Hills. Both Stan Laurel and Oliver Hardy thoroughly enjoyed making **Jitterbugs**. Oliver Hardy even listed **Jitter-**

bugs as one of the top five films of his entire career—a list reserved for bravura character performances of which he was most proud.

The script was written by Scott Darling, another veteran staffer at Fox. Darling was a Canadian whose literary background included editorial posts with two major newspapers, and a three-year stint as a "collaborator" with adventure novelist James Oliver Curwood. Like Mal St. Clair, Scott Darling had silent-comedy credentials: in the 1920s he was the supervising director of Universal's prolific, if undistinguished, comedy unit. Darling's aptitude for polishing the written word led him into movie scriptwriting, which he pursued for the rest of his career.

Darling's editorial experience was the key to his screenwriting skills: he was not so much a creator as an adaptor. He specialized in rewriting and updating existing material. His scenario for **Jitterbugs** was a retread of a 1933 property, **Arizona To Broadway**, which starred James Dunn and Joan Bennett. Darling's version featured a tricky but likable "Robin Hood" character, patterned after "Boston Blackie."

Darling had very little imagination when it came to assigning names to his characters. In **Jitterbugs** he gave the same name (Bates) to two minor roles; one assumes that he named the romantic lead "Chester" after Chester "Boston Blackie" Morris, and a mobster "Malcolm Bennett" after Malcolm St. Clair and Joan Bennett! Darling also had the careless habit of abruptly introducing plot elements and just as suddenly abandoning them. Several characters and incidents are "orphaned" in **Jitterbugs**.

In revising the **Arizona To Broadway** script, Darling was so busy tending to the con-man-outwits-gangsters plotline that he paid only mild attention to Laurel & Hardy. Because he was unfamiliar with the "Stan and Ollie" characters, he wrote dialogue for an eloquent windbag and his lowlife sidekick. (The characters aren't even *identified* in the script; Darling merely indicates when the actors "Stan" and "Babe" speak.) St. Clair and Laurel & Hardy wisely retained the traditional "Stan and Ollie" personalities, throwing out some of Darling's dialogue but using his story situations.

Fox commissioned a songwriting team (Charles Newman and Lew Pollack) and a choreographer (Geneva Sawyer) to contribute three production numbers to the film. One of the studio's more accomplished cameramen, Lucien Andriot, was assigned to supervise the photography. The added production luster was intended for the studio's latest discov-

ery, the 21-year-old Vivian Blaine, an attractive singer in the Alice Faye/
Betty Grable mold. (She was billed as prominently as the stars.) Thanks
to the showcase, Vivian Blaine went on to greater success as "The
Cherry Blonde" on stage and screen.

Another 21-year-old starlet, Virginia deLuce, attracted more attention from the publicity-photos department than she did in the film.
(She is a crowd extra in the carnival sequence of **Jitterbugs**.) The slim,
redheaded dancer appeared in a few 1940s films including **Cover Girl**
and **Diamond Horseshoe**, but made more of an impression in Broadway musicals, notably the stage and movie versions of *New Faces Of
1952*.

Jitterbugs required a leading man, but leading men were hard to
come by in 1943—many were serving in the armed forces. With a limited number of experienced thespians available, the studios picked up
new performers wherever they could. One source of dramatic talent was
radio, where an actor from Chicago named Bob Bailey was recruited.
As a screen personality, Bailey was presentable but had little potential as
a matinee idol. However, his broadcast training gave him a polished
baritone speaking voice, as well as an easy assurance with dialogue. Fox
was pleased enough with his performance to retain him for a second
picture.

With so much hubbub attached to the project, one might think Laurel & Hardy would be overlooked in the confusion, but they thrived
under the new conditions of attentive production and sympathetic direction. Both writer and director were now soliciting Stan Laurel's opin-
ion. "At the end of the working day my dad would huddle with [Darling
and St. Clair] at Fox," says Lois Laurel. "Usually it was confined to on-
the-set after a day of shooting, and concerning the next day's lines and
changes. He would offer suggestions, and the writers changed their tune.
If they didn't really know the Laurel & Hardy style, they eventually
came to realize that my dad knew what worked and what didn't work.
They would want the credit, of course—but they would do it his way."

"His way" was the right way, because the first reel of **Jitterbugs** com-
pares favorably to one of the team's vintage shorts. The boys, with the
screen to themselves, deliver some typical exchanges before any cumber-
some plot complications interfere. Many of the gags in this sequence
weren't in the script.

The **Jitterbugs** script begins with a playfully pretentious title card, worthy of a Cecil B. DeMille epic: "America—1943. This land of ours, last fortress of freedom, still finds daring pioneers who venture into the unknown . . . searching for new frontiers . . . embodying that indomitable spirit which is the heritage of the America of today." Of course, this was the cue for Laurel & Hardy to amble across the screen. Unfortunately, the gag preface wasn't filmed, so **Jitterbugs** fades in on the script's second scene.

The boys' old jalopy, dragging a trailer behind it, sputters to a halt in a western desert "a thousand miles from nowhere," and Stan is sorry. "You were sorry about that redhead in the auto court," Ollie reminds him. "You were sorry about that waitress in the barbecue stand." This dialogue is on the blunt side but it's certainly evocative; it's easy to imagine Hardy tie-twiddling his way out of an embarrassing series of blunders. The *most* embarrassing faux-pas was scripted but not filmed: "You were sorry about getting into the wrong rest room!"

Scanning the open plains for signs of life, the boys notice two skeletons—a fat one and a thin one—lying on the road. When Hardy sits on the car's running board to ponder this grave situation, the hot metal scalds his posterior. Laurel observes Hardy's burned britches through a spyglass, and mistakes them for a passing truck!

Another glance through the telescope yields a miraculous view of a gas station. Ollie tells Stan to push the car, and the trailer attached to it, down the road to the pumps. A moment later Stan joins Ollie in the front seat, and they discuss how well Stan is pushing the car.

The service station turns out to be abandoned, so the boys resort to flagging down the occasional motorist. In true Laurel & Hardy fashion, this fails spectacularly. Fortunately, a smooth character, Chester Wright (Bob Bailey), stops to offer Stan and Ollie the benefit of his miracle product, "The Little Wonder Gasoline Pill." He convinces Stan and Ollie that the fraudulent tablets can transform ordinary water into high-octane fuel, and prevails upon the boys to sell the pills at a nearby carnival. Vastly relieved by their good fortune, Stan and Ollie happily tear up their book of ration coupons—which must have sent groans through wartime theaters as sacrifice-conscious moviegoers watched in disbelief!

The crowd at the fairgrounds is captivated by Laurel & Hardy's exhibition, a "two-man zoot suit band." Stan and Ollie, dressed to the nines in wide-brimmed hats and custom-tailored zoot suits, regale the audience with instrumentals of "I Had The Craziest Dream" and "That's A-

Plenty." Composer Lew Pollack, who collaborated on the original musical score for **Jitterbugs,** furnished "That's A-Plenty" from his personal library; he had written this jazz chestnut in 1914. (The tune may be familiar to TV fans as Jackie Gleason's "traveling music" as he bellowed "And away we go!")

Laurel & Hardy's musical instruments are played by a complex system of robot hands, wires, and gadgets manipulated by the bandleaders. The humor here is literally mechanical but the scene is still great fun to watch, thanks largely to Hardy's exaggerated imitation of a jazz musician. This is the only Laurel & Hardy movie where our heroes are not clumsy or inept at their jobs. Their automated orchestra is quite the professional operation. Once the musical number is completed, however, the band is never mentioned again.

Ollie turns huckster and offers the amazing pills to the astonished throng. Stan Laurel doesn't say a word and barely participates in this scene; Oliver Hardy gets to monopolize the microphone in a character-actor turn and rattle off an impressive high-pressure pitch. The demonstration goes awry and Chester spirits the boys out of town. A young woman, Susan Cowan (Vivian Blaine), tags along to recover a purse that Chester held for her.

The carnival set is very elaborate, but only part of it was used in the film. The unused section of the set included concession stands, one of which was literally a commercial for a major meat packer, with prize hams on prominent display.

Susan's mother has been swindled and Chester, recognizing one of the crooks from a newspaper clipping, resolves to right the wrong. "Money lost through larceny can often be recovered the same way," he murmurs in the best "Boston Blackie" tradition. Some of the romantic leads' dialogue never made it out of the cutting room. In the finished film, Susan is ignorant of Chester's motives and she warily follows his lead, but as originally written Susan clearly sees through Chester, who good-naturedly concedes his larcenous tendencies. They both look upon Laurel & Hardy as helpless dummies:

> *Chester:* Honey, in me you see the great social leveller—I rob the rich to feed the poor.
> *Susan:* Oh! The modern Robin Hood.

> *Chester:* Which reminds me—I wonder how my Merry Men
>   of Sherwood Forest are getting along.
> *Susan:* They're never quite sure of the score, are they?
> *Chester:* Honey—they don't even know what teams are
>   playing.

This demeaning dialogue was removed, along with other Bailey-Blaine exchanges.

Stan and Ollie, having their own involved discussion in the front seat of their car, narrowly avoid a collision with a truck labeled "Dynamite." The "dynamite truck" is actually stock footage from Mal St. Clair's slapstick episode in **Hollywood Cavalcade**. St. Clair remembered that particular piece of film and worked it into **Jitterbugs**.

Chester's objective is New Orleans, but one wonders how Laurel & Hardy's antique car made it from a western desert to the deep South. The script offers an explanation which was filmed but not included in the final print. Laurel & Hardy's band is literally disposed of when they use the phony gasoline pills themselves, and their car blows up. The boys magnanimously donate the wreckage to a bewildered bystander's wartime scrap pile, and ride off with Chester and Susan.

At the Hotel New Orleans, management and guests alike are impressed by the entrance of "Colonel Watterson Bixby of Leaping Frog, Amarillo County, Texas." It's Oliver Hardy with a fifteen-gallon hat and a molasses-thick drawl, pouring on the charm. His imposing entourage attracts two local con artists, Henry Corcoran and Dorcas (well played by vaudeville veteran Robert Emmett Keane and character actress Lee Patrick). They work a badger game by enticing the colonel to the lady's suite, but Stan blunders into the room first. Dorcas, assuming that Stan is the colonel, tries to hold his attention.

Scott Darling has been criticized in print for this scene's scripted dialogue, which has Laurel suavely offering cocktails to Dorcas. Stan seems to turn into a Casanova, with lines like "I will be your cup-bearer, madam," and "Your lips are an intoxication in themselves, madam." Although the dialogue certainly does not fit "Stanley," it *is* appropriate as written, because Stan is pretending to be an English butler who emphatically agrees with everything. One can imagine character actor Arthur Treacher as the butler, reading these lines in a cold, condescending voice. In this context Darling's extravagant prose makes sense. In the film, however, Laurel downplays the Britishisms and recites only one of the scripted lines: "You know, that's a bit of all right."

Someone's at the door, so Stan has to hide under a divan. The Colonel enters, and he and Dorcas coyly cultivate each other. Most of this amusing scene consists of courtly flirtations by Hardy and breathy Southern-belle palpitations by Miss Patrick, with the occasional interruption by Laurel. One of the funniest spots has Hardy attempting to kiss the lady's dainty hand, only to wind up with *Laurel's* hand! As romance carries them away, the husky Hardy whirls the damsel around the floor in a graceful waltz, to the strains of "Lovely Lady."

The script reveals an important detail. It is explained that Chester has coached Ollie to play along with the badger game, and to take every initiative with Dorcas. Ollie follows instructions and forces his attentions on her. But the release print omits the briefing session, so Ollie's sudden transformation into a lady-killer is startling.

When Corcoran intrudes and tries to blackmail the amorous suitor, Hardy stays in character as the Colonel, until he drops the dialect and reveals himself as a county sheriff! In the fracas that follows, Hardy forgets characterization long enough to say "Here, Bob" when he hands a prop to Bob Bailey. Corcoran and Dorcas are locked in a closet, where they presumably languish to this day since the script dismisses them here.

The scene was supposed to end with Chester and Ollie dumping the handcuffed Corcoran onto the divan. Stan would suddenly emerge from beneath the chaise, toppling Corcoran, and leave the scene after removing a coiled spring from his person. The spring-in-the-pants had served only to prevent Stan from moving. Laurel & Hardy hated to waste potentially funny props, so the punchline was changed during filming. Stan tries to run away, but the spring catapults him backwards in a picturesque pratfall.

The next reel is largely devoted to Vivian Blaine. Within ten minutes the singer has two audition scenes. The first song is the best, a simple presentation of "I've Gotta See For Myself." (The song is also used in the main titles.) The second tune, "The Moon Kissed The Mississippi," was intended to be the major musical highlight; the vocalist is supported by six dancers and two chorus boys (and this is just for an *audition*). The number is impressively photographed by Lucien Andriot with good lighting effects.

The man who cheated Susan's mother, Malcolm Bennett (Douglas

Fowley), is trying to mount a nightclub production, and needs someone to invest in the show. Chester gets Stan to pose as Colonel Bixby's childhood sweetheart, the wealthy Bostonian "Emily Cartwright."

The script cuts directly to Stanley having magically mastered the masquerade. Evidently Stan Laurel recognized the gap in the story, so a quick transitional scene was added. Stan, in feminine attire, has no poise and has to be trained by Ollie, who hilariously demonstrates how a lady walks.

Ollie's charm school is a success, because Stan is now fully in character as the society dowager. (He was *too* convincing for his daughter Lois; she recalls walking right past him when she visited the set.) Oliver Hardy is just as comfortable playing the Colonel. The "Colonel Bixby" role gave him a rare opportunity to play a character other than "Stan's friend Ollie," and in Hardy's hands the Colonel is a playfully pretentious rogue who doesn't mind turning a situation to his advantage. This scene makes fascinating viewing, and is an excellent indication of the comedians' skills as character actors. Their straight man here is the underrated Douglas Fowley. Fowley was typecast in gangster roles but often displayed adroit comedy timing (he played the harried movie director in the classic musical **Singin' In The Rain**). When Hardy keeps interrupting Fowley's business proposal, Fowley laughs jovially as he excuses himself from the table—and then rudely shoves Hardy out of earshot! Laurel, exchanging pleasantries with Fowley, giggles, "I feel so gay!" This improvised reference to cross-dressing slipped past the censors in 1943 but gets startled laughs in more enlightened times.

Laurel & Hardy recover the money for Susan, and give it to Chester, who walks off with it. The executive mobster, Tony Queen (Noel Madison), wants revenge when he discovers he's been had. Noel Madison was a familiar face in gangster epics of the 1930s like **Little Caesar** and **G-Men**. By 1943 Madison was working mostly for PRC, the lowest of the low-budget studios. He was about to retire but, having worked with Laurel & Hardy before, he accepted the role in **Jitterbugs**. It was his last film appearance.

One of Madison's henchmen is played by James Bush, who played underworld hirelings in three Laurel & Hardy movies at Fox. Evidently Bush just happened to be around for the shooting, because the tiny role only called for five words of dialogue and anybody could have played it.

Another member of the mob is Tony Caruso, then at the beginning of a busy career playing tough-guy roles in such films as **Hell On Frisco Bay** and **The Asphalt Jungle**. He appeared in the background of only two scenes with Laurel & Hardy but recalls the experience affectionately. "I met the gentlemen, and they were absolute gentlemen. They were two beautiful, beautiful men, and very soft-spoken. Very nicely spoken, and they'd get on the set and be as zany as you see them in movies. **Jitterbugs** was almost one of their last pictures. I don't know whether the boys had that much to say about it or not, except I'm sure in the gags that they did, they controlled every bit of that. [Mal St. Clair] let the boys go, as far as I can remember. He would lay out the situation and say 'all right, what do you think?' and they'd walk through it."

During the riverboat-nightclub scene, Caruso tells one of his cronies (Chick Collins) to fire up the boilers. "Aunt Emily" and "Colonel Bixby" are being held prisoners, and Stan has the bright idea of releasing a hanging weight onto their captor's head. The scheme works too well, as the weight releases the ship's entire supply of coal on top of Ollie.

While Ollie shovels his way out of the coal, Vivian Blaine sings "If The Shoe Fits, Wear It." (The studio's 78-rpm reference disc is labeled "If The Shoe Fits You, Wear It.") It starts as a torch song but turns into a paean to shoe rationing! The song (which only has *four* chorus members this time) dates horribly and sadly disrupts the film.

Stan and Ollie use their "gasoline pills" to incapacitate the crooks, and the mob gives chase. The burly bouncer is Cy Slocum, who resembles Oliver Hardy—and he should, because he often doubled for Hardy in films.

Hiding from the mob, the boys, still dressed as "Emily" and the "Colonel," take to the dance floor and wreck the place with their acrobatic gyrations. The scene is similar to one of Laurel & Hardy's silent-era routines from **Sugar Daddies** (1927), and was almost certainly suggested by the team, since it is not in the script. The band music has been identified by researcher Richard Finegan as a Gene Rose composition, "Just Jive."

The showboat accidentally breaks loose from its moorings and rushes out to sea. As the frenzied guests run riot on deck, Stan and Ollie invade the ship's pilothouse and try to steer the craft themselves. Deleted scenes involved Stan trying to ring a bell hanging above Ollie's head; naturally the bell falls *on* Ollie's head, knocking him out momentarily and leaving Stan to take the ship's wheel—which breaks. Ollie revives and helps his partner foul up the navigation. The only footage retained in this speedy sequence is a few seconds of Ollie clumsily catching the end of Stan's skirt on the wheel. Some of the runaway-boat shots are taken from Fox's 1938 film **Sally, Irene, And Mary**, thus furnishing a convenient climax without straining the budget.

The harbor patrol arrives, with long-lost Chester in tow. Susan is furious with him for having taken the money and run, but Chester innocently explains how he returned the money to her mother. Susan embraces Chester, and shoos Laurel & Hardy away when they try to confront him. The lovers exit, oblivious to Stan and Ollie, and once again the boys have the screen to themselves.

Defiantly Stan removes his "Emily" wig and dashes it to the ground—just in time for the gangsters to spot the boys and chase them over the rail. (The film doesn't explain why the police didn't apprehend the crooks, but the script has the gang boss, inflated by gas pills, floating toward the horizon!) After a mighty splash, the film fades out with Stan and Ollie trying to keep their heads above water.

Many Laurel & Hardy buffs regard this film as the team's finest hour of the forties. In terms of overall production quality, **Jitterbugs** is indeed the best of Laurel & Hardy's 1940s output. It has a host of amusing incidents and diversions, despite the excessively talky script and occasionally confusing continuity. Under Sol Wurtzel's orders to bring the film in under an hour and a quarter, film editor Norman Colbert ruthlessly jammed everything into 74 minutes, occasionally chopping off dialogue in mid-sentence to keep things moving. (At a projection-room tradeshow screening, a viewer noticed that "the transition from scene to scene is often abrupt.") Norman Colbert later became quite adept at trimming overlong comedy films; in the 1950s he had the mammoth task of cutting the raw footage of Groucho Marx's *You Bet Your Life* TV series, compressing the loose, rambling conversations into twenty-four-minute episodes.

Both Vivian Blaine and Tony Caruso recalled making **Jitterbugs** on a "B" schedule. Caruso notes that the timetables for "the big features ran sixteen, eighteen weeks. The 'B' pictures that they used to make were twenty-eight days." The ambitious **Jitterbugs** was allowed five weeks, more time than usual for a Sol Wurtzel production. While technically a "B" picture due to Wurtzel's participation, **Jitterbugs** was sold as a "nervous A," right on the borderline between an "A" and a "B."

It could be played theatrically either way. (**Jitterbugs** premiered on Broadway as a single-feature "A.")

Most exhibitors were expecting a companion feature for double bills, and were pleasantly surprised by the superior quality of the merchandise. Reports from the nation's theaters were unanimous. Oklahoma: "The best picture from this pair in quite some time. Business good." Missouri: "I played this Friday and Saturday on a double bill but my patrons would have supported this one on a single-bill program; they like Laurel & Hardy. Business was extra good." Kansas: "One of their best in a long time, and had my patrons laughing all through the picture. It is just right for the weekend double and makes a swell program that draws the farm trade." Ohio: "Well liked by all. Did extra business for a Tuesday night." South Dakota: "My patrons say they are tired of these two, yet we had the biggest Sunday, Monday, Tuesday in months . . . This is tops for these stars. Not a big special, but very entertaining." The War Department even cited **Jitterbugs** when it played at a California army base: "For a slaphappy comedy, this one was well received. At least it got the [soldier] boys' minds off the war."

Curiously, the trade critics hadn't expected anything out of the ordinary. *The Exhibitor* briefly summed up **Jitterbugs** as a "Laurel and Hardy entry for the duallers [double-feature houses]. This should please the Laurel and Hardy fans. Story is fair, and the comedy situations are amusing." Bosley Crowther of the *New York Times* was indifferent, judging it "neither the worst nor the best of the boys' films. Why do they call it **Jitterbugs**?"

The Motion Picture Herald was more expansive: "A welcome change of pace is offered in the latest Laurel and Hardy comedy with the interpolation of several musical and dance numbers before the joke is carried too far. These, and the attractive Vivian Blaine, should extend the appeal of the film beyond the strictly L & H fans to all who enjoy lightweight, amiable film fare."

In preparing the advertising posters and accessories for the studio's films, Fox's graphic-arts department liked to employ realistic artwork of the stars instead of photographs. The one-sheet poster for **Jitterbugs** is an exceptionally dazzling display, with full-figure portraits of Laurel & Hardy in colorful zoot suits, and a prominent photograph of Vivian Blaine (who was not yet well known enough to be recognizable in caricature).

Jitterbugs was offered to exhibitors as part of a package with two "A" features, **The Ox-Bow Incident** with Henry Fonda and **Coney Island** with Betty Grable. The "important" films were heavily promoted in the trade press; **Jitterbugs** was ignored.

The on-screen advertising was equally sparse; the **Jitterbugs** coming-attractions trailer runs only 105 feet, or seventy seconds. Like M-G-M's **Air Raid Wardens** trailer, it opens with a pompous fanfare and a ceremonious, dignified preface, only to reveal Laurel & Hardy. A title card imperatively commands, "Please keep your seats for an important announcement." The announcer turns out to be Oliver Hardy in his zoot suit, yelling "Come on, hep cats, we're gonna spread a load of jam!" The trailer's soundtrack consists of narration, speedily spoken in verse, and pleasant orchestrations of the film's music. The quick visuals hint at the feature's funny business: Ollie kicking Stan in the pants, Aunt Emily walking in an unladylike manner, and the boys cutting up on the dance floor. Featured player Vivian Blaine is allowed one close-up and eight bars of singing. Billing is reserved for Stan Laurel, Oliver Hardy, and Vivian Blaine; the other cast members (including romantic lead Bob Bailey) are not mentioned.

Laurel & Hardy's later films did not receive worldwide distribution during the war years. There were no special versions available for the continental market until after the war, when Fox's foreign office, Fox-Europa, prepared new dubbed soundtracks.

One of the Fox-Europa releases has recently come to light: the French version of **Jitterbugs**, printed on 16mm film in 1947 for nontheatrical use. The film differs radically from its American counterpart. There are no alternate takes or additional scenes, but 27 minutes of footage have been removed, yielding a skillfully edited 47-minute featurette. This five-reel length was a concession to the 16mm market, where films were often screened in classroom or social situations inside of one hour.

The major casualty of the French **Jitterbugs** is the opening "desert" scene, which is the only section devoted exclusively to Laurel & Hardy. It's a shame, since the team's pantomime would have played well in another country. This new version fades in on Hardy at the carnival, about to launch into a rendition of "That's A-Plenty." Another major comedy scene, the dance-floor melee near the end, is also missing.

Only one of Vivian Blaine's three songs survives: "The Moon Kissed

The Mississippi," which remains in English and is not dubbed. "If The Shoe Fits, Wear It" would have been meaningless if retained for French audiences, dealing as it does with America's rationing policies.

The dialogue is dubbed very well, and recited by a troupe of French actors. The Laurel & Hardy roles are essayed by French-speaking Americans, which lends the spoken word a charming native twang. Frank O'Neil has the bulk of the dialogue and his vocal mannerisms as Hardy are amusing.

Some of the American dialogue had translation problems even in Britain! The original ads for **Jitterbugs** read, "Wait till you hear Stan and Ollie's gut-bucket band!" This slangy reference to Dixieland music totally escaped Fox's British promoters, who changed the ad copy to "Stan and Ollie's lilting, swinging jive band."

The Dancing Masters

Released November 19, 1943 by 20th Century-Fox. Produced by Lee Marcus. Directed by Mal St. Clair. Screenplay by W. Scott Darling; suggested by a story by George Bricker. Photographed by Norbert Brodine. Edited by Norman Colbert. Running time: 63 minutes.

Cast: Stan Laurel and Oliver Hardy (themselves); Trudy Marshall (Trudy Harlan); Robert [Bob] Bailey (Grant Lawrence); Matt Briggs (Wentworth Harlan); Margaret Dumont (Louise Harlan); Allan Lane (George Worthing); Emory Parnell (Mr. Featherstone); Bob [Robert] Mitchum (Mickey Halligan); George Lloyd (Jasper); Nestor Paiva (mob leader); Robert Emmett Keane (auctioneer); Charles Rogers (butler); Harry Tyler (accident victim); Hallam Cooley (auction barker); Edward Earle (airport clerk); Hank Mann (fruit vendor); Daphne Pollard (matron); Chick Collins (anxious bus passenger); Sam Ash (pianist); Sherry Hall (dentist); Charlie Jordan (patient); Alyce Ardell (extra in dance studio).

The Dancing Masters marked a distinct change in the way 20th Century-Fox handled Laurel & Hardy. In the summer of 1943 Fox was establishing a new policy: nothing but "A" product would be produced. The studio expected to spend $41,000,000 on the coming year's slate of features. Intent on promoting these big, new shows, studio spokesmen were loath to admit that "B" pictures (read: Laurel & Hardy movies) were still being made. **The Dancing Masters**, film number three on Fox's 1943–44 schedule, was quietly erased from the list. Only the expensive projects were itemized on the revised list, with no mention of Laurel & Hardy at all.

Fox's new arrangement had its disadvantages—notably a certain loss of prestige for Laurel & Hardy. Less attention was being paid to the team. Even producer Sol Wurtzel busied himself elsewhere while this picture was made. Sadly, the lack of care shows in the finished product. It was slapped together from existing components: leftover sets, contract players, stock gags. When it was released in November, 1943, **The Dancing Masters** emerged as a definite "B" picture.

The comics had made economical films before, but even these had commanded premium rentals and preferred showtimes. Prior to 1943, a Laurel & Hardy film was usually seen as a prime attraction, either by itself or as the top half of a double feature. Now, the nation's theater managers reserved the lower berth for Laurel & Hardy, as the companion to a more pretentious "A" picture.

There was a bigger market for comedy than ever, and Laurel & Hardy were in demand. As **The Dancing Masters** was being filmed, Fox had **Jitterbugs** in circulation and M-G-M was booking **Air Raid Wardens** into neighborhood houses, while RKO shrewdly reissued **The Flying Deuces** and United Artists offered the "streamliner" version of **A Chump At Oxford**. So Laurel & Hardy's new second-feature status was not due to any loss of popularity.

It was the running time of **The Dancing Masters**, a scant 63 minutes, that relegated it to twin bills. Six reels was simply too short to pass off as a major feature. The film originally ran longer, but several sequences were cut before release. **The Dancing Masters** was an embarrassing violation of Fox's new "all-A" policy, which is why it was trimmed. In six reels, it wouldn't be mistaken for one of 20th Century-Fox's new, standardized pictures. (Fox tried to rectify matters with Laurel & Hardy's next movie, by padding the length to seven reels. This did carry the bill in many situations, but it wasn't enough to reverse the second-feature trend.)

The ultimate indignity attendant to Laurel & Hardy's "B" status was the way they were listed in the credits. Their names were no longer accorded the respect of star billing, or even "featured" promotion. For the first time in the team's history, the title of the picture was more important than the comedians themselves. The awful truth may be seen in the final print: "Twentieth Century-Fox presents **The Dancing Mas-**

ters. *With* Stan Laurel—Oliver Hardy." Since the crucial word "and" does not link their names, they aren't even billed as a team.

But there were some advantages. The studio noted the success of **Jitterbugs,** and the comparative harmony of that film's stars, director, and writer. The unit ran smoothly, so Fox kept it intact for the duration of the comedians' contract. The studio executives left the old-timers to make their little slapstick comedies while they concentrated on the making and selling of more ambitious productions.

The filming of **The Dancing Masters** was an informal affair. Laurel & Hardy found supporting roles for new acquaintances and old cronies, and they even had one of their Hal Roach cameramen, Norbert Brodine, assigned to the picture. The atmosphere was more congenial, which made the comedy a bit less strained.

Author Scott Darling was faced with a challenge. **Jitterbugs** had been a rewrite, with the source material already prepared. Now the scenarist had to expand a story by George Bricker into a full-length screenplay, which required more new material. Darling's shooting script offered some original sketches, but too often fell back on familiar routines from older films. As with **Jitterbugs**, Darling introduced various characters and complications, and didn't always resolve them. Laurel & Hardy had to stick to the script, such as it was, but Mal St. Clair allowed them to embellish certain scenes with spontaneous gags.

The producer this time out was Lee Marcus. A former production executive with RKO, he left after his last film, an intended comeback for Gloria Swanson, failed at the box office. Marcus had been associated with RKO's comedy teams, Wheeler & Woolsey and Clark & McCullough, and had worked with limited budgets, so he seemed to be a good match for the Laurel & Hardy unit. For **The Dancing Masters** Marcus cut corners everywhere, using standing sets and cheap special effects to keep the budget down. Marcus appears not to have been a disciplinarian; the finished film wanders aimlessly from one sequence to another, a possible result of Marcus's way of working.

Director Mal St. Clair is equally responsible for the movie's patchwork structure. His technique harks back to the era of silent shorts, and he paces each sequence like a separate one-reel comedy. In **The Dancing Masters**, the first reel takes place in a dancing school, the second in a mansion, the third in a society bedroom (with the boys under the beds), the fourth at a weapons demonstration and an auction, the fifth on a city sidewalk and a construction site, and the sixth on a runaway bus. Small wonder that in 1966 a home-movie distributor was able to slice the feature into four separate comedy shorts.

For the record, the casual composition of St. Clair's work applies not only to his Laurel & Hardy assignments but to his other full-length efforts as well. His 1943 comedy **Two Weeks To Live** is assembled exactly like **The Dancing Masters**: a variety of short sketches, strung together very loosely.

The plot of Laurel & Hardy's previous film may have been sometimes incoherent, but the plot of their new film is often invisible. Although not as sturdy as **Jitterbugs, The Dancing Masters** is a relaxing hour of nonsense with plenty of funny business—and for fans, Laurel & Hardy are in practically every scene.

The Dancing Masters fades in on an exterior of The "Arthur Hurry" School of Dancing. The quotation marks are on the sign, calling attention to the mild pun on dancing teacher Arthur Murray. (This establishing shot was added after the scene had been filmed; a close look at the office interior shows that the frosted glass on the door reads "Laurel & Hardy School of Dancing.") The advanced classes are conducted by Professor Hardy, sumptuously attired in a satin suit with pom-poms, ruffles, and tassels. Ollie prances gaily with a bevy of chorus girls, and he is as light on his feet as ever. Perhaps Hardy's accomplished dance scene with Lee Patrick in **Jitterbugs** prompted writer Scott Darling to try some more terpsichore.

Dissolve to the beginners' classes, under the tender care of Professor Laurel. The concept alone gets a laugh from audiences before they even see the professor. An airy flute and harp selection accompanies the dainty dancing of a prima ballerina. Of course, it turns out to be Stan, tiptoeing around in a ballet gown with a garland of flowers around his head. Laurel is literally floating on air—because he's obviously on wires and being bounced along like a puppet. "Isn't he light?" twitters an impressed observer. "In the head!" mutters a disgruntled matron. The lady is none other than Daphne Pollard, a diminutive Australian comedienne who had co-starred in several of Laurel & Hardy's vintage comedies. Another face in the dance-studio crowd belongs to the equally petite Alyce Ardell, one of Stan Laurel's longtime friends.

The dance-studio reel looks very choppy, with lots of gags and attempted gags, but the elimination of nonessential footage makes it move very briskly. When Laurel leads his students in a series of exercises, he raises his right leg horizontally and plants his foot against a wall. Unfortunately he can't lower his leg because it's stuck. Glue from some unnamed source has found its way onto the classroom floor. This looks like a remnant from one of the film's deleted scenes, which used the glue as a prop. To cover the gap in continuity, a quick insert was filmed of a bucket of glue being upset by an anonymous workman.

Hardy is summoned to rescue his pal (he is interrupted in the middle of an amusingly fluid hula lesson), and when he yanks Laurel away from the wall, it collapses. We see a quick flash of the people on the other side of the wall—a dentist and his aggrieved patient—but the scene suddenly ends as Hardy dismisses the students for the day. A dissolve whisks us to something else while Hardy is talking to his partner. This whole sequence had extra footage, in which L & H encountered their outraged neighbors from the dentist's office (Sherry Hall and Charlie Jordan). Another casualty of the cutting room was Arthur Space, who portrayed the director of the dance academy. He would have appeared near the beginning of the film, when a receptionist is speaking on the telephone. In the final version the picture cuts away from the receptionist and jumps directly to Hardy's dance class. As if to compensate for Space's footage being discarded, he was given a leading role in Laurel & Hardy's next feature.

Stan and Ollie's star pupil (and only paying customer) is played by Trudy Marshall, who was prominently featured in a number of 20th Century-Fox features. "I was one of the top photographic models in New York," she explains. "*Look* Magazine used to take different people to different places and run big stories. They decided they wanted two models, who had to be 'real American-looking.' I was chosen, and they took us to Hollywood."

Miss Marshall was offered a stock contract at a salary of $75 per week, which she declined because her modeling work paid three times as much. Fox matched her modeling salary and promoted her as one of its "Five Stars Of Tomorrow," together with Mary Anderson, Jeanne Crain, June Haver, and Gale Robbins. Trudy's grooming for stardom came to an abrupt end when "I had the audacity to get married. Gale Robbins eloped with someone, got married before I did, and they dropped her *immediately.* They put Vivian Blaine in her place, that's how Vivian got in."

Trudy Marshall took the ingenue role of "Mary Harlan" in **The Dancing Masters**, but Laurel & Hardy knew her as "Trudy" so they addressed her by her real name throughout the picture. She is quite prominent in **The Dancing Masters**; her other films may have been more noteworthy but this one gave her more to do.

Trudy visits the dance studio to make a tuition payment, which Ollie decides to keep in the office safe. The combination—two turns to the left—fails to work for Mr. Hardy, but it's simplicity itself for Mr. Laurel. He takes hold of the safe and physically moves it "two turns" counterclockwise, exposing the safe's contents. Hardy is singularly unimpressed.

The shady offices of the Acme Importing Company are occupied by the firm's shady ringleader, unnamed in the final print but called "Silvio" in the pressbook (master dialectician Nestor Paiva), and his shady hirelings Mickey and Jasper (Bob Mitchum and George Lloyd). Robert Mitchum had just started in pictures, and was then playing small parts in modest features and westerns. His unbilled surprise appearance in **The Dancing Masters** is one of the film's highlights.

The racketeers, who used to sell "protection," are now posing as insurance agents. They intimidate customers into paying heavy premiums for lucrative policies. Their first two prospects are—who else? While the smooth Mitchum discusses the benefits schedule with Hardy, the gravel-voiced Lloyd subjects Laurel to a physical examination (using a ballpeen hammer!). Laurel is declared "a poifect specimen" and Hardy forks over the cash. The con men leave the office, only to be arrested on the spot. That's the last we see of them, as the film speeds off to other events.

Trudy's beau, Grant Lawrence (Bob Bailey, now billed as Robert Bailey), works in her father's munitions plant as a research scientist. His current project is an invisible heat ray that will revolutionize jungle warfare by burning anything it touches. He can't develop his invention without financial backing, which he is unlikely to get from Trudy's wealthy father (Matt Briggs). Father favors Grant's rival, the sneaky George Worthing (Allan Lane, more familiar to horse-opera fans as Allan "Rocky" Lane in Red Ryder westerns, and incidentally the voice of TV's talking horse Mister Ed). Lane plays his villainous role with cool finesse, but he does display a flair for comedy with an exaggerated leap when a blowtorch hits him.

Trudy secretly invites Grant to dinner and asks Stan and Ollie to join the party. Mr. Harlan expressly forbids liquor in the house, so ginger ale is served. The gag has a good setup, as Stan absently aims the bottle point-blank at Ollie. The expected explosion is delayed by Ollie's imperious "Give it to me, *I'll* open it." The comic anticipation hits its peak when Ollie opens the bottle—and nothing happens. "Simple!" notes Hardy pedantically—and *then* the bottle sprays him with foam!

Lounging in the master's study, Stan and Ollie take in the imposing shelves of books and the inviting panel of electrical controls. A rather weak joke in 1943 which referred to a thirty-year-old event (and thus totally falls flat today) had Stan reading the book title, "Boswell's Life of Johnson," and Ollie commenting, "Yeah, I remember the day Jess Willard knocked him out." The gag is supposed to underscore the boys' lack of literary knowledge, but it's just another dumb thing the script forces them to say. The book must have been interesting reading on the set, because it changes positions three times during this sequence.

Ollie, continuing to sample the switches, accidentally reveals a fully stocked bar hidden behind the bookshelves. Stan notices that the wall keeps changing, but Ollie thinks his pal is hallucinating. This trumped-up scene, which plays more like an Abbott & Costello routine, showcases the set more than the comedians. The "hidden bar" was left over from Fox's omnibus feature **Tales Of Manhattan**, filmed the previous year. Mal St. Clair and Buster Keaton had collaborated on a comedy sequence starring W. C. Fields and Margaret Dumont (Dumont made a screen career out of playing ultra-dignified dowagers, often opposite the Marx Brothers). The scene had Fields delivering a variation of his famous "Temperance Lecture" at a society mansion. When the party guests got soused on alcohol-fortified "cocoanut milk," an elaborate bar was revealed. Because the scene ran to almost a full reel, overburdening the lengthy feature, it was completely removed from the final print. (The out-take, recently preserved, turned out to be disappointingly mild, but it still might have lightened the downbeat feature.)

Laurel & Hardy buff Kay Lhota recognized the true origin of the **Dancing Masters** scene: "Perhaps director Mal St. Clair remembered the 'hidden bar' set and figured that, since the general public would never know, why not incorporate it into **Dancing Masters**?" With all the unrelated scenes in the script, Mal St. Clair found a place for the "hidden bar." In fact, St. Clair hired Margaret Dumont to repeat her dowager role, which she essays as "Mrs. Harlan" with fruity hauteur.

A light supper is served, and Trudy offers plates of food to Stan and Ollie. Without a word the boys take the dishes in hand, only to exchange them, pass them back to Trudy, mix them up, entrust one to Trudy while attending to the other, hand their *hats* to Trudy, mix them up, retrieve them, and so on.

Trudy Marshall has fond memories of this scene. While under contract to Fox she generally played statuesque beauties with little inclination toward humor. "In Betty Grable's movies I was always the debutante and she was always the showgirl," she chuckles. Trudy had no experience in physical comedy but had ambitions toward light, sophisticated farce. "I was slated to be an Irene Dunne double, more or less, at Fox," she explains. When she was assigned to work with Laurel & Hardy, "we were sitting talking one day and they said, 'What do you really want to do—what kind of film?' And I said, 'Comedy.' They looked at one another, and they thought I meant *their* comedy, which was marvelous but I meant the Irene Dunne type. Stan said to Ollie, 'Shall we?' and Ollie said, 'Okay.' So they let me do some of the scenes that you see in the movie—going out and having the door hitting Ollie or the ironing board hitting Stan, and I don't think any other girl has ever done any of those with them. They always did their own routines, and would never have anyone else in them." Laurel & Hardy expertly carry out the busy pantomime, and Trudy keeps up with them.

Stan breaks into another bottle of ginger ale with the expected results, and now the victim is Grant, whose trousers are drenched. He stands around in his underwear while waiting for the garment to dry, just as Mr. and Mrs. Harlan return unexpectedly. Bob Bailey gets chuckles with his nervous attempts to conduct a casual conversation, under Harlan's steady glare, while concealing his exposed legs. The jig is up when Mrs. Harlan beholds the underdressed man from the rear. "I got my pants wet," he says sheepishly as Mrs. Harlan registers a horrified take.

Meanwhile Laurel & Hardy are hiding upstairs in the master bedroom, where they are trapped while the Harlans retire for the evening. This sets up another Abbott & Costello-esque situation, as the Harlans blame each other for the random noises Stan and Ollie are making under the beds. The tone shifts to slapstick as the boys attempt to escape unnoticed. Dangling from the bedroom window, Hardy hangs onto the carpet while Laurel hangs onto Hardy. The suspense and laughs build easily to a good payoff—a moving bed catapulting the hapless Harlan into a lily pond. The scene is admirably shot in dim light by Norbert Brodine, and very well scored by composer Arthur Lange.

To this point the film has maintained reasonable continuity, but now it degenerates into random episodes. A brief scene at the boys' apartment has Laurel & Hardy ad-libbing a little fight, with Hardy settling the argument by sticking a feather duster into Laurel's face (as an off-stage crew member laughs aloud). The boys exchange some scripted dialogue with blustery landlord Emory Parnell, in a role perhaps intended for Edgar Kennedy, and then they start improvising again as Laurel invents a tale of woe about an unclaimed bank account.

Having withdrawn their nest egg from the bank, they are enticed into the parlor of an auctioneer (Robert Emmett Keane, making his third consecutive featured appearance with Laurel & Hardy at Fox). Stan and Ollie are asked to keep the bidding going for an anxious audience member. Naturally the boys bid astronomically and get stuck for the bill. This is a rehash of Laurel & Hardy's 1935 short **Thicker Than Water**, with a new coda: they engage the cashier in another "swapping" routine, this time juggling a wad of cash, a receipt, and a hideous piece of statuary. Stan and Ollie didn't get to keep the statue—it was borrowed by Monogram Pictures a few months later. The unique prop became the focal point of Monogram's "Charlie Chan" mystery **The Chinese Cat** (1944).

The auction scene stops very abruptly after Laurel & Hardy's purchase, a grandfather clock, is demolished by a truck. Hardy surveys the wreckage in pantomime and beckons to Laurel, who frowns apprehensively. Hardy signals more insistently. End of scene! As originally conceived, the boys had a run-in with the bellicose truck driver (William Haade), but this was another episode that was thrown out at the last minute.

In the boys' apartment, their demonstration of Grant's super-powered vacuum cleaner ends in disaster. This is followed immediately by a demonstration of Grant's super-powered ray gun, which also ends in disaster. Upon reflection, practically every scene in the second half of the film ends in disaster.

The ray-gun scene has Stan masquerading behind a brush mustache as the foreign scientist, Professor Fendash Gorp. As the professor speaks no English, Mr. Hardy acts as interpreter for Mr. Harlan's benefit, using an impressive, exotic double-talk. It's a funny, vaudevillian sketch, if a little out of character for the comedians. Harlan's imperturbable butler is Charlie Rogers, one of Laurel & Hardy's closest colleagues, who helped write or direct their vintage Hal Roach comedies. At one point Rogers addresses his master as "Mr. Harlem"—perhaps in reference to Hardy's home town of Harlem, Georgia!

With the ray gun in ruins, Stan and Ollie explore other avenues of fundraising. When Hardy recalls that he is the beneficiary of Laurel's insurance policy (remember the first reel?), he tries to get Laurel injured in order to collect a windfall. Fruit vendor Hank Mann, one of the original Keystone Cops, sells bananas for five cents a pound. Hardy wants a pound—and Mann hands him *one* banana. We are then treated to variations of the ancient "banana peel" gag, as it victimizes Hardy and then a cop. (It's the world's fastest police booking: Hardy is fined fifteen dollars before Laurel can finish one bite of banana.)

Next stop is a construction site, which is a likely place for an accident. Hardy climbs a scaffold to release some bricks onto his partner, but the scheme ends—that's right—in disaster. One of the famous L & H gags involves the sudden collapse of a brick structure; as Hardy sits in the rubble, stray bricks belatedly fall on his head. The humor comes from not knowing when the "surprise" bricks will come out of the sky. Mal St. Clair, recycling the bit for **The Dancing Masters**, staged it effectively, but Fox ruined it in post-production. A slide-whistle sound was dubbed in when each brick was *about* to fall—tipping off the joke and totally killing the surprise element. The gag isn't improved by the fake bricks actually *bouncing* after impact!

The romantic leads haven't been heard from for awhile (which is unusual in Laurel & Hardy's later films), but suddenly Trudy informs Grant that her father has discovered George Worthing's true colors, and that he is going to finance Grant's invention after all. They rush off to tell Stan and Ollie, who are still desperately seeking funds.

Ollie learns that an accident victim stood up on a rollercoaster and received a tidy insurance settlement. That's good enough for Ollie, who boards a beach-bound, double-decker bus with Stan. The boys seat themselves on the upper deck while a dog gets into some whipped cream on the lower deck and barks urgently.

"Mad dog!" yells the crowd, and everybody bails out. This scene is more than a little contrived: the bus is jammed with people, yet Laurel &

Hardy have the top seats to themselves; moreover, nobody stops the bus or even slows down while the passengers leap recklessly from the exits.

Realization slowly dawns that Stan and Ollie are alone on the bus as the empty vehicle careens through the streets. Hardy becomes trapped when his foot is caught, so Laurel has to take the driver's seat. ("You wait here," Stan ad-libs.) Stan divides his energies between trying to operate the vehicle and reporting back to Ollie for further instructions! One of Hardy's suggestions is to throw out the gear—which Laurel takes literally. This bit had originally appeared in one of the team's earliest talkies, **Perfect Day** (1929).

The bus conveniently drops Laurel off at an amusement park, where he staggers into a shooting-gallery concession. His head becomes the target for a playful contestant who throws rubber balls with unerring accuracy. Meanwhile, back on the bus, Ollie can't understand why Stan isn't responding to his cries for help. The bus rolls onto a rollercoaster and, predictably, the scene ends in disaster.

The runaway-bus climax boasts of very convincing process photography—you actually believe that Hardy is climbing a rollercoaster—but the scene is another victim of post-production sabotage. The sequence was augmented with inserts of a very obvious toy bus scooting across a model rollercoaster. The close shots of Hardy are great, but the spliced-in "long shots" of the bus are horrible. This miniature is one "special effect" which is neither special nor effective, and the scene would have played much better without it. It was probably Mal St. Clair's idea; the same device was employed in St. Clair's 1943 comedy **Two Weeks To Live**, which intercuts a rocket flight with shots of a toy spaceship.

Hardy's wild bus ride, accompanied by a rendition of Wagner's "Ride of the Valkyries," ends as the bus runs off the rails and into oblivion. The picture dissolves to a fireworks display, and then to a hospital room, where Laurel is visiting Hardy. After this brief echo of Laurel & Hardy's 1932 short **County Hospital**, the film fades out.

This was Bob Bailey's second and last appearance in a Laurel & Hardy movie. He had carried the mature "straight" lead in **Jitterbugs**, only to be handed a smaller, less showy juvenile role as a follow-up. Bailey had good reason to disdain juvenile leads: his boyish looks belied the fact that he was in his early thirties at the time. (Bailey was born in 1913, not 1898 as one L & H reference book has claimed.) "Robert" Bailey hung on for another year at Fox, appearing in five moderately important features: **Tampico, Eve Of St. Mark, Ladies In Washington, A Wing And A Prayer**, and **Sunday Dinner For A Soldier.** His parts in these were minor and undistinguished, and when leading roles eluded him "Robert Bailey" returned to radio. He starred or was featured in dramatic series and serials, and remained a fixture on the airwaves into the 1960s. His best-known broadcasting work was in the detective program *Yours Truly, Johnny Dollar,* "starring Bob Bailey" in the title role of a humorously cynical insurance investigator. Bailey took over the part from another Hollywood actor of the forties, John Lund, and became the most durable of the series's leads, performing the role 484 times between 1955 and 1960. Trudy Marshall remembers Bob Bailey as "a very serious young man, and he came from the east. He had a wonderful voice—he acted more like a radio actor."

The Dancing Masters may have been a mixed bag, but critics gave it a thumbs-up response. *The Exhibitor* predicted that it "should please the Laurel and Hardy perennials," despite its "weak plot and story." "The story is as old as the industry," chimed in Jack Cartwright in *The Motion Picture Herald.* "While the best of the gag lines couldn't be termed new, they'll undoubtedly go over well with followers of the team . . . Mal St. Clair directed for every ounce of characteristic comedy possible." Cartwright's magazine was one of the tougher trade periodicals which often gave "fair" or "average" reviews to program pictures; this film got a "good" rating. Theodore Strauss of the *New York Times* noted that Laurel & Hardy were again "trying to prove that time does not wither nor custom stale the effectiveness of an old joke . . . The only gag overlooked was the tossed custard pie. But if their stock is well worn, the boys still manage to sell it for an occasional laugh."

The coming-attractions preview for **The Dancing Masters** offered a fast-paced collage of highlights (as well as "lowlights"). The trailer was narrated by the jocular Ralph Edwards, a popular broadcaster who played a part in Laurel & Hardy's careers a decade later. Edwards endorsed the film as excellent "family entertainment."

The Dancing Masters did nicely at the box office and played comfortably in double-feature theaters, occasionally as the main event but usually as the co-feature. Laurel & Hardy continued to bring in the customers: "They always draw, and this was a good one," confirmed an Ohio exhibitor. "One of their best, lots of laughs, business good," reported a theater owner from Nova Scotia. A college-town showman, who booked Laurel & Hardy movies regularly, offered a comparison: "This is not as good as **Jitterbugs** from the audience standpoint. If they are not too particular, they'll sit through it. We coupled it with Warner's **Northern Pursuit** to excellent Friday and Saturday business. I hope Laurel and Hardy make more pictures, but not like this one." A fellow who booked the film on the strength of its title was justifiably confused when the print arrived, since Laurel & Hardy appeared as dancing masters for only a few minutes.

The Dancing Masters remains one of the better wartime Laurel & Hardys, no small accomplishment considering the age of some of the material. Yet the picture's flimsy construction embarrassed Stan Laurel, who was becoming aware that Fox was more interested in the progress of Laurel & Hardy's co-stars than in the stars themselves. Laurel was probably surprised that the completed film was missing an entire reel of footage, and the subtle omission of the team from Fox's publicized 1943–44 schedule may well have been another sore point. Laurel never complained to his bosses about it, but privately he considered **The Dancing Masters** the nadir of his 1940s work.

By this time in the forties, more than one reviewer was describing the Laurel & Hardy team as "old." In some quarters the boys were regarded as the last remaining practitioners of the silent-era school of comedy. The lower quality of Laurel & Hardy's later films was indulgently overlooked by moviegoers, who seemed to accept the worn gags and slower pace as being typical of the "old-time" style.

But the "old" stuff was selling, and Fox wanted more of the same, so writer Scott Darling obliged. He was polishing his next screenplay even as **The Dancing Masters** went into release. Producer Lee Marcus resigned his post to accept a position with independent filmmaker Edward Small, so Laurel & Hardy would again be reporting to Sol Wurtzel.

The Studio System

Later generations of Laurel & Hardy admirers have trashed 20th Century-Fox and Metro-Goldwyn-Mayer for refusing to give the comedians more attention. At Hal Roach's small studio, Laurel & Hardy were the whole show, but at the big studios they were part of the sideshow: a little extra attraction alongside the more illustrious stable of stars.

The team might have fared better at a more comedy-oriented company like Universal, Columbia, or RKO, with experienced comedy writers and directors on their busy staffs; in the early 1940s Universal successfully supported *three* comedy teams. Neither 20th Century-Fox nor Metro-Goldwyn-Mayer were dedicated to making funny pictures. This was the direct opposite of the Hal Roach company, which had produced nothing *but* comedy. After fifteen years of working at Roach, Laurel & Hardy would have been challenged by *any* new working atmosphere, but the climate at the comedy-free Fox and M-G-M studios was especially stifling.

Laurel & Hardy were bewildered and frustrated by their new bosses' unwillingness to improve their product. The studios didn't care about the product because, oddly enough, the public didn't care. By the mid-1940s Laurel & Hardy had been screen favorites for so long that audiences warmly greeted them as old friends—and kept buying tickets. For the studios, that meant a dependable source of income.

As was customary with "B" pictures, a Laurel & Hardy film of the forties was rented to theaters for a fixed fee, so its earning potential was relatively limited. It didn't make sense for the studios to spend any extra money on a product that wouldn't bring in any extra money. A Laurel & Hardy picture could be made on 20th Century-Fox's standard "B" budget of $300,000 and earn a considerable profit, so why raise the budget and cut into the profit margin?

Nor did it make sense for Fox's Sol Wurtzel to let the Laurel & Hardy unit work at its own pace when he had other units waiting to use the sets, technicians, and equipment. Trudy Marshall recalls that Wurtzel ran a tight ship: "He was a character. I had three scripts to do in 'B' movies for Wurtzel, and we were going to do one after another. We used to do a scene for the one movie, and they would change the draperies and put the desk in a different place, and shoot the next movie. We did three scripts the same day!"

Another quite probable reason for Fox's resistance to change was Sol Wurtzel's impending retirement. Wurtzel was winding down his activities, and had discontinued all of his feature-film series. The only resident company left in the "B" division was the Laurel & Hardy department. With retirement in sight, Wurtzel may not have wanted to upset production with any experimental policies.

Should Stan and Babe have made their complaints more vocal? Fox already had an object lesson: The Ritz Brothers. In 1939 the Ritzes walked out on the studio, loudly complaining about their latest script. The resulting publicity about Fox's inferior craftsmanship obliged the company to save face. Studio chief Darryl F. Zanuck took personal charge of the Ritz production, adding several important "name" actors to the cast. The film turned out to be a lemon, but it was a handsomely produced lemon. The writing was on the wall for The Ritz Brothers, who vacated the studio for good a few months later.

Laurel & Hardy didn't want to make such a drastic move, although Laurel had done it before. He clashed with Hal Roach over contractual issues in the 1930s, when he was half of Roach's most important property and a key creative contributor. Now, away from Roach, he was a contract actor with less bargaining power. Little would be gained by another well-publicized rift with Hollywood producers.

Things were no better at Metro-Goldwyn-Mayer, where the brass was bigger. The company was top-heavy with executives at every level, and any protest from the lower strata would probably have been bogged down in bureaucracy.

The studios' management technique toward internal problems seems to have been "the squeaky wheel gets the oil." The Laurel & Hardy partnership, always professional, seemed to be a well-oiled, money-making machine—so it was left alone.

Fox didn't have many "low comedians" in its employ. Joan Davis and Milton Berle had left the company; apart from Jack Oakie, who kept busy in "A" musicals, Fox's only comedy stars in 1943 were Stan Laurel, Oliver Hardy, and the cavern-mouthed comedienne Martha Raye. It was only natural that Fox considered various ways to team them.

Raye had been a memorable foil for Abbott & Costello and Olsen & Johnson, and Fox thought she might create similar sparks opposite Laurel & Hardy. But the studio executives didn't realize that the comedians who worked with Martha Raye were just as brash as she was. The antics of the raucous Raye might have clashed with the more deliberate doings of the timid "Stanley" and the courtly "Ollie." On the other hand, Martha Raye was one of the few comediennes who could handle physical comedy as easily as verbal humor, so she could have made her own contributions to a Laurel & Hardy slapstick sequence.

Fox had enough faith in the idea to keep it alive for almost a year. In May of 1943 the studio announced a forthcoming Laurel & Hardy-Martha Raye comedy entitled **By Jupiter**. This was to be an adaptation of a current stage play by Richard Rodgers and Lorenz Hart, a musical-comedy version of the 1932 Broadway production *The Warrior's Husband*, which had starred Katharine Hepburn. Rodgers & Hart's make-over featured the ebullient Benay Venuta in the lead, and a 20th Century-Fox story scout thought Martha Raye could play Venuta's role of Hippolyta, Queen of the Amazons. Raye had been featured in a similar Rodgers & Hart movie musical, **The Boys From Syracuse**.

By Jupiter is set in ancient Greece, where the population is totally dominated by Hippolyta (in the film version, Martha Raye) and her army of female warriors. The male contingent is epitomized by Theseus (Oliver Hardy) and Hercules (would you believe, Stan Laurel), who think this feminine superiority is a deplorable situation. It seems that the queen's power comes from a magic girdle. Theseus and Hercules sneak into the royal residence to steal the vital prize but, predictably, they fail. However, when the women become irresistibly attracted to their male subjects, all's well that ends well.

This period farce was a moderate success on stage, and 20th Century-Fox began planning a film version while the Broadway show was still running. Although the play had no Rodgers & Hart hit tunes, Fox planned to use the show's listenable score in the film.

By Jupiter actually had possibilities as a Laurel & Hardy comedy. The "Stan and Ollie" characters were easily bullied by aggressive women, and their interactions with the formidable Martha Raye had distinct potential for broad humor. The team often fared well in costume comedies, and the plot called for a comic burglary, which was a Laurel & Hardy specialty.

The elegant **By Jupiter** would have been Laurel & Hardy's ticket out of the "B" ranks. Most of Fox's production plans for 1944 came to fruition, but **By Jupiter** was never filmed. The play was still doing business on Broadway, and Fox probably couldn't wait for the show to close before embarking on a movie version. **By Jupiter** was abandoned after three months on the drawing board. (Another idea which Fox put on hold was a musical biography of John Philip Sousa; **Stars And Stripes Forever** gathered dust in the files for nine years.)

Fox and M-G-M found that making Laurel & Hardy pictures was a relatively easy job. Accordingly, they considered writing for Laurel & Hardy to be an entry-level assignment. Don Martin, a former newspaperman and Hollywood publicist, had just joined Fox's writing staff, and was promptly given a Laurel & Hardy project. Judging from the surviving outline, Martin was asked to include a major comedy role for Martha Raye. On January 28, 1944, Martin submitted the outline for a film to be titled **Congratulations**.

Martin evidently screened **Jitterbugs** and was impressed by several elements of its plot (which itself was not originally written with Laurel & Hardy in mind). Martin's outline incorporates the main episodes of **Jitterbugs**: 1) Laurel & Hardy are stranded with their orchestra in a small town; 2) the audience is deceived during their performance; 3) a comical coquette shows amorous interest; 4) one of the comedians has to dress like a woman; 5) criminals intervene and take prisoners; 6) Stan and Ollie spoil a formal function. **Congratulations** tries to be another **Jitterbugs**—it even has a one-word title—but it differs in the details.

Laurel & Hardy head an itinerant vaudeville troupe, including bandleader Tommy Thompson and his girlfriend, Judy. Stan and Ollie overhear an uninspiring political speech by a dull candidate named Ben Watson. Hardy convinces Watson's manager to use the boys' showmanship to attract crowds. (The team's act consists of Stan imitating a singer while Ollie plays a Dick Haymes record backstage!) Stan's performance is so successful that it completely overshadows the candidate.

Bessie "Boss" Topper (the Martha Raye character) is prominent among the local women voters. She falls for the boys' charade and eagerly nominates Laurel for governor.

The "crooked opposition," Michael Meech, sends a girl (named Greta Boop) to Laurel's hotel room to incriminate him. Hardy rescues his pal by impersonating a chambermaid. When Meech arrives to discredit Laurel, he finds the "maid" bouncing Greta on "her" knee.

Ollie forestalls any future embarrassments by having Tommy's girl, Judy, pose as Stan's sweetheart. This only creates more misunderstandings for Tommy, Judy, and Boss Topper.

Meech's mob kidnaps Stan and Judy, and hides them in a haunted house. (Inexplicably, the captives free themselves before Ollie and Tommy can rescue them.)

Laurel & Hardy repeat their record hoax at an important political rally, but are exposed when Meech pulls the plug on the phonograph. The enlightened Boss Topper urges the voters to elect Ben Watson in the name of honest government. Watson pays off the vaudeville troupe, which moves on.

To a Laurel & Hardy fan—and perhaps to movie fans in general—**Congratulations** makes no sense at all. The story poses a number of puzzling questions. First and foremost, why don't Laurel & Hardy behave according to their traditional screen personalities? Martin casts them as hapless hustlers of the Hope & Crosby stripe. Second, a question of logic: if Stan and Ollie's vaudeville unit features an orchestra, complete with a bandleader and an attractive female entertainer, why do they have to resort to faking a Dick Haymes record?

Ollie is the "leader" of the team, so why isn't *he* running for public office (as he did in a 1931 featurette, **Chickens Come Home**)? And why does *Ollie* have to carry out the female impersonation? Every other L & H movie using this gag has Stan doing the masquerade. Where's Ollie when Stan is trapped in the haunted house? Why is there a haunted house in the first place?

Finally, once the plot is resolved with happy endings for the "main" characters, what about Stan and Ollie, who are not even mentioned at the conclusion? Author Martin apparently lost sight of who would be starring in the picture.

The comedy sequences suggested by Martin include a baby-kissing episode, in which a midget smacks Laurel in the nose, and a romantic burlesque with Laurel having to "sing" to Boss Topper. The punchline has Hardy rushing in to explain that his friend has a sore throat.

If these were the comic highlights, it's easy to see why 20th Century-Fox had no cause for **Congratulations**. The outline stayed in the studio files, and further plans to team Laurel & Hardy with Martha Raye were dropped.

Whenever Fox commissioned a Laurel & Hardy project, none of the writers ever came up with anything suitable. Sol Wurtzel handed the team back to Scott Darling; at least Darling knew who Laurel and Hardy were. Darling's scripts may not have been fresh, but they did contain some recognizable comedy and they were better than anything else Fox had handy.

Scott Darling approached his writing assignments in a thorough, methodical manner: he'd brush up on his subject and use his findings in the script. His "Charlie Chan" screenplays of the late 1940s were rewrites of old "Mr. Wong" mysteries, but Darling hit the books, borrowing dialogue from Earl Derr Biggers's original "Chan" stories. At first glance this method would seem inappropriate to the spontaneous Laurel & Hardy style, but Darling was told to write a Laurel & Hardy screenplay, and where inspiration failed, imitation succeeded. As part of his research Darling screened some old L & H comedies and lifted entire scenes for his new script.

One thing can be said for Scott Darling: he knew his priorities. When he wrote (or more accurately, rewrote) for Laurel & Hardy, he kept them front and center. His scripts contained less romantic subplotting and more emphasis on the star comedians. But he seldom gave them anything novel to do, and forced them to re-enact any number of weatherbeaten gags. Critics couldn't help noticing the age of the material, coupled with the comedians' own advancing age. They pointed to the sameness of the proceedings and shrugged their shoulders. Exhibitors didn't mind, however, because the neighborhood moviegoers still came out for Laurel & Hardy.

Thus Scott Darling's next script turned into a hit, in spite of itself. It went before the cameras on March 27, 1944.

The Big Noise

Released October, 1944 by 20th Century-Fox. Produced by Sol M. Wurtzel. Directed by Mal St. Clair. Screenplay by W. Scott Darling (with uncredited additional dialogue by Frank Fenton). Photographed by Joe MacDonald. Edited by Norman Colbert. Running time: 74 minutes.

Cast: Stan Laurel and Oliver Hardy (themselves); Arthur Space (Alva P. Hartley); Esther Howard (Aunt Sophie Manner); Bobby Blake (Junior); Veda Ann Borg (Mayme Charlton); Frank Fenton (Charlton); Robert Dudley (Grandpa Hartley); Philip Van Zandt (Dutchy Glassman); James Bush (Hartman); Doris Merrick (Evelyn); Jack Norton (lush); George Melford (Muggeridge, the butler); Harry Hayden (Digby); Selmer Jackson (Manning); Edgar Dearing (policeman); Francis Ford (railroad agent); Charles Wilson (train conductor); Julie Carter (cab driver); Beal Wong and Louis Arco (officers aboard submarine).

The Big Noise was a landmark film of sorts when first released. In the trade it was noted as the last production of Fox's veteran "B"-keeper, Sol Wurtzel, who selected a Laurel & Hardy project to end his thirty-year career at the studio. The film has since achieved "landmark" status of a different kind: it is regarded by many critics as Laurel & Hardy's worst movie. It even made one list of the "Fifty Worst Films of All Time."

Laurel & Hardy fans who have read such unflattering things about **The Big Noise** have taken the critics at their word—until they actually see the film, and then they are pleasantly surprised and amused. **The Big**

Noise isn't as bad as its detractors have claimed; while it misses as often as it hits, there are enough little touches to satisfy the team's followers. This picture is certainly more worthwhile than **A-Haunting We Will Go**, and it has a higher laugh count than even some of the vintage Hal Roach productions, which relentlessly milk a single situation to the point of tedium. In 1954, when the team's old two-reelers were sweeping the country on television, 20th Century-Fox decided to reissue a representative Laurel & Hardy comedy to theaters—and chose **The Big Noise**.

Even Stan Laurel admitted to a fondness for **The Big Noise**. According to Bob Burns, Stan's friend and frequent visitor in later years, this was the only Fox film Laurel singled out for honorable mention. "They weren't his favorites, and he never said they were glorious films, but he *never* said he hated them," says Burns. "**The Big Noise** he thought was okay, because there were funny routines in there."

The boys reprise no fewer than eight of their familiar routines in **The Big Noise**. There is plenty to please a Laurel & Hardy fan—and for first-time viewers there is plenty to *make* them Laurel & Hardy fans. Production values are decent, the direction by Mal St. Clair is capable, and there are several excellent deep-focus compositions by photographer Joe MacDonald.

The supporting cast is adequate but unexceptional. Arthur Space, who specialized in playing small-town fathers, lawyers, farmers, or bankers, is the pleasantly eccentric inventor Alva P. Hartley; it is the biggest role of this prolific character actor's career and he makes the most of it. Esther Howard is pleasantly fluttery as a society matron. Starlet Doris Merrick, billed immediately below Laurel & Hardy, does not appear until halfway into the picture, and then only briefly; she is decorative but incidental to the plot.

The female lead in the *first* half of the picture is Veda Ann Borg. Whenever a Hollywood film of the forties needed a worldly, wisecracking "broad," the blonde Miss Borg was usually hired. Unlike her featured roles in other comedies, her "gangster's moll" in **The Big Noise** has very little to do. She has no flippant dialogue, and shares no scenes with the stars.

This happened by accident, because she joined the cast after filming had begun. Her role was originally taken by Helene Reynolds, a Brussels-born actress who had played supporting roles for 20th Century-Fox since 1941. Miss Reynolds apparently balked when she was assigned to the new Laurel & Hardy comedy, because she was removed from the cast during shooting. (She made no further films.) The vacancy was hurriedly filled by an experienced "temp"—Veda Ann Borg. All of Miss Borg's scenes were shot consecutively, independently of the Laurel & Hardy sequences.

The production was untitled until filming started, and then it was tagged **Good Neighbors**. After one week it became **The Big Noise**.

Author Scott Darling received an assist from Frank Fenton, a dependable, witty screenwriter who had several collaborations to his credit, including the popular "Saint" and "Falcon" mysteries. Actors were hard to get in 1944, so Fenton played the part of the criminal mastermind himself.

One would very much like the film to be better than it is. The thing holding **The Big Noise** back from greatness (or even goodness, as some might claim) is its labored scenario.

Darling plotted his new script along the lines of **The Dancing Masters**: a collection of old comedy routines with the required minimum of romantic subplot. His derivative script features another struggling inventor determined to aid the war effort. The role may well have been written for Bob Bailey, but Bailey had graduated to bigger pictures. The role went instead to Arthur Space, who had "graduated from a reputation as one of the best bit players in Hollywood," according to Fox publicity.

Scott Darling, having gotten away with inserting old sketches into **The Dancing Masters**, now called attention to his playful plagiarism. He included certain inside references to Laurel & Hardy movies which are unfunny and pointless—it's as if the writer were showing off how much homework he had done. A policeman lecturing a speeding motorist barks, "You out-of-state drivers think you can go *hog wild*," the italicized words being a vintage Laurel & Hardy movie title. Stan Laurel, discussing the finer points of detection, uses the term "habeas corpus" (another old L & H title). Hardy's rather lame comeback ("Habeas Corpus is the name of a town in Texas") is saved by a beautiful look into the camera, as if to ask the moviegoer, "Are you buying any of this?"

The Big Noise holds the record for the number of "camera looks" Oliver Hardy directs to the audience. There are at least twenty of them in the 74-minute feature. What makes them more than usually amusing is that most of them are thrown away. Customarily the camera will dwell on a close-up reaction shot of a disgusted Mr. Hardy. In **The Big Noise**, however, the "camera looks" are not confined to close-ups. Hardy darts conspiratorial glances at the audience in two-shots, and even in ensemble long-shots. Neither the editing nor the direction calls attention to the "camera looks"—Hardy just sneaks them in to punctuate a sentence whenever he feels like it. When Hardy is asked if he enjoyed his dinner of tiny food pills, his vehement and deliberate "I'm stuffed" is immediately followed by an "oh-what-a-liar-I-am" grimace. Hardy's reaction lasts less than one second and is one of the funniest things in the picture.

Hardy had good reason to "insure" his dialogue with pantomime, because Darling had an unfortunate tendency to *explain* his jokes. When inventor Hartley displays a valuable painting by Van Dyck (pronounced "Van Dyke"), Laurel says, "Oh, yeah—my uncle had one. But he had to have it shaved off." Yet the script compels Hardy to explain, "Van Dyck was a painter, not a beard." An earlier scene has Grandpa Hartley (Robert Dudley) recounting a stirring military episode, mixing up the battle of San Juan Hill with the Charge of the Light Brigade. Hartley says, "And your history's bad," as if to clarify why Grandpa's details were garbled.

Suddenly Hartley and Grandpa see a villainous burglar lurking at the window—and merely acknowledge that there are "enemy spies" around! No alarm, no pursuit, no logic. At least it serves to bring detectives into the story (who might investigate why Hartley, consulting the classified phone book for a detective agency, immediately looks under "J").

In any case, the Jones Detective Agency employs two janitors who wear bowler hats and answer telephones in their boss's absence. Hardy, as usual, takes command of the situation and accepts Hartley's lucrative commission. Part of this scene is photographed in a fairly tight two-shot which makes a nice portrait. The years have mellowed the boys and this shot presents them virtually as "living caricatures." Laurel is thin, vacuous, and worried; Hardy is fat, confident, and masterful. In fact, Hardy is heavier than ever, and his chubby cheeks, rounded chin, squinted eyes, and spit-curl hair give "Ollie" more character and visual appeal.

Scott Darling works in another reference to **Habeas Corpus** by including one of its sight gags. Night has fallen (or at least the cameraman tries to convey this illusion), so the boys can't read the street signs. Hardy climbs a tall lamppost, only to find that the sign reads "Wet Paint." The script calls for the actual street names to be painted on the curb, which would be a motorist's nightmare. (In the original version of this gag, filmed in 1928, the street name is where it belongs, at the top of the pole.)

Hartley's obnoxious little nephew (Bobby Blake) misses nothing in the Hartley household. He sees the boys coming and in a few seconds' time manages to rig up a phony doorbell buzzer and a remote loud-speaker system to confuse the boys. Whether Junior is an electronics wizard or just happens to have these devices on hand is not made clear. The only genuinely funny bit in this silly scene is the time-honored "mixed-up hats" routine, where Laurel & Hardy lose their derbies and try to put them back on, only to constantly wind up with the wrong-sized hats. This looks suspiciously like an ad-lib which Laurel & Hardy tacked on after the scripted scene was supposed to be finished, and direc-tor St. Clair kept the camera rolling. Once again Laurel & Hardy tried to sneak a little of "their" business into a weak sequence, and to their credit, they succeeded.

Convenience is a hallmark of the Hartley home—as well as of Scott Darling's script. When Hardy arrives at the inventor's door in disarray from his "Wet Paint" encounter, Hartley's ingenious paint-remover ma-chine just happens to be sitting in the living room. Hartley shows the detectives a variety of offbeat inventions (although one of his futuristic ideas, a "motorized toothbrush," wasn't so impractical after all!). His push-button humidor dispenses cigars from the mouth of a bird statue. (The script called for a live duck to deliver the cigars, but the gag was too troublesome to film.)

Hartley's latest brainstorm is a powerful explosive called "The Big Noise," which is intended to help the nation's war effort. Laurel & Hardy are to remain at the house and guard the bomb closely.

Stan and Ollie's room has all the comforts of home—but is totally empty. Hartley proudly pushes a series of buttons, and various bed and bath furnishings emerge from the walls and floor. Needless to say, the boys fail to master the control panel at bedtime, and the machines go haywire. Hardy's bed retreats into the wall while Laurel pushes every button but the correct one to rescue him. The *agitato* music by Emil Newman and the fast cutting by Norman Colbert do not completely disguise the fact that there isn't that much comedy content here. These scenes must have had science-fiction overtones for 1944 audiences, and they get high marks for set construction if not for gag construction. The "automated" set was actually operated manually by nine stagehands.

A full-course turkey dinner is served, and the butler ceremoniously unveils the entrées—which instead of being appetizing poultry and steaming vegetables, turn out to be little concentrated capsules. It's a good "flash" gag, amusing for the moment, but the script extends it beyond its worth. Each menu item is served individually, so the "capsule" gag is essentially being repeated over and over. Even the musical background, a bouncy rendition of "You're My Little Pin-Up Girl," keeps repeating. Laurel & Hardy have very little to do beyond looking quizzical, although these reactions are good for a few chuckles. A neat improvisation has Laurel about to tuck his napkin under his chin when he observes Hardy fastidiously spreading his serviette over one knee. So Laurel does the right thing: he places his own napkin on Hardy's *other* knee. The punchline, which reads funnier than it plays, has Hardy offering Laurel one final capsule: a bicarbonate.

Hartley's flirtatious sister-in-law, Aunt Sophie (Esther Howard), makes a beeline for Hardy, who oozes gallantry and charm. Sitting cozily beside Oliver (Stanley has been chased away), she displays portraits of her former husbands, who all resemble Hardy. ("And they're all dead," explains Grandpa, lest we miss the point.) This sets up an old Laurel & Hardy sketch from **Oliver The Eighth** (1934), but the scene shifts to something else before we can see it. Apropos of nothing, Aunt Sophie comments that Mr. Hardy looks very much like Romeo—and the picture match-dissolves to Hardy in Shakespearean costume. An elaborate gag, to be sure, but a long way to go for such a small payoff.

After dinner the boys return to their room. An old gag has Hardy carrying the key on a chain attached to his belt. When the door won't open, Laurel takes the key and pushes the door inward, tearing Hardy's pants. Any other comedian would react loudly and abusively toward his partner, but Hardy just stands there, quietly fuming while waiting for Laurel to extricate the key. This is another example of the boys "taking over" with their pantomime when the script would let them.

The boys put their traveling bag on the table and, like magicians, pull out an impossibly long string of objects from the valise. The joke doesn't entirely work because a close shot hides the tabletop (which gives away the "secret" behind the bottomless bag), but it's a good try.

A totally unnecessary scene has the boys accompanying the inventor to a remote location to test the explosive. (Hartley must have an expendable duplicate!) Of course, it's only a matter of time until the comedians bungle the job and set off the bomb. The framing of the shot admirably telegraphs the gag, zooming out from the principals to reveal the detonator box in the right foreground. When the explosion is triggered, the trio is scattered across the landscape. Hardy, with his head encased in the folds of a camera bellows, looks like an enraged rogue elephant.

The next major comedy sequence returns us to the **Oliver The Eighth** sketch, in which the not-so-merry widow walks in her sleep and threatens Hardy with a knife. The sinister mood of this sequence is undermined by the exaggerated musical score (a playful orchestration of "Did You Ever See a Dream Walking?") and by the boys' deadpan reactions. Instead of being unnerved by the weapon-wielding woman, they merely stare at her as she passes. And Grandpa, who has followed the somnambulist during her deadly procession, does nothing to wake her up!

The criminal gang next door plans to rob the Hartley mansion. In a gallant display of patriotism, the ringleader bypasses the valuable new explosive and concentrates instead on the family jewels. Two disgruntled members of the gang decide to steal the bomb on their own. The malcontents are played by James Bush and Philip Van Zandt. Bush played an identical role in **A-Haunting We Will Go**, that of a hoodlum posing as a butler. Van Zandt was also typecast as a thug or henchman in feature films (including **Air Raid Wardens**), but he played a wider range of roles in comedy short subjects, from pompous headwaiters to mad scientists. In **The Big Noise** Van Zandt's character is named "Dutchy," in playful reference to his ancestry. It is a simple gangster role, but he makes it count in his first scene with Laurel & Hardy. The crooks have come for Hartley's bomb. Van Zandt wants information, and holding Stan and Ollie at gunpoint, he orders them to start talking. Stan asks Ollie what he wants to talk about. Ollie amiably asks Stan what *he* wants to talk about. Stan doesn't care, and so on until Van Zandt bursts in with an exasperated roar at precisely the right moment. He gets into the spirit of the scene, relaxing to the point of addressing James Bush by his real name instead of his character name. (The character name is "Hartman"—Scott Darling couldn't think of many surnames besides "Hartley"!)

Stan has concealed the explosive inside his concertina. He outwits the insistent Van Zandt by telling him that the bomb is in the closet. When

Van Zandt and Bush investigate, the boys lock them in. However, this is probably the only instance in motion-picture history where *the closet has a window.* (Logic is not a strong point of this script.) Instead of shooting their way out of the closet, the villains merely go out the window.

The boys decoy the crooks by taking a train to Washington, so Hartley, who has the bomb in his possession, can travel unmolested on his own. It develops that Hartley does not have the explosive—it's riding with Laurel & Hardy on the train.

The scene of the comedians undressing in a cramped upper berth was originally used in **Berth Marks** (1929), and for once the update improved on the original. The scene was filmed over Stan Laurel's objections; he wanted to update the gag by using an airplane setting. But Fox stuck to the script, which at least embellished the old sketch with new complications, including the noisy concertina, irate passengers, and a comic drunk. The "drunk" idea had been used in **Our Relations** (1936), where L & H and a barfly found themselves trapped in a telephone booth. The "suspense" angle should have been explored further, perhaps with shots of the bomb hidden inside the little accordion. As filmed, the concertina gets knocked around the boys' berth, but without any added build-up.

At one point Laurel places a hot-water bottle under his blanket. The presence of this prop in a Laurel & Hardy routine usually means that sooner or later it will accidentally become uncorked, either spraying or soaking somebody. This time the hot-water bottle is in the bed but the "wet" payoff never comes (this was evidently one complication too many!).

Laurel & Hardy spend several minutes getting in each other's way. (Laurel mischievously tries for a gag by poising his foot near Hardy's face, but Hardy reacts before it makes contact!) Observant viewers will notice a seldom-seen part of Stan Laurel's costume: his professional footwear. The heels are missing from Stan's shoes; Laurel removed them to emphasize his character's comic walk.

The upper-berth really *looks* cramped, as shot by Joe MacDonald. The scene is largely played in pantomime, but there is no musical accompaniment (it would have clashed with the railroad sound effects). The long, static take is broken up with old stock shots of trains, cutaways of the crooks in pursuit, and reaction shots of surly passengers who *loudly* demand quiet!

When happy-go-lucky souse Jack Norton intrudes upon the proceedings, the scene brightens considerably. There is barely enough room for Laurel & Hardy in the berth, and now a total stranger is settling in with them. The genial lush even thinks Stan and Ollie are enjoying *his* hospitality. He insists on conversing with the boys, who are trying to sleep, and his constant outbursts are very funny. (Crowded next to Hardy, Norton incredulously asks Laurel, "Is this all one person?") When the train conductor announces the boys' stop, they scramble out of the berth and gather their belongings while trying not to disturb the drunk. The sight of L & H and Norton thrashing around in hurried chaos was too much for the camera crew—one can hear the crew members laughing in the background!

Strangely, at the end of the scene the script drags in a totally unrelated punchline. It comes from another 1929 two-reeler, **Perfect Day**, in which Laurel & Hardy are hailed with endless "good-byes" from friendly neighbors. In **The Big Noise** it is no longer a running gag so the joke, told without build-up, falls flat. Moreover, the "good-byes" are coming from *angry* neighbors, nullifying the comic effect completely. This is another instance of Darling putting his "homework" in the script, regardless of whether it belongs there.

After driving all night, the crooks intercept Stan and Ollie—who escape when a motorcycle cop detains the villains. He is none other than Edgar Dearing, the same cop who rousted the boys in **A-Haunting We Will Go**, and whose motorcycle was demolished many years earlier in the Laurel & Hardy film **Two Tars**. Incidentally, one of the inserts showing the gangsters in their car features an incongruous palm tree in the background. The process shot was chosen with little regard for the topography of the eastern seaboard!

Stan and Ollie, looking for a place to hide, board an airplane sitting peacefully in an open field. Meanwhile, a battery of Army fusiliers prepares to fire upon the plane for target practice. Stan and Ollie take off, and their craft is brought within gunnery range by remote control. The stern young actor playing the commanding officer is miscast; the scene could have used an Edmund-MacDonald-**Great Guns**-sergeant type, gloatingly encouraging his troops to blow the plane out of the sky. Again, the situation reads funnier than it plays, but there is enough hectic airborne confusion to salvage the scene. There is no music until *after* the climax, when Laurel & Hardy bail out to the strains of "The Man on the Flying Trapeze."

Scott Darling still has one final script complication up his sleeve, and from here on the film plays like an animated cartoon! Hardy, parachuting to earth (why are there two parachutes in an unmanned target plane?), produces a pair of binoculars (from heaven-knows-where) and spies a shipboard conference between two heavily accented naval officers while a staccato Oriental theme is heard in the background. Ollie yells up to Stan that an enemy submarine is below them (odd, since they were flying above an open field a moment ago). Stan opens the concertina and drops the bomb. For once Mr. Laurel does something accurately, because the bomb actually hits its target. (In 1944, patriotic theater audiences cheered when Laurel & Hardy scuttled the sub.)

This incredible scene dissolves to the film's improbable closing gag. It is another capricious whim by Scott Darling, thrown in without rhyme or reason, but this one works. The gag itself is a non sequitur: Laurel & Hardy are contentedly sitting on a buoy at sea, with Stan playing "Mairzy Doats" on his concertina as a school of fish dances around them. On paper it must have looked pretty flat and somewhat bizarre, but on screen it plays beautifully, and sends the audience out smiling. It's one of the most charming fade-outs in the Laurel & Hardy canon.

The original ending, filmed but not used, had Arthur Space and Doris Merrick in formal attire, looking on proudly as a civic leader (Ken Christy) thanks Laurel & Hardy for their public service. The camera reveals the boys dressed as Boy Scouts leading Bobby Blake's troop. This scene was removed at the last minute; actor Christy still receives billing in the pressbook. The deletion made the difference in timing the film to Sol Wurtzel's "hour-and-a-quarter" specifications; the 76-minute working print was trimmed to the Wurtzel-approved 74 minutes.

The best thing in **The Big Noise** is its theme music. Composer David Buttolph came up with a delightful variation on Laurel & Hardy's "cuckoo" theme song. "The Sappy Sleuths" might be described as "the theme song with hiccups." The loping, rhythmic tune fits Laurel & Hardy exceedingly well; it complements the main titles and is used as underscoring throughout the movie. It became their new unofficial theme, as it was used very briefly in their next Fox film.

Speaking of main titles, either Stan Laurel or Oliver Hardy (or both) lodged a complaint with the front office regarding their "star" billing, because they're back above the title in **The Big Noise**. Their names are on a separate introductory panel, with the film title itself on the following card. And they're billed as a team again: "Stan Laurel *and* Oliver Hardy." Fox paid extra attention to the main-title footage, and it's an especially handsome job. Three-dimensional lettering dominates a medium-gray background, with endearing artwork of Laurel & Hardy (in deerstalker "detective" costumes) casting long shadows against the credits panel.

Publicity releases for this film stated that Laurel & Hardy, in a gesture reflecting wartime attitudes toward rationing, elected "to reduce destructive scenes to a bare minimum." In 1995 Fox's video packagers reprinted this fictitious item, claiming that the video release of **The Big Noise** "contains no pie-throwing, clothes-ripping or furniture busting"—a dubious endorsement for a slapstick comedy. The blurb also reprinted the fabrication that Laurel & Hardy starred in 177 pictures as a team. (They actually appeared together in 106, and not always as a team.)

One of the pressbook's statistics humorously indicated which half of the partnership had more screen mishaps. According to wardrobe master Clinton Sandeen, Oliver Hardy had gone through six navy blue suits while under contract to Fox, while Stan Laurel was still using the gray flannel suit he was issued in 1941!

In the unfilmed story **Congratulations**, Laurel & Hardy shared the spotlight with popular singer Dick Haymes. Their paths actually crossed during the filming of **The Big Noise** when Haymes, working on an adjacent soundstage, took frequent breaks to visit the comedians. Studio publicity chief Harry Brand reported that Fox eventually retained a special messenger, whose sole duty was to keep escorting Haymes back to his own set.

The original advertising posters featured prominent caricatures of Laurel & Hardy with a sputtering bomb. This artwork was retained for the film's Spanish-language release, titled **La Bomba**.

The Big Noise was filmed in a fast three weeks; the shoot wrapped up on April 18, 1944, but the film was shelved until October. Hollywood's movie-merchandising season began in the fall, when the studios announced their most promising properties to entice the exhibitors. Fox used **The Big Noise** to help kick off its 1944–45 schedule.

Critical reaction was mixed when the film came out, and much of the backlash was aimed at Scott Darling's overripe script. *Variety* sniped,

"Practically every gag the fat boy and his partner use in this melange has been used on the screen before, either done by themselves or others [and] Mal St. Clair is a much better director than his job in this one would have you believe. But even they were hampered by an obviously poor screenplay." *The Exhibitor* graded **The Big Noise** as "routine," but noted that "several of the sequences are funny, and inasmuch as L and H have provided some surprisingly high grosses in the past, the same opportunity is present here. Audience reaction was good." *The Motion Picture Herald* expertly summed up the film's off-and-on belly laughs with a three-word headline: "Explosions and Duds."

The film played to satisfied customers. "This picture can be played on your best dates," advised an Indiana showman to his fellow exhibitors. "It is full of good old slapstick comedy that hits the funnybone. The upper berth scene is a knockout." "Just the stuff for a small town," agreed an Oklahoma exhibitor. "Business was above average in spite of rainy weather and flooded roads." An astute Minnesota theater owner reported that this Laurel & Hardy adventure was "only fair but one scene in an upper berth was worth the price of admission."

With producer Sol Wurtzel's departure, the Fox management had to reorganize its production units. The studio announced that a relatively low total of 27 features would be produced during the year ahead, with an additional twelve "B" pictures being "contemplated." Fox was too busy adapting expensive stage plays and dramatic novels to compete in the field of comedy. In 1944, RKO led the studios in feature-length comedies with seventeen; Universal came in second with nine. Twentieth Century-Fox ranked dead last with *one*: **The Big Noise.**

While Wurtzel's office was vacant, and **The Big Noise** was still on the shelf, Fox had no immediate plans for Laurel & Hardy—so they adjourned to M-G-M.

Nothing But Trouble

Released March, 1945 by Metro-Goldwyn-Mayer. Produced by B. F. (Bennie) Zeidman. Directed by Sam Taylor. Screenplay by Russell Rouse and Ray Golden; additional dialogue by Bradford Ropes and Margaret Gruen (with uncredited additional material by Buster Keaton). Photographed by Charles Salerno, Jr. Edited by Conrad A. Nervig. Running time: 69 minutes.

Cast: Stan Laurel and Oliver Hardy (themselves); David Leland (King Christopher); Mary Boland (Mrs. Elvira Hawkley); Henry O'Neill (Basil Hawkley); Philip Merivale (Prince Saul); John Warburton (Ronetz); Matthew Boulton (Prince Prentiloff); Chester Clute (employment agent in 1944); Garry Owen (employment agent in 1932); Johnny Berkes (informant); Eddie Dunn, Joe Yule, Robert Emmett O'Connor, Robert Emmett Homans (policemen); Connie Gilchrist (Mrs. Flannagan); William Frambes (shipboard interviewer); Paul Porcasi (outraged Swiss restaurateur); Jean DeBriac (outraged French restaurateur); Gino Corrado (party guest Mr. Kittredge).

Immediately after **Air Raid Wardens**, M-G-M prepared another script for Laurel & Hardy. Novice writer Russell Rouse submitted an outline, and veteran comedy writer Ray Golden was assigned to work with Rouse in developing the screenplay. Rouse and Golden remained partners, and went on to collaborate on the classic film-noir drama **D. O. A.** in 1949.

To some Laurel & Hardy enthusiasts, **Nothing But Trouble** has about as many laughs as **D. O. A.** Like **The Big Noise** immediately before it, **Nothing But Trouble** has a terrible reputation among comedy lovers. Some of this reputation, unfortunately, is justified: the story is about a lonely boy king in exile who is targeted by assassins. The script might have had a chance as a straight political-intrigue drama, but it isn't a good framework for Laurel & Hardy gags.

As with **Air Raid Wardens**, this film tries to create a feeling of warmth for the leading players, who are misfits in a hostile world. Unlike their roles in the Fox films, Stan and Ollie aren't stupid, just naive.

One wants to sympathize with poor King Christopher, but it isn't always easy. The film might be more palatable if the juvenile role were entrusted to a more accomplished actor of British manner, like Roddy McDowall, Peter Lawford, or Freddie Bartholomew. However, the role is taken by American-born David Leland, age 13, who instead of being gentle and sensitive seems prissy and delicate. In some scenes Leland is fine; in others he comes off badly. Some of Leland's dialogue had to be re-recorded for technical reasons, and in the dubbed tracks he overdoes the British accent, which may explain the inconsistency of his performance. In fairness to Leland, he does deliver his lines with conviction. (Imagine M-G-M's "Our Gang" youngsters, whiny Bobby Blake or earnest Froggy Laughlin, as King Christopher!)

The supporting cast is otherwise solid. Mary Boland, who had years of experience starring in domestic comedies, makes a good foil for Laurel & Hardy as a socially ambitious matron who stops at nothing to impress her guests. Henry O'Neill, who had appeared as a spy ringleader in **Air Raid Wardens**, is the lady's beleaguered husband. Philip Merivale and John Warburton are effective as the king's evil guardian and his accomplice. The large cast includes familiar faces down to the bit roles: hilarious Paul Porcasi as an excitable Alpine innkeeper, stuffy Matthew Boulton as a befuddled potentate, mousy Chester Clute as a harassed clerk.

Nothing But Trouble was hardly the most important release of the year, but the studio still gave it the trademark M-G-M gloss. From the opening frames, it is obvious that this is a Metro-Goldwyn-Mayer production. Dozens of extras are on hand to dress the scenes. The hotel and ballroom sets are so large that the dialogue echoes (again, some of it had to be redubbed). The set decorations and props are scrupulously crisp and clean; the pipes under a kitchen sink are glistening. There's a scene

set in a charity mission, where even the dining hall and its humble in-
habitants are tidy. Such a refined, almost sterile atmosphere would be a
good place to turn Laurel & Hardy loose, but at M-G-M civility had to
be maintained at all costs.

The feature gets off to a good start as Stan and Ollie, trying to find
jobs as chef and butler in Depression-ravaged 1932, are trampled by the
masses at the local employment agency. After Stan suggests looking for
work in some other countries, we hear some very funny tirades from
apoplectic continentals. Laurel & Hardy return to America in 1944, and
the manpower shortage has caused another crush at the employment
agency, this time of people *offering* jobs. One desperate applicant wants
to hire a waitress, "that Keaton girl." (This is an obvious reference to
Buster Keaton, then employed as a gagman at M-G-M. Keaton contributed to the **Nothing But Trouble** script during its development.) Stan
and Ollie arrive just in time to be rushed again by the greedy crowd.

They are drawn away from the mob by Mrs. Elvira Hawkley (Mary
Boland), whose predatory glances unsettle the boys. She eagerly loads
them into her automobile and speeds off. "I know you're going to enjoy
every minute of it," she hungrily promises. "The last man I had stayed
for several years." Stan and Ollie look worried. "He'll tell you I was
most accommodating!" she boasts. Stan starts to get out of the moving
car!

At this point the "straight" plot intervenes. Young King Christopher
is bored with signing government documents and attending to affairs
of state. He would much rather learn to play football. Christopher has
embraced the democratic ways of America, but his treacherous uncle
Prince Saul is the heir apparent, and wants to accede to the throne. "Our
good people of Orlandia are not ready to rule themselves," says the
prince. He and his accomplice, Ronetz, plot to do away with Christopher.

"Orlandia" is a vaguely European country, even though its citizens
all have distinct British accents. To make sure that no actual foreign
power was slighted, M-G-M's technical advisor Felix Bernhardt created
a fictitious coat-of-arms and regalia for Orlandia, using elements from
various countries' flags, emblems, and uniforms.

After this dramatic scene, the story reluctantly shifts back to Laurel &
Hardy as though they were merely comedy relief. Mr. Hardy is piling
an ominously large stack of dishes onto Mr. Laurel's hands. Mr. Laurel

leaves the room as Mrs. Hawkley starts prattling about the dinner menu. Off-screen crash. The lady continues unabashed, until she hears another crash. Each time Mrs. Hawkley resumes, there's a more violent crash. Mary Boland and Oliver Hardy, two masters of mugging, wince apprehensively at each disturbance.

King Christopher, wearing a formal suit and hat, goes out to meet the people, and joins a playground football game in progress. He is grudgingly allowed to play, despite his effete manner. (He rubs "common clay" on his face tenderly.) When the referee has to leave and the game is abruptly called off, Christopher looks like a hurt dog. Stan and Ollie are returning from a shopping trip, and Christopher pleads with them to referee the game. The boys oblige, and spend the next few minutes trying to stay out of the way of the hyperactive kids. This scene resembles one of M-G-M's "Our Gang" comedies, and was probably staged by assistant director Herbert Glazer, who had directed nine "Gang" reels.

Mrs. Hawkley is giving a dinner party for the Orlandian regents, but Stan and Ollie have forgotten to procure a steak for the main course. Passing through a neighborhood zoo (?), they see an exceptionally tempting sirloin in a lion's cage. (This drooling shot must have sent ravenous, rationing moviegoers into a panic.) The steak is horsemeat but the boys don't know that. They try various means to grab the steak, including hypnosis and female-feline impersonation, but the lion is triumphant. That is, until Christopher, who now tags along with the boys and calls himself "Chris," makes off with the steak himself.

Chris, wanting to stay with his new friends, tells them that he can't go home, because he is often starved and beaten. As Prince Saul arrives for dinner, Stan and Ollie agree to conceal Chris from their employers. The boys offer Chris an exotic food that he has never seen: a salami.

The Hawkleys' dinner party reaches low for laughs, but does furnish some amusement. Butler Stan enters the dining room and screams the name of each entree at the top of his voice. He struggles with his partner's precise instructions to serve the "Mock Turtle Soup a la Hardy," placing dishes on the table and shuffling them around to their "proper" positions. When the perplexed diners finally get a chance to sample the soup, they immediately wish they hadn't. Tasting the cook's creation, Mrs. Hawkley tells her guest that "Oliver is a . . ." (pause, grimace, face falls) ". . . genius." The entire scene is based on gastric disturbance: the guests are trying to conceal their distress while Chris, hiding nearby, is suffering from too much salami. Through it all, Laurel & Hardy go about their duties utterly deadpan.

Bringing out the specialty of the house, "Steak a la Oliver," the chef strenuously attempts to carve it (even tearing it apart with his bare hands), while the dazed host and hostess strenuously attempt to make small talk. The dinner is ruined, the Hawkleys are disgraced, and the boys are discharged.

At the local all-night mission, the boys are deflated by their dismissal. Ollie ponders his beloved chef's hat and muses, "I guess I'll never wear that again." Chris tries to cheer him up, but Ollie will have none of it: "We're failures." Stan agrees, "Yeah, we're just no good, that's all." This is one M-G-M "low point" that is a *new* low for Laurel & Hardy. "Stan and Ollie" always had their dignity, but never in the team's history were the characters robbed of their self-respect.

Chris is recognized from a news photo and restored to his guardian. Stan and Ollie show up at the king's hotel headquarters, expecting to see someone else, when they see King Christopher greeting important dignitaries. Chris is overjoyed to see the boys, and vice versa—until Prince Saul informs Stan and Ollie that their young friend is royalty. Ollie is shocked and Stan is stunned, and they meekly depart. "We know how it is," says Stan bravely, fighting back tears. "He's a king and we're . . . we're just nobody." One self-pitying scene is bad enough, but this is the only M-G-M comedy with *two* low points, as Laurel & Hardy are totally humiliated.

Things brighten, however, when Prince Saul asks them to serve tea at a reception for the king. Their professional standing restored, Laurel & Hardy happily go to work.

A toxic capsule is planted among the appetizers, and Prince Saul confidently expects Laurel & Hardy to poison the king. Thanks to still another variation of Laurel & Hardy's "mixed-up hats" routine (this time involving salad plates), the scheme is foiled. Because this is a stately M-G-M movie, everybody at the luncheon eats *quietly*, and the great hall is oddly silent—except for party guest Mrs. Hawkley, who obliviously chatters away.

In a last-ditch murder attempt, Prince Saul forces Christopher out on a high window ledge with Stan and Ollie. Chris manages to escape safely, but the boys aren't so lucky, losing their balance and dangling precariously in midair above the city traffic. This climactic sequence is exceptionally well photographed by Charles Salerno, with convincing process shots indicating dangerous height. There's one especially harrowing shot of Stan and Ollie taken from overhead, looking straight down! A subtle but effective touch is a wind machine adding to the realism of the scene. It's so realistic that all we hear on the soundtrack are Stan's terrified shrieks; the climax could have benefited even more from a musical setting. The authorities arrive, our heroes are saved, and Chris is freed from his uncle's clutches.

Sam Taylor was yet another director from bygone days who was given a Laurel & Hardy picture to keep him occupied. Taylor had worked with Harold Lloyd in the 1920s and knew how to stage the climactic thrill sequence. The effective windup of **Nothing But Trouble** allowed Taylor to retire on a reasonably high note.

Compared to the speedy **Big Noise** schedule, the **Nothing But Trouble** shoot proceeded much more calmly. Throughout the six weeks of production the picture was known as **The Home Front**, a wartime expression which was a close cousin to the successful **Air Raid Wardens** title. Filming concluded in August, 1944, but the completed feature was shelved for several months.

At the time, the motion-picture industry was faced with a severe shortage of film stock. Vaults all over Hollywood were bursting with completed pictures that couldn't be released until the laboratories could furnish prints. Eleven studios and 189 films were affected.

Many of the accumulated pictures were war stories. With the end of the global conflict in sight, the producers gave priority to films with a short shelf life. The military-themed movies were unloaded first, to recoup their costs while they could, as less topical entertainments sat on the shelf. By the time M-G-M was ready to release its new Laurel & Hardy comedy, the film needed a new title. The "home front" expression had become dated, so the more neutral **Nothing But Trouble** was coined in its place.

Nothing But Trouble was ultimately shipped out in March, 1945, when the venerable team of Laurel & Hardy was practically an institution. The tone of each review heralding a new L & H comedy was simply "they're back again." In the *New York Times* review, titled "Very Old Acquaintances," Bosley Crowther referred to Laurel & Hardy as "those two old-time slapstick cut-ups . . . mostly engaged in dropping things, including themselves, out of windows and generally gumming the works. If you go for that sort of clumsy clowning, you may find some pleasure in this one. Mary Boland plays the rich dame very broadly and the boys are their own inimitable selves." *The Exhibitor* looked upon the film as more of the same: "A typical Laurel and Hardy entry, this will slide into the duallers, and their fans will probably get laughs out of it. Production, etc., are up to the usual standard."

Variety, however, was more accurate: "Latest Laurel and Hardy comedy is geared for mild returns on duals in most situations. Story, contrasting employment void in '32 with big demand for help in '44, seems to have something, but after the introductory reels it gets lost in the shuffle . . . Laurel and Hardy project their stock tricks throughout, managing to garner laughs here and there but not as socko as some of their previous stanzas."

Nothing But Trouble, like most Hollywood films at that time, was packaged with other movies and sold in a set. It was the seventh film in a block of seven (the number-one selection was **The Thin Man Goes Home**).

As the public anxiously waited for the war to end, the tense political climate weighed heavily on people's minds. M–G–M reminded trade buyers, "Laughs sell seats! Never was the American public so in need of relaxing comedy! Sell the laughs! It's their most riotous film and a natural for live-wire promotion."

Exhibitors who took the bait were generally pleased, since moviegoers were so eager to laugh. "Typical Laurel & Hardy," said a Missouri moviehouse man. A Georgia showman "played this on a double bill. This could have played alone for one day here as my crowd enjoys this pair immensely." In Minnesota, an entrepreneur advised his brethren, "If your crowd likes this pair you have a natural. It has several amusing spots and closes with a bang. For the present it is a natural—an escapist picture."

But for some of the team's loyal followers, **Nothing But Trouble** was a discernible step down. "Not so good," reported an exhibitor from California. "This was off the beam. Even the children noticed the difference."

According to his daughter Lois, Stan Laurel was concerned with the way the current Laurel & Hardy films were being merchandised. "He thought at that time that they were just aiming at the kid market, rather than family entertainment. He mentioned, 'They only think we're good enough for the kids.' Always a Saturday matinee for kids."

During the filming of **Nothing But Trouble**, M-G-M's publicity department prepared a list of the company's thirty-three star performers under contract. Abbott & Costello, like Laurel & Hardy, made only occasional films for M-G-M, but A & C were on the star list. Laurel & Hardy, once the studio's leading laughmakers, were not mentioned, nor were they asked to make additional features for the studio.

There was one unintentional joke on the advertising posters for Laurel & Hardy's final M-G-M film. In 1944 and '45, all the M-G-M features were being promoted with the studio's name immediately before the title. Thus there were "M-G-M's **Kismet**," "M-G-M's **National Velvet**," and "M-G-M's **Dragon Seed**." In the case of this below-par Laurel & Hardy comedy, it seems like an editorial comment: "M-G-M's **Nothing But Trouble**."

The Bullfighters

Released May, 1945 by 20th Century-Fox. Executive producer (uncredited): Bryan Foy. Associate producer: William Girard. Directed by Mal St. Clair and (uncredited) Stan Laurel. Screenplay by W. Scott Darling (with uncredited additional material by Stan Laurel). Photographed by Norbert Brodine. Edited by Stanley Rabjohn. Running time: 61 minutes.

Cast: Stan Laurel and Oliver Hardy (themselves); Richard Lane (Hot-Shot Coleman); Ralph Sanford (Richard K. Muldoon); Diosa Costello (Conchita); Irving Gump (Gump); Edward Gargan (conventioneer, unidentified in the film but listed as "Mr. Vasso" in the pressbook); Rafael Storm (desk clerk); Jay Novello (headwaiter Luis); Carol Andrews (Larceny Nell); Emmett Vogan (prosecutor); Gus Glassmire (judge); Max Wagner (farmer); Margo Woode (Señorita Tangerine); Hank Worden (Mr. McCoy); Ralph Platz (Pancho); Frank McCown/Rory Calhoun (matador in café, unidentified in the film but listed as "El Brilliante" in the pressbook); Cyril Ring (masked café patron); Lorraine De Wood (one of Don Sebastian's admirers).

Back at 20th Century-Fox, in the late fall of 1944, Laurel & Hardy found that the "B" unit was in limbo after Sol Wurtzel's departure. Someone had to make the few low-budget films still on the schedule. The studio hired Bryan Foy to temporarily fill the void. No one knew more about "B" pictures than Foy, who made dozens of efficient programmers for Warner Brothers, Columbia, and Fox. "Brynie" Foy worked fast and cheap: one of his first new endeavors, a movie version of the radio show *Take It Or Leave It*, was an especially flagrant quickie padded out with old film clips.

A former vaudevillian, Foy was partial to comedians and gave Laurel & Hardy more creative freedom than they had formerly enjoyed at Fox. The team's nominal producer was William Girard, a staff producer since 1943 who monitored a handful of "B" mysteries and dramas, including a pair of Scott Darling screenplays. Girard was responsible for the picture staying on schedule, but the executive decisions were actually made by Bryan Foy.

The Bullfighters is the only L & H Fox in which the team has center stage, with no romantic leads in sight. This is a "Laurel & Hardy picture" instead of "a movie with Laurel & Hardy." **The Bullfighters** ranks with **Air Raid Wardens** as the closest the 1940s films came to being "traditional" Laurel & Hardy comedies.

Unfortunately, by this time the Laurel & Hardy unit was such a low priority that the studio actually used it as a *threat!* Helene Reynolds bowed out of her contract after Fox assigned her to **The Big Noise**. When Joan Bennett was reluctant to appear in Fox's production of **Nob Hill**, the studio gave her a choice: she would have to do either **Nob Hill** or a Laurel & Hardy picture. She opted for **Nob Hill**, but told film historian Steve Randisi that she wished she'd appeared with Laurel & Hardy instead.

The Bullfighters was a "throwaway" movie, not because Laurel & Hardy's contract was running out, as some authors have stated, but because Fox's "B" unit was closing down at the end of the year. The company's plans to produce a dozen new "B" pictures were suddenly dropped, and the studio's current commitments were hastily fulfilled. Laurel & Hardy's contract called for ten features over five years, but Fox called a halt to things with film number six, after just three-and-a-half years.

The care that was lavished on the comedians' first Fox film is absent from their last Fox film. Gone is the large company of established stock players; this time the only strong support is furnished by Richard Lane and Edward Gargan. Nor is there much script support; the "original screenplay" by Scott Darling is little more than a virtual textbook of familiar Laurel & Hardy routines. The movie's grade-B running time is just over an hour. Even the main titles were done in a hurry: instead of the usual artwork of Laurel & Hardy on the credit panels, now it's merely a simple line drawing of a bull. However, the casual production works in the film's favor, because the stars are left to their own considerable devices much of the time.

Another reason for Fox's easygoing attitude was the approaching holiday season of 1944. The **Bullfighters** crew began filming just after Thanksgiving and finished just before Christmas. The Fox bosses, preparing for the holidays and reshuffling production plans, were too busy to closely supervise Laurel & Hardy's last "B" movie, so Mal St. Clair's gang took advantage of the relaxed rules and had a good time.

At last there is an "official" connection with "Boston Blackie." Smooth-talking character actor Richard Lane was familiar to moviegoers as "Inspector Farraday" in the "Blackie" mysteries. In a 1978 interview with Jim Neibaur, Lane recalled that his good friend Mal St. Clair hired him for **The Bullfighters**. Lane, who went into the project expecting the sullen atmosphere of **A-Haunting We Will Go**, was pleasantly surprised by the new conditions. Laurel & Hardy were now offering suggestions to make the scenes funnier, there were a lot of on-the-set jokes, and it was a very happy assignment for Lane. He reported to the set even when he wasn't needed, and watched the fun from the sidelines. Dick Lane got along so well with Laurel & Hardy that they worked him into one of their "mixed-up hats" routines. The comedians went out of their way to give special opportunities to Lane and three other members of the supporting cast, finding places for "their" scenes.

Diosa Costello, of the musical stage, recalls that "**Bullfighters** had already been in production two weeks before I even was in the picture!" Brynie Foy ran into her while she was visiting friends at the studio, and offered her a specialty role on the spot. "And I wound up being the only female, practically, in the movie."

The burly Ralph Sanford was hired to play the villain, Muldoon. Sanford was a big fan of Laurel & Hardy's work and was thrilled to appear with them, according to Dick Lane. Sanford was also pleased to have a major supporting role instead of the smaller character parts he usually played. Sanford's participation seems to be more of a friendly gesture than an inspired bit of casting, because he just isn't colorful enough to carry the role. A more menacing presence, like Sheldon Leonard or Mike Mazurki, would have lent the role both chills and chuckles. (One only wishes Leonard or Mazurki could have delivered the foreboding line, "First the little one . . . then the big one!") Even comic adversary Ed Gargan, who is the foil in the "fountain" scene, would have been more acceptable as Muldoon.

Now that the imposing Sol Wurtzel was gone, Stan Laurel regained some of his former on-the-set authority during shooting. "As you see in the movie," comments Diosa Costello, "the big guy is the tough one and the other one is meek. In person it was just the opposite. The big guy sits in a little corner, he doesn't say a word, he waits for a cue. *Laurel* is the boss. He's the genius, the one that does the whole thing. Wonderful people."

Dick Lane confirmed that two slapstick set-pieces, one involving eggs and the other a hotel fountain, were contributed by Stan Laurel, and that *Laurel directed both scenes himself.* He staged the actors' movements and camera placements while Mal St. Clair stood back. St. Clair got along famously with his stars and encouraged their participation. Laurel offered suggestions and was permitted to work them out; Hardy also made observations which Laurel enthusiastically endorsed. This was the most creative challenge Laurel & Hardy had experienced in years, and on screen they're enjoying every minute of it.

A choice moment occurs in the hotel-lobby scene. After Dick Lane warns them about his vengeful friend Muldoon (quoting "first the little one . . . then the big one . . . I'll skin them both alive"), he gleefully chortles "Good day, gentlemen" as he departs. The boys pause to digest this, and the worried Hardy invites Laurel to sit down. Laurel absently sits down *immediately*—on Hardy! Hardy, not expecting the ad-lib, rumbles "Over—*here!*" as he roughly jostles Laurel into place. Then he tops the laugh with his familiar catch-phrase, "Well, here's another nice mess you've gotten me into!" This is the old-time Laurel & Hardy, all right, and it's good to see them in form.

The boys' renewed enthusiasm is obvious and they indulge in their specialty—pantomime—far more than usual in their later films. The opening scene has Laurel & Hardy trying to hail a taxi, only to have a mob crowd them into the cab, leaving Laurel sprawled out on the road and Hardy wearing the door. St. Clair tries a variation of the "bottomless valise" gag from **The Big Noise**: this time a cab pulls up, the door opens, and a dozen people pile out. Again, the joke is only mildly successful because the staging doesn't entirely conceal the trick.

At the Hotel El Matador, the boys approach the registration desk. This is a familiar setting from the L & H comedies of yore, and we may expect some time-honored bit of business. In this case it's a reprise of a gag from **Way Out West** (1937): Ollie whispers a juicy morsel of confidential information to the man behind the counter—which Stan didn't hear so Ollie finds himself reciting the news all over again. At this point viewers conversant with the L & H canon realize that they're in for a comfortable hour of déjà vu.

The boys are sitting quietly beside the lobby fountain while conventioneer Ed Gargan, attired in formal wear, rehearses a speech. Laurel notices a faucet and turns it on, causing a spray of water to hit Hardy. Hardy assumes Gargan is the culprit and sprays *him*. (Hardy waits for Gargan to acknowledge the insult before he nods defiantly.) Gargan retaliates by splashing him back with more water, adding a Hardyesque nod of his own before resuming his reading. Hardy, needing something that will hold additional water, soaks a handkerchief and plops it on Gargan's head. Gargan strikes back with an even larger water receptacle. The battle escalates in true Laurel & Hardy fashion, with both sides taking turns piling on the ammunition, saying nothing all the while. At last the hotel desk clerk intervenes, only to be greeted with a few gallons of water. The scene ends with Laurel explaining how the whole thing started—and Hardy getting drenched all over again.

The boys are obliged to change clothes after this soggy episode, so for most of the film their traditional raiment is reversed: Laurel is now wearing a dark pinstripe while Hardy is sporting a light gray coat with an abbreviated necktie. Their hairstyles are different, too, with Laurel's unkempt hair plastered down and touched up with dye, and Hardy's spit-curl bangs combed back out of sight. The comedians' new look is neat and novel, but doesn't completely disguise their ages.

Sports promoter Richard K. Muldoon (Ralph Sanford) and his publicity man Hot-Shot Coleman (Richard Lane) are sponsoring a bullfight featuring the premier Spanish matador Don Sebastian. (Not exactly an original thought by the screenwriter: Eddie Cantor's famous comedy **The Kid From Spain** had the star impersonating "Don Sebastian the bullfighter." The Cantor film was playing theaters in reissue at the time, so one wonders whether Scott Darling spent a night at the movies doing "research.") Anyway, *this* "Don Sebastian" bears a striking resemblance to a little guy with a derby who has a fat friend with a derby. Muldoon grimly explains that twelve years ago Laurel & Hardy, private detectives, testified against him in court, and he was sentenced to hard labor. After five years the guilty party confessed and Muldoon was released, but thanks to Laurel & Hardy his life was ruined, and he had to flee to Mexico. He swears that if he ever sees them again, he'll skin them alive.

Laurel & Hardy have changed their clothes just in time for another messy slapstick episode, this one being the egg bit from **Hollywood Party** (1934). In the original performance of this scene, Laurel & Hardy are rudely attacked by the temperamental Lupe Velez, and they respond by using the armament at hand, a bowl of eggs. The new version pits Laurel & Hardy against blonde starlet Carol Andrews as "Larceny Nell," a fugitive the boys have been trying to capture and arrest. This scene was left to Stan Laurel to supervise, so St. Clair simply lets the cameras roll. Laurel & Hardy run through the routine with clockwork precision, and Miss Andrews plays by the rules of battle: she does the give-and-take in pantomime, and tops it off with a decisive nod. Unfortunately, the jokes were tampered with in post-production. Every time one of the protagonists gets splattered with eggs, the soundtrack bursts into "clucking" sound effects or random musical phrases like "Yankee Doodle" and "Dixie"!

The two scenes Stan Laurel personally contributed were basically the same in structure. It is unusual to find two separate Laurel & Hardy "battle scenes" in the same movie, and it is unprecedented to find them within fifteen minutes of each other. Why would Laurel submit a second scene so similar to the first? Probably to accommodate Carol Andrews, who was worked into the action. There aren't many L & H routines which involve a woman as a key player, and evidently when Carol Andrews was assigned to share a scene with Laurel & Hardy, Stan Laurel had to come up with some simple business "for three." Hence the old Lupe Velez bit. Miss Andrews was only allowed the one scene because that's the last we see of her: the boys' hunt for "Larceny Nell" is never mentioned again.

When it becomes apparent that the famous matador's arrival will be delayed by passport problems, Hot-Shot prevails upon Mr. Laurel to impersonate him for publicity purposes. The boys fear the worst and refuse. This scene was only sketchily written so the three actors start improvising; Dick Lane's oily patter contrasts nicely with Laurel & Hardy's agitated reactions. Hot-Shot reaches for the telephone and asks for Muldoon. Laurel covers the phone with his hands just before Hardy hangs up the receiver—on Laurel's hands! A few moments later the gag is repeated with Laurel hanging up the receiver on his *own* hand. Hot-Shot finally convinces them that Stan will not have to fight any bulls, and the deal is clinched.

Hot-Shot shows off "Don Sebastian" at a nightclub, where Stan ineptly tries to cope with taking theatrical bows and posing for flash pictures. When Muldoon shows up, Hardy snatches an adjacent merrymaker's party mask and conceals himself. Muldoon can't get over how strongly the matador resembles Mr. Laurel, and refers to Laurel's friend as "a human hippopotamus." Hardy's face is totally obscured but he still conveys a worried reaction for the camera! This is an example of Oliver Hardy's technique which made an impression on co-star Dick Lane: "Hardy never stopped acting." He stayed in character on-camera even when he wasn't the center of attention. Lane noticed that whenever "Ollie" looked at "Muldoon" there was genuine fear in his eyes.

The floor show begins, featuring a song specialty in Spanish, "Bim Bam Bum." Diosa Costello plays the fiery entertainer Conchita. Señorita Costello's dance scene, by her own admission, was "too hot." She says, "In my dancing, they were there checking to see how I moved: 'Don't do this bump! Don't shake this way!' " As presented in the final cut, the torrid dance movements are interrupted at crucial moments by cutaways of Ralph Sanford and Stan Laurel. The reaction shots are redundant and serve no purpose other than "reducing the temperature." When Señorita Costello shows a series of dance steps to Ralph Sanford, an entire sequence is missing—she demonstrates four dances but only three survived the cutting room.

Meanwhile Ollie is hiding from Muldoon in a telephone booth, and keeps trying to call Stan without success. This is a variation of a gag in Laurel & Hardy's **Blotto** (1930). When Muldoon heads for the booth himself, Hardy gets flustered and tries to find his way out of the small enclosure. The booth tips over onto Muldoon, permitting Hot-Shot to spirit the boys away.

The next day Muldoon and Conchita review this year's selection of fierce bulls. "No, no," says Conchita, "*thees* one. *Beeg* fighter." Diosa Costello didn't care for this dialogue: "In those movies they make you have a very thick accent. I used to say to them, 'I have a natural accent. Why do I have to say *thees, thees*?' "

Hot-Shot takes Laurel & Hardy to the local livestock farm to select a non-threatening bull. (Laurel is wearing an ornate matador's outfit—

with his derby!) The three of them get involved in a "mixed-up hats" routine, capped with a ridiculous bulb-horn sound effect as Laurel's hat is knocked off. When a quiet bull suddenly shows alarming signs of life, Hot-Shot seeks refuge behind some hay while Stan and Ollie clamber up a stack of bales. The stack sways precariously and finally dumps the boys into a hay wagon. Their wagon runs wild through the countryside and crashes into a cactus field.

This elaborate sequence is a noble attempt by Fox to put some physical action into its comedies. Some of the backstage shenanigans, however, weren't very funny to Stan Laurel when production suddenly came to a standstill. Laurel was annoyed by the infighting between the studio's union laborers. Union gardeners delivered several loads of fresh hay to the **Bullfighters** location, but by the time the scene was completed, the hay had thoroughly dried out and was strewn all over the set. The gardeners, who had originally furnished a "green" product, claimed that the dessicated straw was now a prop, and should be handled by property men. The property department denied responsibility, and the frustrated filmmakers could not continue shooting until the hay had been moved. It took the Fox bosses half a day to decide how the hay would be classified.

The final quarter of **The Bullfighters** takes place at the arena. Sunday arrives but Don Sebastian hasn't, so Stan will have to fight the bull himself. Hot-Shot breezes into the star's dressing room for last-minute preparations. These include pouring Stan a shot of potent Mexican liquor to bolster his courage. The booze is so strong that Stan sprays it out instantly, but his reaction is interrupted by the sudden arrival of Muldoon and his girlfriend. (Laurel's mind was always working when it came to props. He hurriedly puts his hat on *vertically* like a British admiral, but repositions it at the last minute.) There is an effectively photographed match-dissolve when Muldoon suspiciously regards Stan, whose Mexican headgear transforms into Stan's usual derby and back again. It was easier to switch hats in close-up than to have Laurel change his costume completely! Under Muldoon's merciless glare Stan self-consciously turns to see what Muldoon is looking at—or perhaps he's wondering where the eccentric sound effects accompanying the dissolve are coming from!

The real Don Sebastian arrives by taxi, and thanks the driver. The word "Gracias!" is dubbed in by a booming baritone! Whenever the matador speaks, it's in this re-recorded Spanish voice, except in one instance which the sound engineer overlooked, so Don Sebastian says "gracias" in Stan Laurel's own British-accented voice.

Don Sebastian always wears a hat, except for a quick flash where he bows to the crowd. His hair is slicked down and parted in the center. We see it for only a moment, but it shows Stan Laurel's attention to characterization. It also explains why "Stanley's" hair is slicked down, because one would not expect Stan's double, a Spanish matador, to sport Stan's unruly mop of hair.

An indignant bull cannot be contained by the arena staff, so Don Sebastian steps in to subdue the beast. The medium shots of Laurel passing the matador's cape don't match the long shots of a professional bullfighter, although the close-ups of Laurel looking intense are impressive. Everyone in the crowd loves the daring display except for Ollie, who is unaware that the matador risking life and limb is Don Sebastian and not his friend Stan.

Meanwhile Stan has been sampling the dressing-room firewater and staggers up to Ollie for a showdown. (Laurel begins to recite his dialogue but pauses to interject his childlike trademark "You know what?", so Hardy plays along: "What?") Stan reaffirms that he is *not* going to fight any bulls. "Get back in that ring!" orders Ollie, pushing Stan into combat. Now there are *two* Laurels in the arena. Stan is drunkenly oblivious, Don Sebastian is taken aback, and the bull is thoroughly confused. There is a surprisingly funny "take" by the bull, flabbergasted by this incredible spectacle.

The actor Ralph Sanford was *genuinely* confused. He points to the fake matador and cries, "That guy's *Hardy* . . . and the other one's Laurel!" Movie fans sometimes couldn't keep the boys' identities straight, but this is the only time one of their *co-stars* made such a mistake.

The bulls are turned loose in the arena, and the crowd rampages. Fox had toyed with the idea of filming the bullring sequence in Mexico; many Hollywood productions of the period had Latin-American themes and locales. The location trip never got beyond the planning stages, so the **Bullfighters** crew had to make do with homegrown material. The Laurel & Hardy footage was garnished with crowd shots and atmospherics from Fox's 1941 feature **Blood And Sand**, plus newsreel scenes of an arena riot. Film editor Stanley Rabjohn did his best, juggling long shots of hundreds of people and new inserts of dozens of people.

(There's a memorable close-up of the panic-stricken Laurel in the middle of the crowd, hiding his face to make the trouble go away.) These new scenes were shot outdoors in the middle of December, which is why the spectators are wearing long-sleeve shirts and jackets in "sunny Mexico." The plot resolution also gets lost in the crowd, as the boys never do capture "Larceny Nell." Carol Andrews reported in costume to the arena location, and posed for publicity stills, but does not appear in the bullring sequence.

Ollie finds his pal and they make a hasty retreat, while Muldoon gets butted in the rear by an errant bull. At the hotel, the boys are back in their traditional costumes (Laurel in gray and Hardy in dark blue). They open their closet door and find Muldoon waiting for them with his trusty knife: "First the little one . . . then the big one." Laurel & Hardy are so galvanized that they don't even resist. Laurel, removing his clothes, cautions Hardy not to get the hat dirty!

Dissolve to a classic Laurel & Hardy wrap-up gag. Many of the vintage L & H comedies had weird, surreal endings which showed Stan and Ollie stretched, squashed, bloated, tied in knots, bent out of shape, or otherwise outrageously contorted at the fade-out. **The Bullfighters** adheres to this peculiar tradition, and shows two skeletons walking toward the camera with Laurel & Hardy's talking heads intact! Fred Sersen's special-effects work is ingenious, and it brings this film and the comedians' career at Fox to a fitting conclusion.

Fox made some confusing and bewildering corporate decisions regarding the Laurel & Hardy unit in the 1940s, but the most baffling one occurs in **The Bullfighters**: *why* does Margo Woode get featured billing? She speaks only three lines in the entire film and contributes nothing to the picture, apart from a few cover-girl close-ups. Yet she is billed above everyone in the cast except Laurel & Hardy. Diosa Costello, who has the major feminine role, is billed sixth, after Carol Andrews (another starlet, who at least does something—the egg bit). And Ralph Sanford, who plays the villain, doesn't get any billing at all! Perhaps an obliging executive arranged for Margo Woode to be in **The Bullfighters**; it's probably the most expensive screen test ever made. Neither Margo Woode nor Carol Andrews set the screen ablaze, and they made no other movies. (Margo Woode is not to be confused with Marjorie Woodworth, another former model who appeared in several Hal Roach comedies of the early 1940s.)

The Bullfighters was completed in December, 1944 but, like The Big Noise and Nothing But Trouble, it stayed on the shelf for months. Exhibitors who had profitably presented The Big Noise were clamoring for more Laurel & Hardy, but prints of their newest movie were not yet available. Fox serviced the demand with old prints of The Dancing Masters, which did excellent business through the spring of '45. In May, when the film-stock crisis abated, The Bullfighters emerged from the labs.

Twentieth Century-Fox was celebrating its thirtieth year in business, and each of its 1945 releases was given a special advertising tag line: "It's A 20th Century-Fox 30th Anniversary Picture." The Bullfighters was technically part of the "anniversary" series, which included twenty-four features. Significantly, Fox publicity mentioned only *twenty-three* features. More attention was paid to a 19-minute patriotic short which played alongside The Bullfighters as a gift. Fox released The All-Star Bond Rally at no charge, and spent money on full-page magazine ads.

The studio regarded its Laurel & Hardy pictures as reliable but unremarkable products; they weren't worth publicizing. If 20th Century-Fox had been a fast-food chain, it would have devoted its advertising budget to all of its deluxe, triple-decker sandwiches with catchy names and fancy ingredients—never calling attention to the simple hamburger, an almost-forgotten staple of the industry.

The Bullfighters, despite its lack of promotion, was an immediate success. The critics smirked knowingly at the old comedy sketches; Thomas M. Pryor of the *New York Times* wryly commented that "Mr. St. Clair didn't need a script; he must have had the whole business down pat in the back of his memory, but we note that a script is credited to W. Scott Darling. And in a case like this, an author deserves all the notoriety he can get." *Variety* concurred that "the comics and director Mal St. Clair have added nothing novel to the exasperation, etc., routines on which Laurel & Hardy have been cashing in, with result that except for locale, Bullfighters differs little from earlier efforts . . . and should do no better and no worse than previous films starring the duo." *The Motion Picture Herald* led its review with a charitable but inaccurate comment about the team's longevity: "Currently celebrating their 20th year as film partners, this marks the 177th picture together of those hardy madcaps, Laurel and Hardy. Those who go in for the team's familiar brand of slapstick and tomfoolery will find this one of their better vehicles."

Exhibitors agreed. "Silly, but what do I care as long as my Sunday crowd was pleased," grinned a Georgia exhibitor. "Only complaint was that it was too short. Hope to have more of this comedy team soon."

The short running time actually enhanced the film's desirability for moviehouse double features. Laurel & Hardy's little Fox film was often used as a light companion for another studio's overstuffed dramatic opus. The average "B" picture played first-run for a maximum of two weeks; **The Bullfighters** played for four. The film proved to have tremendous staying power, and was making worldwide theatrical rounds into 1947. In Kobe, Japan, to promote one of the film's final first-run engagements, a bull was borrowed from a local zoo and led through the city streets by an Oriental "toreador."

Time has been kind to **The Bullfighters**. Unlike the other Laurel & Hardy films of the forties, this one was free from wartime references or dated American settings, so it remained "active" with theatrical bookers. **The Bullfighters** is the only L & H Fox film that stayed in continuous circulation; fifty years after its premiere, it was still being offered to theaters in the 35mm format.

Theatrical Reissues

There is a forgotten postscript to Laurel & Hardy's films of the forties. Only nine films were made, but dozens more were released—via the reissue route.

After their production unit closed, Stan Laurel and Oliver Hardy withdrew from the motion-picture scene, but their films did not. Postwar theater attendance had boosted the movie industry to a new prosperity, and in 1946 practically every film made money. This fact was not lost on several enterprising salesmen in the "small time" of the industry, who revived a number of old Laurel & Hardy comedies that year.

In the days before television, movies could stay in theatrical circulation for up to five years. Some of the more popular films were periodically re-released. Since their old productions still had earning power, the major movie studios weren't about to let someone else profit from their property. Salesmen on the fringe of the industry often had to secure their wares from independent producers. The United Artists library, housing films produced by Hal Roach, Samuel Goldwyn, and Alexander Korda, was a frequent source of material.

The minor-league movie merchants were a closely-knit group, often renting office space a few blocks away from each other (or sometimes a few *doors* away). The market was relatively limited, and the friendly competitors were much like rival television stations. If a popular TV series goes off the air on one station, another outlet is likely to pick it up. So it went with the independent distributors: after one company shelved an old negative, another firm would grab it.

Moe Kerman operated a reissue business named Favorite Films. He and his associates, J. J. Felder and Leo Seligman, opened an office in February, 1946. Among Favorite's first acquisitions was a Hal Roach-

United Artists package, which included a pair of short Laurel & Hardy features (**A Chump At Oxford** and **Saps At Sea**). To save money, Kerman reprinted the original 1940 publicity kits, substituting the words "Favorite Films" for "United Artists"—but in one instance he overlooked the cover artwork, which contained a blatant "UA" plug! (A similar Roach-UA reissue package was handled in England by Renown Pictures.)

Three years later these Laurel & Hardy films returned to theaters from the unlikely source of Sam Katzman. Katzman was one of Hollywood's premier low-budget producers; over three decades he released dozens of inexpensive features and serials through Monogram Pictures and Columbia Pictures. At the end of 1949 Katzman experimented with the idea of distributing films himself, and circulated **A Chump At Oxford** and **Saps At Sea** under the "Kay Pictures" banner.

Oxford was originally released in America as a 42-minute featurette; an alternate "European" edition included an additional 21 minutes of footage. The Kay print was an inexplicable hybrid; it was longer than the domestic version but shorter than the continental version. A Massachusetts moviegoer recalled that the picture abruptly jumped from Laurel & Hardy entering an employment office to a fade-in on the boys as street sweepers. A lengthy dinner-party sequence was suspiciously absent. "Some of this picture was cut out," confirmed an Arkansas exhibitor. "It wasn't long enough."

The smaller distributors usually had to scramble for Laurel & Hardy material, since most of it was reserved by a company called Film Classics, Inc. In June of 1943 Film Classics acquired the rights to the entire Hal Roach library of 1929–38 product. The eleven feature films and over 200 short subjects had originally been released by M-G-M. The package included most of the Laurel & Hardy comedies, as well as dozens of two-reelers starring Charley Chase, Thelma Todd, and Billy Gilbert, among others. The reissue agreement was made by Edward Peskay, representing Hal Roach, and by George Hirliman and Irvin Shapiro, representing Film Classics.

Film Classics had only been in business for a matter of weeks when Hirliman and Shapiro clinched the Roach deal. Hirliman, a former film-laboratory operator, achieved some success in the late 1930s as an independent producer. Many of his features were released by Grand National Pictures, an ambitious company of the day. He promoted a color-film process and used it in his features (including a Spanish-language series that was released by M-G-M). He also supervised a string of George O'Brien westerns for RKO.

Shapiro, a former RKO publicist and booking agent, had slight production experience but was more at home in the sales area. He left Film Classics to open a film-exporting concern in 1945.

Film Classics aggressively scoured the vaults for any vintage films that were independently produced. Immediately after securing the Hal Roach wares, Film Classics went after the prestigious feature productions of Samuel Goldwyn, David O. Selznick, and Edward Small. Hirliman and Shapiro devoted their energies to marketing these opulent, star-packed favorites, while the humble Roach features (mostly Laurel & Hardys) languished on the shelf for almost two years. The Roach shorts and featurettes fared better, going into circulation sooner.

During Film Classics' first two years of activity, the company revived only one Roach feature, the 1937 Cary Grant comedy **Topper**. The situation bothered Hal Roach, who wasn't seeing many profits from his film library. Roach threatened to sue Film Classics for $50,000 in damages for mishandling **Topper**. Film Classics mollified Roach by agreeing to market more of his works. The first of Roach's Laurel & Hardy "features" to be reissued was actually a 37-minute featurette, **Beau Hunks** (1931), officially released on New Year's Day, 1945. **Sons Of The Desert**, **Pack Up Your Troubles**, and **Pardon Us** followed.

When Film Classics re-released a movie, the advertising materials were updated, often with a topical slant. The 1931 Eddie Cantor musical **Palmy Days**, reissued in 1944, billed The Goldwyn Girls as "The Goldwyn Doughgirls." Laurel & Hardy's comic operetta **The Bohemian Girl** (1936) was trotted out again ten years later, when the atomic bomb was very much in the news; the new posters heralded the film as "a full-length ATOMIComedy." The poster also dispensed with the "corny" artwork of L & H in operatic costumes and used "civilian" poses from **Way Out West** instead. Film Classics also played up the "timeless" quality of their revivals; their slogan was "Good Pictures Like Good Books Never Grow Old."

Film Classics' ad art is often very attractive, often improving on the original first-run ads. M-G-M's **Way Out West** ad of 1937 is cluttered and difficult to read, while Film Classics' 1947 graphics are much cleaner. (They goofed on the one-sheet poster, though. It was common practice to tint black-and-white photos for multi-colored posters; in the **Way Out West** sheet, Laurel & Hardy's barely distinguishable outfits are colored totally in black, so outlines are obscured.) In general, the Film Classics lobby accessories did L & H proud.

One only wishes Film Classics lavished this kind of care on the films themselves! While the company furnished theaters with new prints and posters, it stopped short of making up new coming-attractions reels. The original-release 35mm trailers were put back into circulation, and they were much the worse for wear by the mid-1940s. The slick merchandising techniques of the wartime movie industry were nowhere to be found in these relics of another day. A Virginia exhibitor who had booked several Film Classics revivals railed against their antique previews: "The trailer [for **Topper**] looked like it was made a century ago. Sound was terrible and advertisements made it look out of date." This penny-pinching on Film Classics' part did nothing to sell Laurel & Hardy to new audiences.

Film Classics was initially very careless in removing and replacing the films' original titles and logos. In an economy move, new title sections were printed on inferior film stock and physically spliced onto the original footage. The shoddy grade of celluloid used by Film Classics deteriorated in time; forty years later when archivist Michael Agee went through the vaults to reprint **Sons Of The Desert**, he found that the badly decomposed Film Classics footage had contaminated and spoiled the first 100 feet of the original film. (The president of Film Classics once owned a major film laboratory and should have known better!)

Pioneer talking pictures had the soundtracks on phonograph discs. (This process was abandoned in 1931 in favor of the sound being printed directly on the film.) The soundtrack discs went into storage until Hal Roach donated them to wartime scrap drives; Film Classics transferred the tracks to film. Much of Hal Roach's 1929 output contained dialogue, so the sound was relatively easy to synchronize. Where there wasn't dialogue, however, there were problems.

Laurel & Hardy's 1929 short **Liberty** was originally a silent film released with music and sound effects on disc. Film Classics inherited the picture and soundtrack elements some fifteen years later and attempted to combine them. The original title section ran 32 seconds; Film Classics' rephotographed version ran only 17 seconds, so the film was fifteen seconds out of synchronization. Film Classics apparently noticed the

problem too late, and tried to correct it in half-hearted fashion, according to Michael Agee. One of the silent-film captions was "frozen" for
an interminable length, while the soundtrack was allowed to catch up
with the delayed picture. This only served to throw off the synchronization the *other* way, so the sound ran *behind* the picture for most of the
movie, then the sound raced *ahead* of the picture near the finish!

Film Classics prepared new prints of one other Laurel & Hardy silent-
with-music, **That's My Wife** (1929). The rarest Film Classics prints
are **Two Tars**, **Big Business**, and **Double Whoopee**. These films were
originally released in 1928–29. Film Classics was all set to reissue the
films—until someone realized that they were silent, and that no soundtrack discs ever existed. The aborted reissues were dumped onto the
home-movie market instead, where they were reprinted on silent 16mm
and 8mm film.

The first wave of Film Classics releases was riddled with errors.
Chickens Come Home was mislabeled **Chicken Come Home**. Sound-
man Elmer Raguse was usually billed as "Roguse" and actress Mae
Busch emerged as "May Bush." **Beau Hunks** has a gag cast list which
was totally massacred by Film Classics: the credit for "1921 native Swede
guides" became "1944 natives Swede guilders." Various technical credits were transposed or omitted. Perhaps the most glaring example of
Film Classics' haphazard technique is the 1944 reissue of Hal Roach's
1937 comedy **Topper**. The glossy animated titles were scrapped, and
replaced by plain white lettering on a plain black background. Screenwriter Jack Jevne was misbilled as "Levne," cameraman Norbert Brodine was listed as "Robert Dorbine," and featured player Arthur Lake
was omitted altogether.

One of Hirliman's earliest title designs became a trademark as familiar
as Laurel & Hardy's derby hats: the "Film Classics plaque." This title
card, heralding the arrival of Laurel & Hardy on the screen, has remained
a welcome sight to moviegoers and television viewers over the years.
The words "Hal Roach presents" appeared above a marbled plaque, on
which was embossed the names "Stan Laurel and Oliver Hardy." Beneath the plaque, in very small print, was a copyright notice, dated 1933,
crediting Metro-Goldwyn-Mayer. This legal formality was incorrect on
two counts: because the stock "plaque" title was used on practically
every L & H film, the "1933" notice appeared on films dating from any

other year; also, the original copyright was held by Loew's Incorporated, not Metro-Goldwyn-Mayer.

The "plaque" format was retained for Film Classics' other Hal Roach reissues, with other comedians' names etched on the plate. Charley Chase's name was misspelled "Charlie," and ZaSu Pitts's name was mis-printed "Zazu." For Roach's "All-Star" comedies (which had no stars to speak of), the film title itself went on the plaque.

The Film Classics plaque supplanted the imaginative graphics used in the original M-G-M title frames of the 1930s. Latter-day film buffs, unable to see the older titles, had to be content with the plaque. The first four Laurel & Hardy feature reissues were handled just like the shorts, with the plaque tacked onto the titles.

Fortunately for the purist, Film Classics adopted a different technique in 1946. A still photograph was made from the original title frame, and the M-G-M trademark was airbrushed out. The doctored photo was then refilmed, and this footage was inserted back into the old film. This process preserved the original titles and made any tampering less obvious. A charming if somewhat unusual example occurs in **On The Wrong Trek**, a Charley Chase two-reeler. The M-G-M lion has been removed, but the ornate border framing the trademark remains! Curiously, Film Classics did not put its own trademark on the feature-film title frames. A separate credit was attached to the film leaders.

Film Classics was not above re-editing the old films. For the reissue of **Pack Up Your Troubles**, five minutes of disagreeable domestic-abuse scenes involving a brutish villain were deleted. Laurel & Hardy were not involved in part of this sequence, and the cuts had no effect on the film's continuity. For forty years, every print of **Pack Up Your Troubles**—for theaters, television and home movies—had the Film Classics edits.

For the earliest talkies, Film Classics sometimes substituted music tracks in the title sequences. In reissue, **Men O'War** (or **Man O'War**, as Film Classics called it) had the incongruous sound of a buzzsaw rasp-ing through the main titles—because the theme music was lifted from the carpentry-shop comedy **Busy Bodies**. **Night Owls** used a produc-tion number from **Sons Of The Desert** as an opening fanfare. **The Hoose-Gow** borrowed a pop tune from a Charley Chase short, **The Real McCoy**.

Exhibitors of the 1940s were pleased that Laurel & Hardy's famous hits were back in circulation. The full-length six- or seven-reelers made ideal companion features; in Boston theaters of 1946, three Laurel & Hardy features competed against each other. The films were such audience-grabbers that many exhibitors would book a Laurel & Hardy featurette running 25 to 37 minutes (**Be Big, Oliver The Eighth, Beau Hunks**, etc.) and advertise it as a co-feature. With Laurel & Hardy added to the bill, single-feature offerings turned into novel double features; double features became even more exotic *triple* features.

The Laurel & Hardy shorts were equally popular, and played alongside many major screen attractions. Two-reel comedies had dwindled in quantity and quality since the L & H films were made; vintage episodes of only average quality now seemed like masterpieces, compared to contemporary product. A Wisconsin exhibitor sang the praises of the two-reeler **Any Old Port**, which was then fourteen years old: "The most hilarious short we have ever played. The crowd never got its breath. Will bring in more customers than any features."

The Film Classics Laurel & Hardy comedies were perennials of all-comedy shows and kiddie matinees. The two-reelers were also packaged with other Hal Roach shorts, giving exhibitors ready-made children's programming. Film Classics issued several editions of its "Funz-A-Poppin' Comedy Carnival," beginning in 1946.

Hal Roach wasn't laughing; he observed his old films' new success with dismay. In late June of 1946 Roach filed another lawsuit against Film Classics, in an attempt to nullify the licensing agreement signed in 1943. Roach claimed that the contract had been made for "inadequate compensation." Edward Peskay, the man who signed the papers on Roach's behalf, was named as co-defendant. Roach wanted more money than was originally agreed upon; Film Classics continued to market the Roach comedies during the litigation period, until the original license was revoked.

Film Classics dabbled in film production in the late 1940s, when the major studios lost their monopoly on the nation's theaters, but the small company's homegrown product, mostly talky, stage-bound mysteries, made little impact. Within two years the financially troubled company merged with the Eagle-Lion studio. The new company, Eagle Lion Classics, distributed independent productions for first-run and art-house theaters, obliterating Film Classics' original reissue policy. When Eagle Lion Classics was absorbed by United Artists, Film Classics briefly came to life again as a joint venture with Jack Broder's Realart company, but didn't last long.

Ron Ormond, a show-business entrepreneur whose activities included vaudeville presentations and carnival acts, was releasing Lash LaRue westerns through Realart. In 1951 he assumed the distribution chores himself, doing business as "Western Adventure Pictures." Some of the Laurel & Hardy Film Classics reels were sent out to theaters yet again by Western Adventure. Ormond had never bothered with the promotion of short subjects, but for the Laurel & Hardys he gave exhibitors a moderately expensive full-color poster. The Western Adventure "stock sheet" featured a simple cartoon caricature of Laurel & Hardy (cribbed from one of Moe Kerman's "Favorite Films" posters!) and a blank field which was reserved for whatever title was being screened.

One of Film Classics' closest competitors in the reissue field was Astor Pictures. Astor, founded in 1933 as an import-export house, became a reissue specialist in 1940. Astor's president, Robert M. Savini, had wide experience in the managerial aspects of the film industry. Savini's flair for showmanship extended the life span of any number of films which had seen their day. Savini secured the rights to these "exhausted" titles—many were obscure or independently produced pictures—and he successfully revived them under the Astor banner. Astor's New York exchange was managed for a time by Moe Kerman, whose "Favorite Films" company also enjoyed success with Laurel & Hardy releases.

Four of the most familiar Astor reissues are Laurel & Hardy comedies, although in fact there was only one L & H film produced outside the studio system. Boris Morros had released **The Flying Deuces** through RKO in 1939 and the rights reverted to him after the film's successful runs. Morros followed up his auspicious debut with an ambitious Fred Astaire musical, **Second Chorus**. (RKO was no longer interested, having just discontinued Astaire's contract, so **Second Chorus** was distributed by Paramount to indifferent response.)

When Morros sold both **The Flying Deuces** and **Second Chorus** to Astor Pictures in 1948, Astor was obliged to remove the studio trademarks. Savini's technicians carefully airbrushed the Paramount logo out of **Second Chorus**, but they were less finicky about **The Flying Deuces**. The original title footage was discarded, and a new card was filmed with the producer misbilled as "Boris Morris." Astor offered the

Morros productions to theaters and later to television, where they were frequently shown.

Because the film's copyright has lapsed, **The Flying Deuces** is perhaps the most familiar of all the Laurel & Hardy films. Over the years, numerous film and video distributors have manufactured copies of widely variable quality. These public-domain prints have been "duped" again and again, with a loss of definition each time. Some prints of **Deuces** are horribly murky, with tinny soundtracks and grainy, indistinct images. This is in no way typical of the quality of Astor's own first-generation prints, which were beautifully sharp and clear.

The excellent response to this Laurel & Hardy comedy prompted Bob Savini to try to provide more of the same. This wasn't easy, since Film Classics held most of the Laurel & Hardy backlog, and what remained was controlled by major studios beyond the reach of independent distributors. Yet the canny Bob Savini gained a firm grasp on the elusive prize, by special arrangement with Metro-Goldwyn-Mayer.

How did M-G-M's profitable Laurel & Hardy features "escape" to Astor? In 1941 Hal Roach, who originally produced the films, was embroiled in a legal battle with M-G-M over money due him from his releasing arrangement with the studio. Roach's $1,263,993 breach-of-contract suit dragged on for several years. A "compromise" settlement was finally reached when M-G-M offered to buy a handful of Roach's feature films outright. This way, Roach would receive the money due him as a sales transaction, and M-G-M would no longer be charged with improprieties. Roach accepted the terms of the buyback, and M-G-M, which had no intention of doing anything with the films, put the cans on the shelf.

Enter Astor's Bob Savini, who knew of the films' whereabouts and offered to reissue them himself. M-G-M didn't care—by then the films were about fifteen years old and of limited value. These Hal Roach comedies weren't "true" M-G-M productions, so the studio evidently regarded them as "poor relations." The deal went through, with the stipulation that Astor could not use the films' original titles or trademarks. M-G-M would retain the negatives and copyrights.

Savini eagerly agreed, and three films were rushed out. The re-release was engineered so quickly that Astor prepared only one advertising poster, an inexpensive two-color "stock sheet" which included photos of Laurel & Hardy from various films. The all-purpose poster did triple duty, promoting three different pictures.

The Devil's Brother was based on the operetta *Fra Diavolo*. Savini rechristened the film **Bogus Bandits**.

Bonnie Scotland, a military comedy, was revived by Astor as **Heroes Of The Regiment**. The advertising campaign was cheaply but effectively mounted, with press copy taken from the original 1935 lobby accessories, and the coming-attractions trailer reprinted almost intact, except for the title and studio name changes.

Pick A Star was a musical-comedy film which only featured Laurel & Hardy incidentally, in an unbilled guest appearance. Yet the film was ballyhooed by Astor as a full-fledged Laurel & Hardy comedy, **Movie Struck**. The few photographs of their participation were reprinted as lobby cards, to further the illusion that Laurel & Hardy were the stars, and not merely guest artists. Astor changed the main title but left the production credits alone—so Laurel & Hardy didn't get screen credit this time, either!

These Astor versions of the Laurel & Hardy comedies have caused some confusion among enthusiasts. Astor closed its doors in 1962 and most of the abandoned prints found their way into nontheatrical and television libraries. The Astor Laurel & Hardys, however, could not be released again, since M-G-M still maintained the copyrights. So the films were withheld from theatrical, television and home-movie circulation for years, while fans eagerly awaited their chance to see these rare movies. The films were available only in truncated "highlights" versions for television, their identities obscured by false titles.

A home-movie distributor reprinted **Movie Struck** in the 1960s and offered it to the collectors' market, where it was regarded as a curio, although the presence of Laurel & Hardy in the cast guaranteed a certain degree of interest. It wasn't until 1980, when home-movie-quality prints of public-domain pictures were released to low-budget TV stations, that **Movie Struck** became familiar to Laurel & Hardy buffs. Like **The Flying Deuces**, it was presumed to have no copyright status, so it was widely sold as a cheap video offering. The other Astor titles, **Bogus Bandits** and **Heroes Of The Regiment**, stayed off the dealers' market, out of respect for M-G-M's ownership of the original products.

In 1992 a budget-price video dealer published **Bogus Bandits** under his own public-domain label, perhaps reasoning that these particular reissue versions had no copyright status. The film's original title was omitted, the artwork on the packaging was derived from Astor's movie poster, and the source print ran five minutes shorter than the original. (In stores, the **Bogus Bandits** video was often displayed directly alongside M-G-M's "authorized" tape of **The Devil's Brother.**)

While the Film Classics reissues have become familiar to Laurel & Hardy fans, the Astor enterprises are strangely forgotten. Relatively few Laurel & Hardy comedies were revived by Robert M. Savini, but thanks to his efforts some choice comedy footage was rescued from obscurity.

Boris Morros, who had sold **The Flying Deuces** to Astor, was also responsible for the next major Laurel & Hardy reissue. In 1945, together with producer William LeBaron, Morros founded Federal Films, an independent production company. In January of 1946 Morros and LeBaron announced a full-length animated version of Victor Herbert's **Babes In Toyland**, featuring director George Pal's "Puppetoons." The partnership with Pal fell through, but Morros and LeBaron tried to revive the property. In 1948 they revealed plans to remake **Babes In Toyland** as an ambitious live-action production. Perhaps it wasn't *too* ambitious, since it was to be made in Cinecolor, a cheap photographic process then in vogue which offered a pleasing but limited spectrum of colors. The new **Babes In Toyland** was promised to the nation's exhibitors for the 1949 season.

Federal had planned to release its remake through Screen Guild, a prolific B-movie studio operated by California exhibitor Robert L. Lippert. Lippert had held a Film Classics franchise in the mid-forties, and subsequently branched out into production. In February of 1949 he merged Screen Guild with his new company, Lippert Pictures, Inc.

The remake was abandoned, because there was nothing wrong with the original. When Morros and LeBaron bought the rights to **Babes In Toyland**, they assumed ownership of the earlier motion-picture version. However, because the 1934 film had been part of the Hal Roach–M-G-M "buyback" deal, it could not be exhibited under its original title. In November of 1948 entrepreneur Joe Auerbach paid a mere $10,000 for 35mm and 16mm reissue rights for all world markets (except 35mm in North America). He labeled the film **Revenge Is Sweet**, carefully refraining from mentioning the original title or source.

When the legalities were ironed out, Lippert Pictures released Laurel & Hardy's **Babes In Toyland** in 1950 under the new title **March Of**

The Wooden Soldiers. Most prints of **Wooden Soldiers** are six minutes short; some non-Laurel & Hardy material has been removed. The
missing footage is a "storybook" prologue with "Mother Goose" (Virginia Karns); a vocal duet by "Little Bo-Peep" (Charlotte Henry) and
"Tom-Tom, the Piper's Son" (Felix Knight); and a harmless scene of
Bo-Peep falling asleep next to Tom-Tom. Laurel & Hardy buffs have
always assumed that these scenes were thrown out by Lippert. Actually,
the Lippert negative was fully complete, except for a revised set of titles,
and the company manufactured 79-minute prints for the nontheatrical
market. The trims were made in the theatrical edition, so it would be of
standard double-feature length (shades of 20th Century-Fox's old
"hour-and-a-quarter" policy).

Marie Wilson, who played a small part (with one line of dialogue),
had gone on to bigger things, and in 1950 was starring in the "My
Friend Irma" radio shows and movies. Lippert boosted Marie Wilson's
billing for the reissue, but did not update the credit for co-star Henry
Brandon. He was billed under his former, real name, Henry Kleinbach.
Co-director Gus Meins was misbilled "Mines," and composer Victor
Herbert was forgotten entirely.

Lippert's elaborate presskit included handsome new posters which
stressed Laurel & Hardy and the family appeal of their vehicle. The
publicity department dug up a still of "Little Miss Muffet," enlarged it
for the posters, and listed Marie Wilson's name prominently. It probably
fooled a good many theater patrons—Wilson did not portray "Little
Miss Muffet" at all, but for ballyhoo purposes the young blonde actress
on the posters (Alice Dahl) was close enough.

These successful reissues kept Laurel & Hardy in the public eye, but
they had a negative side effect: they branded the team as "old." The
dated films fostered the belief that the stars were no longer current.
Laurel & Hardy had been visibly aging in their wartime films. Now that
they weren't making pictures any more, fans thought they had retired in
1945, after making **The Bullfighters**.

Leaving Hollywood

Stan Laurel said in later years that he kept hoping 20th Century-Fox would eventually let Laurel & Hardy make films their own way, and when conditions kept deteriorating they got out. Laurel didn't care to discuss this phase of his career at great length, and it was convenient for him to sum up his three-and-a-half years at Fox in a few curt sentences. The fact is, however, things were going better at Fox than Laurel indicated. Both Stan Laurel and Oliver Hardy had considerable input during **The Bullfighters,** and Laurel was even allowed to direct. (He was probably the only star on the Fox payroll who was extended this courtesy.) The team might have enjoyed even more freedom in their next picture, had the "B" unit continued without interruption.

Stan and Babe had been off the Fox lot for about six months when **The Bullfighters** became a surprise success. Fox offered to sign the comedians for another five years—quite a bold and flattering move, considering that the studio would have essentially been reopening the "B" unit just for them. Laurel & Hardy declined, and the unit remained closed. Fox released a few independently-made programmers in 1947–48, with producer Sol Wurtzel and director Mal St. Clair contributing their talents, but **The Bullfighters** was the last "B" actually made by Fox.

History fails to record whether Laurel & Hardy were offered a slot in the 1947–48 schedule. Stan's daughter Lois does not recall any such proposal being made. If Laurel & Hardy were approached, they were forced to refuse for any of the following reasons: the team had stage commitments overseas for most of the year; Stan Laurel was disabled by a temporary illness in 1948; Sol Wurtzel could no longer afford the team, since his new pictures were made on modest budgets, with inexpensive featured players instead of established stars; and the comedians' indulgent **Bullfighters** producer, Bryan Foy, would not be with them, having left 20th Century-Fox.

Stan Laurel later went on record as refusing to stay at Fox, although an alternate version has gossip columnist Louella Parsons using her influence to have the comedians released from their contract. Parsons had asked the team to appear gratis on her network radio program, and Laurel is said to have refused unless he and his partner were paid. The outraged Parsons then had a word with Laurel's employers and that was that, as the story goes.

Parsons had tremendous clout at 20th Century-Fox. In 1944 she sold her autobiography, "The Gay Illiterate," to the studio for a handsome sum; Fox had no intention of actually producing a film version, but made the investment as a public-relations move. While Parsons's intervention in the Laurel & Hardy matter is likely, since Stan and Babe received no other bids from major studios after they left Fox, the comics were not released from their contract until their unit actually suspended production.

"Louella Parsons didn't like Laurel & Hardy," says Lois Laurel, "because they didn't send her presents every Christmas. She only put publicity in her column about who she was getting presents from."

The studio had taken its comedy breadwinners for granted, and their sudden absence was noticeable. "When they left Fox they were appreciated more," recalls Lois. "I remember my dad and stepmother Ruth Laurel telling me that the studio was sorry, that they thought they could have gone on and done some very nice things at Fox."

Laurel & Hardy could have kept working in Hollywood, but not on their own terms. Their production company was active on paper but dormant in reality, owing to a lack of capital. They weren't the only performers who wanted to be their own bosses, and at least one studio was sympathetic. Monogram Pictures, a prolific distributor of low-budget fare, offered special opportunities to actors-turned-producers. Lou Costello, Leo Gorcey, Arthur Lake, Sidney Toler, and Kay Francis launched personal projects at Monogram, but the studio was apparently too minor for Laurel & Hardy to consider. Time was money to the independent companies, and Laurel & Hardy would have had to rush through quickie production schedules.

The other available avenue was a return to short subjects, which by this time were far less important and prestigious than in bygone days. Jules White, who produced Columbia Pictures' slapstick shorts, often came to the rescue of unemployed actors and technicians. He found work for comedy craftsmen who were at liberty, like Buster Keaton, Harry Langdon, and Bert Wheeler. White was a big fan of Laurel & Hardy's brand of comedy: "I would have jumped at the chance to hire them," he once admitted. Laurel & Hardy might have survived in the two-reeler community for another ten years, but fortunately for the comics' artistic reputations, they never worked in Columbia's strenuous, slam-bang shorts.

With the Hollywood moguls adopting a "hands-off" policy regarding Laurel & Hardy, the team accepted an offer to make personal appearances in Europe. Producer Bernard Delfont arranged a six-week tour of England's top theaters in 1947. The public's reaction was strong and spirited. European theaters have always been havens for American performers whose careers were faltering. Buster Keaton went the same route in the late 1940s, as did rock-and-roll pioneers Bill Haley and Buddy Holly a decade later.

The tour was a triumph. The comedians were booked into the palatial London Palladium, but they had a stop to make beforehand. "The first place they played was Newcastle," recalled Laurel's future son-in-law Tony Hawes, "because George and Alfred Black, who were producers, and their father Alfred Black, had grown up with Stan's father. They made a deal: if they ever came to England, the first place they'd play was Newcastle."

The London Palladium announced a new policy: six weeks of variety shows. Laurel & Hardy got the short end of the stick financially, thanks to the Palladium's inflexible salary ceiling. Hawes explained, "Top of the bill at the Palladium, whether you were Tito Gobbi or Gracie Fields, was one set fee, which was £1000 a week. Headlining the first three weeks was George Formby, who got £1000 because he was England's greatest comedy-film actor. The boys followed George Formby for the second three weeks, March 10 to March 31. They were top of the bill, and they got £1000 *between* them." Laurel & Hardy could be thankful they weren't being employed by a lesser theater; the London Casino, for example, only paid £750 for big-name acts. According to Hawes, Laurel & Hardy showed unusual consideration to the theater staff and autograph seekers: "They would go out and buy apples by the *barrel* every week, and put them at the stage door, wherever they went."

The team revived a stage sketch from the prewar *Laurel & Hardy Revue*. The premise had Mr. Hardy trying to renew his driver's license, but with Mr. Laurel doing the driving—driving the clerk crazy, that is, with his "helpful" assistance. The routine was as effective as ever.

In 1947 Tony Hawes was working as a cartoonist for the London *Daily Mail*. As a promotional gimmick the *Daily Mail* artists appeared at the "Ideal Home" exhibition, a popular showcase for postwar building and gardening accessories. "All the cartoonists had a big drawing board and they'd draw their famous cartoons for the crowds," Hawes recalled.

March 14 was a red-letter day for the young artist. "I was sitting there, drawing away, and there was this incredible cheer. Crowds were gathering, people were running—I thought they were all coming to see the drawing I had done! I turned around, and Stan and Babe were walking onto the stage and signing autographs. The applause was incredible. There was quite a crowd for Queen Mary [when she appeared at the exhibition], but nothing like Laurel & Hardy."

Many show-business celebrities visited the exhibition and signed autographs. From America the guests included Robert Taylor, Barbara Stanwyck, and the comedy team of Ole Olsen and Chic Johnson. England's venerable performers Tessie O'Shea, Vera Pearce, and Fred Emney posed with Laurel & Hardy for photographs and newsreels. These three Britons were entertainment heavyweights in more ways than one. When they all joined Oliver Hardy, their imposing physiques dwarfed the slightly-built Laurel and Hawes. Stan looked at Hawes, then at the cavalcade of corpulence opposite him, and said, "I think we'd better get off the stage!" Hawes accompanied Laurel down the steps, to the great amusement of the crowd.

Hawes was asked to escort Laurel & Hardy around the tradeshow booths, which he delightedly did for the next two hours. Stan and Babe paused for refreshment at a beer concession. "We went to the Guinness stand—which is the black muck that they drink in England!—and Babe loved that. Then we went to the Biro stand—that was the first ballpoint pen that had come out, and a pen was £36! Which was about a $150 pen. And Babe and Stan were given two gold ones."

Laurel & Hardy followed their Palladium booking with week-long engagements at South London's Wimbledon and Lewisham's Hippodrome theaters. Bernard Delfont brought the comedians back to the city, for an "incredible" four weeks at the London Coliseum in St. Martin's Lane. This was quite a coup for Delfont; the Coliseum was the showplace where Broadway's most famous musicals made their London bow.

Newsreel cameras covered the comedians' stay in England. The film crews were delighted by Laurel & Hardy's on-camera antics, and gave them far more attention than ordinary news stories. Wherever the newsreel camera caught them—dining aboard a railway car, arriving at their theater, being summoned from their dressing room—Stan and Babe assumed their screen characters and performed miniature comedy pantomimes. The obliging newsmen staged these scenes like film comedies, complete with reaction shots and close-ups.

Babe Hardy always left business details to his partner, but he agreed to be the team's spokesman in public. He proudly explained for the newsreels that he and Stan were going to make a new film. "What is the picture going to be called?" asked the interviewer. Hardy turned to Laurel and asked, in all seriousness, "What's the name of the picture?"

The title Stan gave was simply **Robin Hood**. Perhaps he envisioned a quick variation on their 1933 costume-banditry comedy, **The Devil's Brother**, which he would write and direct himself. Tony Hawes explained that the idea came from the old story *Babes In The Wood*: "Robin Hood is the hero, Maid Marian is looking after the Babes, and the boys are the robbers." Laurel was wary of film deals after his Hollywood experiences, and he backed out when the producer outlined too many production difficulties.

Laurel & Hardy now had time on their hands, time which was eagerly seized by Bernard Delfont. Theater managers throughout England had heard about the team's drawing power, and deluged Delfont with bookings far and wide. The six-week tour was constantly extended, ultimately lasting seven months.

The last two stops on the tour were the Empire theaters of Finsbury Park and Chiswick. The sketch was so well established that the final week should have been the easiest phase of the tour. It turned out to be the toughest, but it points up the comedians' dedication to their art. Tony Hawes told the story: "On September 22, 1947 they were at the Finsbury Park Empire, and Allan Jones was at the Chiswick Empire. At the first band call, Allan Jones was taken ill and they cancelled his show.

The booking artist for Moss Empires, Cissie Williams, went over to Finsbury Park Empire and said to the boys, 'Could you double for us tonight?' You could never do it today, of course. At Finsbury Park, there was a 6:25 and an 8:40 show, with an interval [intermission] in between. Chiswick also had two shows, with 6:20 and 8:30 curtain-up.

"At Chiswick Laurel & Hardy would go on about quarter to seven. They did the first half of the show at Chiswick, and were on stage for twenty-five or thirty minutes for the whole act. Johnnie Riscoe and his wife Violet Terry, a radio comedy team who did songs at the piano, had the closer. They went into the second half of the show, [while] Stan and Babe got in a car and went to Finsbury Park, to do the *second* half of the *first* show. When they got there the intermission would be over, the first couple of dancing acts would be over, and they'd be in time to go straight onto the stage and do their sketch again. The theater put a desk there quickly, and the boys did 'Getting A Driving License' without the backcloth.

"At the intermission they came *back* to Chiswick, and did the first half of the *second* house, and went *back* to Finsbury Park for the second half of the second house. And you should look on a map how far that is." It's some twenty miles, going through the heart of London.

The extraordinary four-performance stint was only intended for the one night, until a replacement could be engaged. But Allan Jones was sent back to America, and word of mouth around Chiswick caused such public demand that Laurel & Hardy were asked to repeat the grind for the whole week! Stan and Babe dutifully shuttled back and forth between Chiswick and Finsbury Park every night, and added an extra trip for the Saturday matinee.

The actors scarcely had a chance to rest after this grueling finale. Delfont arranged a new tour of the continental cities: Copenhagen, Stockholm, Paris, Brussels, and other stops along the way. Living conditions in war-torn Europe were far from ideal; battle-scarred buildings, political riots, labor strikes, and food shortages haunted the team's itinerary. Laurel & Hardy continued to perform the driver's-license sketch in English, but audiences ignored the language barrier and enjoyed the pantomime.

Stan and Babe returned to the United States in 1948. The European trip had affected their health. Fortunately for Hardy, his ration-imposed diet caused him to shed ninety pounds, and he felt happy and fit. Unfortunately for Laurel, his extreme symptoms of exhaustion were diagnosed as diabetes, and he was temporarily unable to work.

Babe Hardy joined several friends from the Masquers Club actors' society for a production of the play *What Price Glory?* It was a community-theater show, which Hardy did for fun. He brought so much humor to his character role that the play's leading man, John Wayne, asked him to play his sidekick in an upcoming movie. Hardy didn't want to fuel rumors that he and Stan Laurel were dissolving their partnership. He finally accepted the job when Laurel, sidelined by his illness, urged him to work on his own.

Hardy played a hearty frontiersman opposite rough-and-ready John Wayne in Republic Pictures' **The Fighting Kentuckian** (1949). He followed this up with another favor to two other friends. Bing Crosby and Frank Capra were doing a remake of Capra's 1933 film **Broadway Bill** (using a good deal of footage from the original). In the new version (**Riding High**, released by Paramount in 1950), Hardy played a chronic horseplayer who falls victim to bad tips.

Babe enjoyed his fling as a character actor; he was extremely pleased with **The Fighting Kentuckian**, and looked upon his work with personal pride. John Wayne offered him a permanent job as his screen sidekick, but Hardy didn't want to leave his own sidekick. When Laurel was ready to resume work, Hardy was ready to rejoin him.

In the spring of 1950 Laurel & Hardy were approached to star in a big-budget motion picture, with location shooting on the French Riviera. They signed for the film immediately. The production looked like it was going to be one big party.

It was actually something of a surprise party.

Atoll K

A Franco-London Films production, in association with Fortezza Film *(Italy)*, Les Films Sirius *(France)*, and Films E. G. E. *(France)*. Released by Les Films Sirius in November, 1951. Produced by Raymond Eger. Directed by Leo Joannon. Screenplay credited in the French print to Rene Wheeler and Pierro Tellini. Screenplay credited in the American print to John Klorer, Frederick Kohner, Rene Wheeler, and Pierro Tellini, with dialogue by John Klorer, Monty Collins, and Isabelle Kloucowsky, based on an idea by Leo Joannon, and "gags by Monty Collins." Photographed by Armand Thirard and Louis Nee. Edited by Robert Isnardon. Music by Paul Misraki. Running Time: 100 minutes.

Released in Germany circa 1952 by Internationale Film-Union A. G., under the title DICK UND DOOF ERBEN EINE INSEL. Running time: 87 minutes. Screenplay credited to Rene Wheeler and Pietro [sic] Tellini.

Released in the United Kingdom in September, 1952 by Franco-London Films, under the title ROBINSON CRUSOELAND. Running time: 82 minutes. Screenplay credited to John Klorer, Rene Wheeler, Pierro Tellini, and Paul Kohner.

Released in the United States in December, 1954 by Exploitation Productions, Inc. (Jack H. Harris) under the title UTOPIA. Running time: 82 minutes. Screenplay credited to John Klorer, Frederick Kohner, Rene Wheeler, and Pierro Tellini, with dialogue by John Klorer, Monty Collins, and Isabelle Kloucowsky, based on an idea by Leo Joannon, and "gags by Monty Collins."

Cast: Stan Laurel and Oliver Hardy (themselves); Suzy Delair (Cherie Lamour); Max Elloy (Antoine), Adriano Rimoldi (Giovanni Copini); Luigi Tosi (Lt. Jack Frazer); Michael Dalmatoff (Alecto, the agitator); Felix Oudart (mayor); Robert Murzeau (Capt. Dolan); Suzet Mais (Mrs. Dolan).

Laurel & Hardy's old movies were in scattered release, but the first-run filmgoer hadn't seen Stan and Ollie for five years. When broadcasting's "Ship's Reporter" Jack Mangan interviewed Stan Laurel (for radio) and Oliver Hardy (for television), he announced that they were "back together again in some of those wonderful pictures." Hardy proudly corrected him, "Well, we've never been *apart*, Jack," although he conceded that people might have confused them with other teams who had split. "Stan and I have been together for twenty-three years and we're still friends. I think that's a record."

The team was about to set sail for Paris, to make a new picture called **Atoll K**. "It sounds very atomic," observed Mangan. "It is about the atom bomb in a sense, then, isn't it?" "Well, it's uranium," clarified Hardy. "We think we've discovered this island with uranium, and the different countries start bidding for our favor to get the island. Eventually we find out that it *isn't* uranium, so the country passes up and leaves us sitting on this island!" Hardy's optimism about the topical premise indicated a successful continuation of the team's motion-picture career.

According to Tony Hawes, "Once they got to France [in 1947] they decided that they were going to do an extended version of the 'driving license.' The sketch had never been put on film. And Stan said, 'Hey, let's find uranium.' I know that came from Stan." This was a conscious effort to modernize the act, to "get them off the old routines, people say they're old-fashioned." Laurel's daughter Lois confirms that the comics looked forward to putting the idea on celluloid: "They thought they were going to have a good time, going abroad to make a film."

It turned out to be the last picture Laurel & Hardy ever made.

The production took almost a year to complete. Because the film was financed by French and Italian companies, the crew had to include a certain number of French and Italian actors and technicians, which made communication difficult. The French government, hoping to revitalize the postwar film industry, offered official funding. This attached considerable "red tape" to the project and dragged out the shooting schedule. Government sponsorship allowed the crew members to drag out their salaries as well. The director, Leo Joannon, was self-indulgent and in-competent, and often spent days merely photographing scenery.

The team of writers could not agree on the direction the storyline would take. In fact, the original release print and the subsequent reissues carry different sets of writing credits. The version that premiered in Paris attributed the screenplay to a French author and an Italian author. Later editions divide the credit among as many as seven writers, and the British and Danish releases credit an author's agent whose *brother* actually collab-orated on the script.

Confusing? Imagine how Laurel and Hardy felt, stuck in a chaotic production with technicians who couldn't speak English and no one in charge. Laurel enlisted the aid of two veteran comedy specialists, direc-tor Alfred Goulding and writer-comedian Monty Collins, both of whom had a wealth of silent-comedy and sight-gag experience. Collins's con-tributions got into the film (with a special credit for "gags"), but Gould-ing was not allowed to interfere with director Joannon.

The final blow, dooming the project, was serious illnesses to the stars, brought on by the arduous location shooting. The intense heat ex-hausted Oliver Hardy and gave him heart problems, while Laurel con-tracted dysentery from the food and lost over fifty pounds. In the final print, Hardy appears robust but for the most part Laurel looks terrible. Various degrees of Laurel's illness are visible in the film; in some scenes he is spry and relaxed; in others his clothes hang on a skeletal frame, and his face is lined and worn. Laurel's voice remains strong but, because **Atoll K** was shot out of sequence, his appearance is inconsistent. The audience is at least spared the spectacle of watching Mr. Laurel deterio-rate as the film unwinds. (He did recover after the film was completed.)

Atoll K is as leisurely as the tropical setting, but that's good—one would hate to see the boys subjected to anything too strenuous. The film doesn't have the cut-and-dried, mechanical look sometimes found in their lesser films. Had Laurel been in condition, **Atoll K** would be a very pleasant adventure. As it stands, it remains a curiosity which never realized its potential. Some Laurel & Hardy fans, troubled by Stan's ap-pearance in the opening scene, are unwilling to give the entire film a chance. Once the viewer gets used to Stan's new appearance, it's easy to adjust to the boys' new surroundings.

While not a success, the film is a good try, because Laurel & Hardy are the whole show. All they have to depend on in this messy project is each other, so Laurel feeds gags to Hardy and vice versa. Their team-work, after so many years, is a pleasure to see. Stan and Ollie dominate the picture, so much so that one resents the "plot" when it appears. **Atoll K** was supposed to be something of a political satire, with pointed statements about unfair taxation and government intervention (a daring premise, considering that government grants were paying for the film's production). One of the film's distributors cut out most of the political rhetoric and a good deal of the romantic subplot, totalling eighteen min-utes of footage. What remains is a choppy, sometimes muddled narrative about life away from civilization, or *Gilligan's Island* with Laurel & Hardy. The shortened, eight-reel edition of the film doesn't always make sense, but that is the version that is usually seen (under the title **Utopia**).

The best presentation of this film is the German release, **Dick Und Doof Erben Eine Insel** ("Laurel & Hardy, Heirs Of The Island"), an intelligent compromise between an overlong print and an abbreviated one. This German-dubbed, 87-minute version maintains satisfactory continuity but dispenses with the long-winded dialogue scenes.

Atoll K opens in an attorney's office, where three international law-yers award Mr. Laurel and his "financial exchequer" Mr. Hardy an in-heritance. This scene is very talky, and the mismatched, awkward English dubbing doesn't help. Laurel's millionaire uncle didn't believe in banks, and left all of his money in cash. Before the boys can figure out how much they have coming, the lawyers greedily deduct various fees and taxes, stuffing their own briefcases with bank notes. The boys are left with a pittance, but they do get an island in the South Seas (where, happily, there won't be any taxes), and a yacht.

At the port of Marseilles, the continentals continue to take advantage of the innocents abroad. A dockhand overhears Laurel's remark about taxes and collects the boys' last dollar. Broke again, the boys decide to examine their new luxury yacht.

The boat is neither new nor luxurious, but it seems seaworthy. There's a lot of traditional Laurel & Hardy silliness as they board the boat, and there aren't any annoying dubbed characters to distract from the stars. Laurel tests the controls, upsetting Hardy; Laurel examines his bunk, disrupting a noisy litter of cats; Hardy tries to activate a water faucet with his usual results. Loading food aboard the boat, Laurel throws produce at his partner—regardless of whether Hardy is ready to catch it! Stan finally dusts his pal's posterior with a legume.

A Laurel & Hardy fan could watch this sort of thing indefinitely, but unfortunately it's time to introduce the plot and return to the primitive dubbing. The port authorities inspect a shipping crate bound for a zoo. The cage contains a mild-mannered man named Antoine (Max Elloy), who claims to be a monkey. (The voice of Paul Frees is *not* heard as the film's narrator, as documented in prior filmographies. In fact, Frees provides the dubbed voice for Antoine.)

Antoine is constantly victimized by a political boondoggle: he isn't allowed to land without a passport, and he isn't allowed to *get* a passport if he can't land. This makes him a "stateless man" with no nationality, so no one will let him off the ship.

An Italian stone mason, Giovanni Copini (Adriano Rimoldi), is doing his best to get *on* a ship, away from authority of any kind. His attempts to stow away are constantly foiled. (The uncut **Atoll K** includes two brief clips of Antoine and Giovanni negotiating with dock officials.)

One of the officials unloads Antoine onto Laurel & Hardy's boat, where Giovanni has gone into hiding. Antoine proves to be a master chef, and prepares a hot meal for his benefactors. Every time Laurel or Hardy turns his back, Giovanni reaches down from the skylight and filches the food. The boys' bewilderment turns to mutual suspicion and then anger, which is only mildly defused when Antoine proposes a toast to friendship.

The engine stalls, so Laurel & Hardy try to fix it. Thanks to their usual powers of concentration, the motor parts fall into the ocean! For that matter, so does Hardy when the boys unfurl the sail and discover Giovanni. Mr. Laurel helpfully throws his friend a life preserver—which immediately sinks!

Drifting along, the four passengers discuss the reasons they went to sea. Wistful Antoine longs for a place to call home, while brusque Giovanni rails against authority. (The full-length print includes a long harangue by Giovanni about how an ungrateful businessman criticized his artistic labors.)

A storm erupts, and the crew goes into action. Below deck, Stan opens a cabinet and an inflatable life raft falls out. It expands at an alarming rate, and traps Stan in its folds. (An undercranked camera helpfully speeds up Stan's movements.) He finally stabs the raft into submission, as a cloud of dust cloaks Stan, but the joke doesn't entirely pay off. One is confused by the editing; there is a flash of a bag of flour, but the shot is too quick to register at first.

As the squall passes, an island rises from beneath the sea. Laurel eagerly disembarks—into Hardy's coat! Unpacking a cargo of books, Laurel gives a stack to Hardy. A ball of rope falls on Hardy, knocking down both him and the books. Laurel obliviously pushes a *second* stack of books toward Hardy, and everything plummets to earth.

A narrator informs us that "weeks . . . months . . . years have passed. This island has become a real paradise." The four castaways have cultivated the land and are fully self-sufficient.

Meanwhile, at the Cockatoo nightclub in Tahiti, singer Cherie Lamour (Suzy Delair) is auditioning for a steady job. As the camera lens scans down her shapely legs, the narrator confirms that "she's got plenty of brains . . . and culture." Her audition song, "Come and Get It," is dubbed in English. (This is the catchy, calypso-accented melody used in the main titles.)

Cherie's fiance, the self-assured naval lieutenant Jack Frazer (Luigi Tosi), is impatiently waiting for her to arrive at their wedding ceremony. He is less than overjoyed to hear that she got the nightclub job. He doesn't want his wife to be a "come-on girl in some clip joint." "I'm an artist, not a bum!" snaps Cherie, as the mayor (Felix Oudart) tries to restore order and perform the ceremony. Cherie gives Frazer time to think it over, and if he doesn't show up for her nightclub act, he'll never see her again. (In the **Utopia** print, the scene is cut to its bare bones, eliminating the musical number, his personal insult and part of her ultimatum. The couple merely squabbles briefly, and then Cherie suddenly says "He'll never see me again.")

Fade in on another dubbed musical interlude, the torch song "Can You Guess." Both Cherie and the mayor keep looking anxiously at the club's entrance, hoping that each new arrival will be Frazer. Frazer's friend, Captain Dolan (Robert Murzeau), catches the singer's eye and shakes his head. The sad news puts new fervor into Cherie's love song, and she leaves the stage on the point of tears.

Cherie insists that Dolan take her as a passenger on his ship. "Hey!" he protests as she departs. "There's also my wife! Ai-yi-yi-yi," he mutters in defeat as the scene fades.

Next we see the captain's wife (Suzet Mais), a no-nonsense type who carries such domestic accessories as a pith helmet and a shotgun. She orders Cherie off of her husband's boat. Suzy Delair's screen character was once described by *Time* magazine as "a Mae West who really *means* it," and true to form she reacts flirtatiously. The jealous wife doesn't trust her husband to row her ashore, so Cherie is left to steer her own boat.

Back on the island, Stan has seen and heard a boat, but nobody believes him. Antoine and Giovanni exchange views: "Stan certainly received his share of stupidity." "Yeah, no one person could be really such a block-head." Stan is vindicated when Cherie suddenly appears in their midst. "You might say I was dropped by a witch," she explains. "This one used a shotgun."

Only a fragment of this sequence was retained for **Utopia**. Besides the second song being cut, most of Captain Dolan's footage and all of Mrs. Dolan's footage were removed, which renders the sequence meaningless. Cherie just shows up on the island without explanation. Antoine and Giovanni's remarks about Stan were also deleted, so when Ollie tells him "You are absolutely right," we don't know why.

Cherie is captivated by the island, as Stan endorses life in the tropics: "It's swell. You don't have to shave or anything." Cherie is curious about how the men got there, so Mr. Hardy melodramatically recounts his thrilling adventure on the high seas. "It was as dark as pitch," he says. Mr. Laurel adds to the mood: "It was so pitch you couldn't see your hand behind your back."

Cherie is given her own quarters, while the men double up. This is a variation of the three-in-a-berth gag from **The Big Noise**, only now it's four in a bunk, and Hardy is larger than ever. In another joke from **The Big Noise**, Hardy decides that he and Stan should sleep in shifts, and once again Stan fails to grasp the idea.

A bat flies into the bedroom, and Stan tries to chase it away with a broom. Stan's broom makes contact with Ollie and his roommates, but misses the bat. (This scene was not dubbed, so one can hear the continental actors' actual voices in the confusion.) Maneuvering the intruder to the wall, Stan opens the window—and more bats fly *into* the room!

Comes the dawn, and the men are anxious to make a good impression on the new girl in town. (Laurel tries for a "mixed-up hats" routine but Hardy doesn't take the bait!) When they call on Cherie, they are unpleasantly surprised to learn that she already has a boyfriend. The men cry uncontrollably when the boyfriend's favorite dish is served to them.

The boyfriend has orders to investigate the island that came out of nowhere, and he confronts Cherie coldly. Neither he nor Cherie will budge from their stands on marriage and career.

Frazer's surveyors detect uranium on the island. Frazer wants to know which country the island belongs to, but since stateless Antoine was the first to land, no country can claim the uranium rights. The new mineral source is classified and identified as "Atoll K."

Laurel & Hardy hear news flashes about "Atoll K" on the radio (one wonders what their power source is). To protect their island from other nations, the castaways decide to form their own government. Inspired by the resourceful fictional character Robinson Crusoe, Ollie draws up a constitution which declares that "Crusoeland" will have no laws, no taxes, no money, no passports, and no prisons. President Hardy selects his cabinet: Cherie is his vice-president, Antoine is his foreign minister, and Giovanni is his minister of construction. Meeting adjourned. Stan is confused: "What about me?" "Stanley," replies the President patiently, "*you* are the *people*."

News of Crusoeland being a lawless, wide-open country attracts refugees from all over the world. Stan and Ollie are astonished to find a Scotsman in kilts parading past them without a word. Then an American Indian in full regalia comes into view. As hundreds of people storm the beach, the boys think their country is being invaded. The light, humorous tone of the story instantly evaporates, as heavy political statements overshadow the comedy.

The new population of Crusoeland lives freely: a mother uses the country's makeshift flag to clean her children's faces. Laurel & Hardy open a restaurant, the Cafe Crusoe, where Ollie is the host and Stan is the bartender. This is a free country, so they give a delighted patron two free bottles of spirits. A stereotypical gangster, complete with slouch hat, dark shirt, and white tie, shoves the patron aside. "I brought this liquor out here so I could sell it," he snarls. Another unruly upstart, Alecto (Michael Dalmatoff), shoots bottles off the bar and pushes the gangster away. (Both the gangster and the brawl are missing from the shorter **Utopia** print.)

When Alecto takes liberties with Cherie, Stan is outraged: "We'll have you imported!" Giovanni points out that they would have to change the laws of the island. President Ollie leaves to call an emergency cabinet meeting.

Meanwhile, Alecto and his cronies plot the government's downfall. "This island is a paradise governed by idiots," Alecto grumbles. He plans to put himself in power, organize a few demonstrations, and tell the people how they should think. (This politically charged scene is not in **Utopia**.)

The president has decreed that there will now be law and order in Crusoeland. Alecto angrily tears down the proclamation and leads a lynch mob against the island leaders. "You will have a fair and honest trial," Alecto assures the accused, "and then you will be hanged at sunrise." But Cherie will be spared, as Alecto suggestively promises, "I will take you under my . . . personal protection." The film's American distributors resented Cherie's being under Alecto's anything, and deleted the line, along with his gleeful announcement of the execution: "And now, let's get the principal actors for our opera!"

Cherie hides a stone in her handbag and powders a flower with pepper. When she attracts the boys' guards, they sneeze, and she knocks them out. Cut to the other side of the wall, where all the boys hear are a sneeze, a bump, and a loud thud! The extras playing the victims get into the spirit of the scene, mugging and then collapsing comically.

The founders of Crusoeland are about to be hanged when another, more violent storm engulfs the island. The terrified crowds depart as the atoll begins to sink beneath the waves. The hangman's scaffolding breaks loose and floats out to sea. (The scene is just a jumble of clouds and crowds, but it works anyway.) The castaways are rescued by Frazer and his shipmates.

The narrator returns to tell us what finally happened to the principals. Cherie and Frazer got married and are still squabbling. Giovanni went back to Italy and is humbly building fences. Antoine tried to sneak aboard a ship in another animal cage, but all we see of him are his boots—next to a contented lion. This is a most unsuitable ending for the sweet, hapless Antoine; one wishes the gag was written for Giovanni, who is angry and unpleasant throughout.

The film has a slightly different ending than the one Oliver Hardy had outlined to Jack Mangan. The boys have finally landed on their own island, and Frazer and Cherie have promised to send fresh stocks of food and supplies. "At last all of our troubles are over," says Ollie. A uniformed officer begs to differ: the island is being taken over by the government (*which* government?) for non-payment of taxes. The boys watch helplessly as their provisions are carted away, leaving them nothing.

Ollie turns to Stan, in the last scene of the last Laurel & Hardy movie, and says for the last time, "Well, here's another nice mess you've gotten me into!" And Stan starts to cry as the film irises out into a miniature. Stan and Ollie shrink into oblivion as their familiar "cuckoo" theme plays them off.

Atoll K was not a success in theaters. The uneven screenplay, overlong running time, and distracting dubbing worked against it. A reviewer for *Variety* caught the first-run, 100-minute screening in Paris on November 13, 1951: "An improper mixture of fantasy, satire and slapstick does not leaven this into palatable comedy for upper case U.S. slotting. With comics Stan Laurel and Oliver Hardy in the cast and an exploitable theme this could do for special situations and duallers. A basically sound comedy idea is overloaded by co-production exigencies necessitating that French and Italian participants have an equal footing with Laurel and Hardy . . . Hardy's resigned double takes and the Laurel crying binges do not register for heavy yocks. However, there are some good moments . . . Direction does not give the comedy the pace it needs." Incidentally, the first-run prints of **Atoll K** billed the stars by their surnames only, with the full names of Suzy Delair and director Leo Joannon printed in equally large type.

The Exhibitor published a short summary of Franco-London Films' 1952 edition, retitled **Robinson Crusoeland** and cut to 82 minutes: "A lot of money was spent on production, but the slapstick antics of Laurel and Hardy will appeal most to the kids." Franco-London had very little money for promotion, but enlisted the services of a sympathetic printer; the "color" lobby cards for **Robinson Crusoeland** were simply blackand-white stills, physically pasted onto a stenciled block print, inked in red and blue.

The New York premiere, which didn't occur until December of 1954, found the 82-minute version of the film now titled **Utopia**. A. H. Weiler of the *New York Times* summed it up in a few brief lines: "The Messrs. Laurel and Hardy are awkwardly involved in some hectic silliness on a South Sea atoll they've inherited . . . Oliver Hardy is the standard globular and exasperated type he has portrayed so many times before. Mr. Laurel appears woefully haggard. No wonder. The boys never should have left home."

The film failed to catch on, resulting in scattered, hit-and-miss exposure. The fact that it received *any* exposure came as an unpleasant surprise to Stan Laurel and Oliver Hardy, who never expected to see the finished film. Lois Laurel recalls, "My dad was very upset about **Atoll K** being released in the United States. To his knowledge, it was only going to be shown in Europe. He thought, 'At least, thank God, it's not going to be shown in the U. S. A.'"

Utopia, it seems, was destined to always play "late." After its belated Broadway opening, the film sneaked in and out of neighborhood moviehouses for the next several years. A 1956 engagement at Chicago's modest Empress Theatre was quietly announced in the newspapers, but after five days of indifferent response, the management started to advertise **Utopia** as an Abbott & Costello comedy! The film opened in Boston for a brief run in the late fall of 1957.

Like the film's unfortunate Antoine, **Utopia** soon became "stateless." No one claimed any copyright to the picture, so it was widely copied and re-copied for 16mm and 8mm home-movie use. These mediocre amateur prints found their way to low-budget television stations in 1980, and these were duplicated again and again for bottom-of-the-barrel discount videotapes. **Utopia** is sadly one of the most readily accessible Laurel & Hardy movies, but the master print looks and sounds a lot better than these muddy, muffled copies. The 35mm materials still exist, and original-quality prints can still be struck from the negatives.

In 1986 **Utopia** was packaged for television as part of the syndicated *Laurel & Hardy Show.* For some strange reason (perhaps to insure copyright protection), the pleasant, tropical theme music was replaced with stock music from the 1938 feature **Block-Heads**. The end title from **Block-Heads** was also added.

Atoll K is almost an afterthought in the Laurel & Hardy history. It's so unlike any of their earlier studio products that it stands apart from their main body of work, and not just chronologically. Like **Atoll K**, the attempted comebacks of other venerable comedians—**Love Happy** with The Marx Brothers, **A King In New York** with Charlie Chaplin, **Kook's Tour** with The Three Stooges—were all far from typical, all independently made, and all financial fiascoes, but they all have their moments for the devoted fan.

Atoll K deserves at least a polite round of applause for being something different, and Laurel & Hardy deserve equal credit for trying something new at such a late stage in their careers.

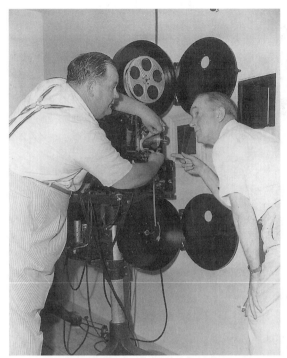

Babe Hardy, who used to be a professional projectionist, threads up a reel for Stan Laurel. (But Stan shouldn't be smoking near flammable nitrate film!)

Making a date with destiny, the boys trade their janitors' jobs for detective assignments in *The Big Noise*.

An oldie but goodie: Laurel & Hardy's "mixed-up hats" routine in *The Big Noise*.

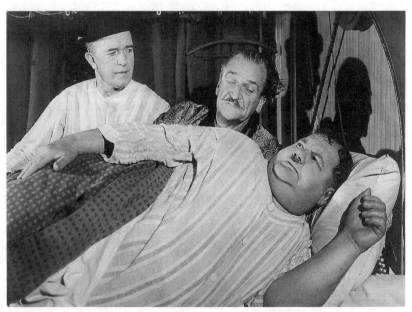

Lush accommodations: The inebriated Jack Norton shares an upper berth with Laurel & Hardy in *The Big Noise*.

LOOK OUT! DANGER!
YOU'LL LAUGH YOURSELF TO PIECES!

Stan LAUREL
Oliver HARDY
in
THE BIG NOISE

A 20 CENTURY-FOX PICTURE

with
DORIS MERRICK · ARTHUR SPACE · VEDA ANN BORG
Directed by Mal St. Clair
Produced by Sol M. Wurtzel
Screen Play by W. Scott Darling

A pressbook ad from *The Big Noise*.

In Spanish-speaking countries, *The Big Noise* was known as *La Bomba*.

Good help is hard to find, so Mary Boland and Henry O'Neill pamper their new servants in this posed shot from *Nothing But Trouble.*

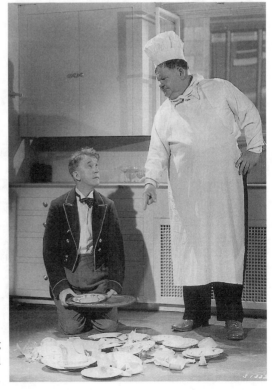

Stan was just following orders—he was supposed to finish the dishes.

Has Stan wrecked the royal luncheon? David Leland and Ollie have their suspicions.

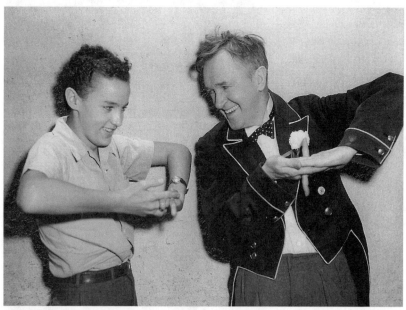

One of Stan Laurel's famous hand games, the "finger wiggle," is demonstrated to eager pupil David Leland between takes during filming of *Nothing But Trouble.*

M-G-M's ad campaign stressed the escapist comedy of *Nothing But Trouble.*

In *The Bullfighters,* the boys' "new look" accentuated their ages, but the "Stan and Ollie" characters were their usual selves.

The Battle of the Fountain in *The Bullfighters,* staged by Stan Laurel, has Ed Gargan as the boys' antagonist.

During the "egg" bit in *The Bullfighters,* again directed by Laurel, the boys try to clap the handcuffs on Carol Andrews.

Stan and Ollie politely refuse the business proposition from Richard Lane and Irving Gump in *The Bullfighters*. This posed photo was squeezed in during a break from filming—note the cigarette in Lane's hand.

Laurel & Hardy filming inserts on Fox's process stage, December 1944. Here is where the close-ups for the hay-wagon chase were done, with the scenery projected on a screen.

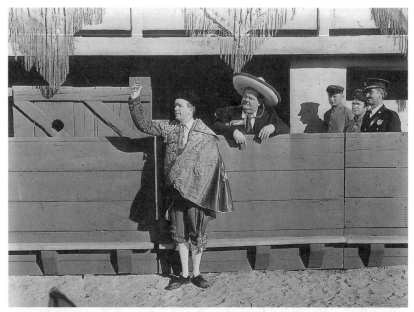

Don Sebastian greets the aficionados in *The Bullfighters,* but it's a lot of bull to Ollie.

The Bullfighters was the only "30th Anniversary Picture" that Fox didn't talk about.

Film Classics re-
released several vintage
L & H features in the
late 1940s.

The familiar "Film Classics plaque."

A lobby card advertising an Astor reissue.

Lippert Pictures prepared this colorful poster for the 1950 reissue of *Babes in Toyland*, now retitled *March Of The Wooden Soldiers*.

A formal studio portrait of Stan Laurel and Oliver Hardy, from the 1940s.

Ida (pronounced "E-da") Kitaeva Laurel, Stan's wife, shares a laugh with the boys on the boat-train to Waterloo during their first night in England, February 10, 1947.

Posing for the press at their hotel, February 1947.

"Ship's Reporter" Jack Mangan chats with Babe Hardy about *Atoll K*.

The cast of *Atoll K:* Adriano Rimoldi, Max Elloy, Stan Laurel, Suzy Delair, and Oliver Hardy.

Despite serious illness and drastic weight loss, Stan Laurel carried his half of the comedy in *Atoll K.*

The bench says "No Loitering." From the looks of policeman Leslie Spurling, Ollie and Stan have some explaining to do in *A Spot Of Trouble* (1952).

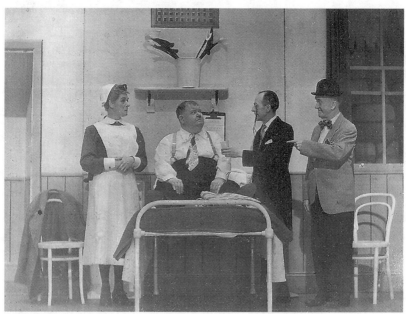

The hospital sketch: *Birds Of A Feather* (1953).

Cowboy Stan has a price on his head. Actually it's a merchandise tag from a clothing store. This was Laurel & Hardy's last personal appearance (1954).

The Laurels and the Hardys pose at the Hal Roach Studios, where *This Is Your Life* erected a plaque dedicating "Lake Laurel and Hardy." The boys weren't smiling much *during* the Ralph Edwards telecast.

The canny Jack H. Harris used caricatures instead of photographs to sell *Utopia*. (This is a reproduction of Harris's original 1954 paste-up; note the scissored outlines around each art component.)

The team's final photo session, at Stan's home in Santa Monica, California, July 20, 1956.

Robert Youngson.

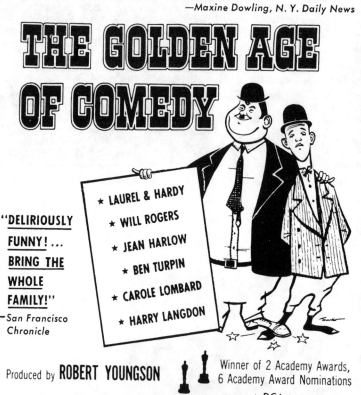

"HILARIOUS! THE SPECTATORS SHAKE WITH LAUGHTER!"
—William K. Zinsser, N. Y. Herald Tribune

"SOME OF THE FINEST SIGHT GAGS FROM THE FUNNIEST PICTURES EVER FILMED!"
—Life Magazine in a two-page picture spread

"THE GREATEST LIST OF STAR COMEDIANS EVER, IN THE BEST COMEDY BITS OF THEIR LONG CAREERS!"
—Maxine Dowling, N. Y. Daily News

THE GOLDEN AGE OF COMEDY

"DELIRIOUSLY FUNNY!... BRING THE WHOLE FAMILY!"
—San Francisco Chronicle

★ LAUREL & HARDY
★ WILL ROGERS
★ JEAN HARLOW
★ BEN TURPIN
★ CAROLE LOMBARD
★ HARRY LANGDON

Produced by **ROBERT YOUNGSON**

Winner of 2 Academy Awards, 6 Academy Award Nominations

A DCA Release

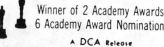

T H E A T R E

Laurel & Hardy stole the show in Robert Youngson's *The Golden Age of Comedy.*

When Comedy Was King (1960) chronicled the history of silent-movie comedy.

"Mexican Spitfire" Lupe Velez's egg battle with Laurel & Hardy was the highlight of M-G-M's *Big Parade Of Comedy*.

These colorful home-movie cartons were often displayed in camera shops and department stores.

Americom brought "talkies" to silent-projector owners.

In 1972 LBJ Films modern-
ized the 1950 pressbook ads
for *March Of The Wooden
Soldiers.*

A sensitive and thought-
ful ad for *The Crazy
World Of Laurel & Hardy.*

The international Sons Of The Desert organization takes its name from a Laurel & Hardy movie.

The Fifties

The beginning of the new decade, like the one before it, brought new opportunities for Stan Laurel and Oliver Hardy. During the summer of 1950 they were offered featured roles in a major motion picture, then in the preparation stages, called **Two Tickets To Broadway**. According to the film's earliest press releases, RKO Radio Pictures intended this Tony Martin-Janet Leigh vehicle to be "the mightiest Technicolor musical of them all," with tunes composed by major songwriters and dance numbers staged by Busby Berkeley. RKO's studio head, Howard Hughes, had enough confidence in **Two Tickets To Broadway** to schedule its release a full year in advance; it was to be RKO's Christmas-week attraction for 1951.

The extravagant Hughes allowed a twenty-week shooting schedule (enough time to make *five* Laurel & Hardy movies in the forties). Laurel & Hardy had had good luck with RKO before; their feature **The Flying Deuces** had been a certified hit. A successful appearance in a new Hollywood movie, plus plenty of Howard Hughes's splashy publicity, would open new doors for the veteran comedy team. It seemed certain that Stan and Babe would complete **Atoll K** and return to Hollywood in plenty of time to report to RKO.

When RKO was ready to turn the cameras on **Two Tickets To Broadway** in November of 1950, Laurel & Hardy were still in France, four months behind schedule, struggling to finish **Atoll K**. They were replaced by vaudevillians Smith & Dale, who garnered the comic honors in **Two Tickets To Broadway** and extended their own careers. The film's director, James V. Kern, received excellent critical notices for his work, and continued to prosper in his field. It seemed that the film, although it wasn't the record-breaker that RKO planned, was helpful to everyone except Laurel & Hardy.

While Laurel & Hardy were away, a technological monster had overtaken Hollywood. It was called *television*. In 1950 very few Hollywood movies were available to television stations; major studios refused to supply films to their small-screen competitors. Early TV schedulers, desperate for product, bought up as much film programming as they could. The reissue dealers saw their chance.

As early as 1946 George Hirliman, founder of Film Classics, saw great possibilities in the new medium, and discontinued his theatrical enterprises. He correctly predicted that the independent film peddlers would be the first to furnish material, using economical 16mm film stock. Hirliman's old production company was called "Regal Productions"; he reclaimed the name for his new video concern.

The farsighted Hirliman had secured the TV rights to Film Classics' Laurel & Hardy comedies, which had already been through the reissue mill. When Regal Television Corporation packaged the team's old films, Laurel & Hardy became the first widely syndicated stars of television. Their films were played and replayed "so often that the sprocket holes of the film have worn out," in the words of one industry insider.

The demand for the thirty-nine shorts was so great that Regal actually manufactured fourteen more. Ten of Laurel & Hardy's feature films were edited into twenty- and twenty-five-minute abridgements. This made sense at the time. Pioneer television broadcasts generally ran fifteen or thirty minutes each, and anything that ran longer was often serialized over several days. The condensed Laurel & Hardys were tailor-made for limited time slots.

To avoid confusion with the original feature films, these truncated versions were assigned new, often peculiar titles. The first portion of **Block-Heads** became a TV two-reeler called **Better Now**. The prison comedy **Pardon Us** was rehashed as **Whatta Stir**, and **A Chump At Oxford** resurfaced as **Alter Ego**. **Saps At Sea** was split into two TV shorts, **Where To Now** (a singularly bizarre reissue title) and **Horn Hero**.

The original six- and seven-reel features were abbreviated with varying degrees of success. **Sons Of The Desert** was intelligently compressed into two reels (as **Fun On The Run**), and **Way Out West** was sensibly streamlined into three reels (as **The Whacky West**). Most of the other features, however, barely survived the perils of the cutting-room floor.

The new "shorts" were prepared as cheaply as possible. Key scenes from the features were crudely patched together in "workprint" fashion, merely to indicate the sequence of shots without regard for scene transitions or optical effects. Regal refused to spend additional money to refine the workprints, so the rough edges remained in the final copies. Not only were the cuts and splices very visible, they were audible, too—dialogue was often chopped off in mid-sentence. The freshly minted title footage failed to mention Laurel & Hardy's names, and the production credits were also overlooked. There wasn't even a soundtrack on the TV titles, which were accompanied by nothing but hiss and static.

A rival distributor, Governor TV Films, offered their own "Laurel & Hardy shows," taken from the trio of Astor/M-G-M reprints. **The Devil's Brother** was sliced into four twenty-minute chunks (only one of which, titled **Cry Babies**, made any sense). **Bonnie Scotland** was divided into three episodes. **Pick A Star** yielded only one extract: the few minutes of Laurel & Hardy footage were retained and most of the rest was junked. The print quality was good, even if the editorial continuity was not. For many years, the only way a Laurel & Hardy fan could see any of these rare movies was via one of these random remnants. At least the stars received billing (not under their full names, but as "Laurel & Hardy"), and Hal Roach was credited as producer and director, which in these cases wasn't always true. The titles did use Laurel & Hardy's "Cuckoo Song" theme—in an odd xylophone-solo rendition, pulled from the track of **Bonnie Scotland**, where the visual had been a blacksmith's anvil! These Governor reels were soon lumped together with the Regal TV condensations for syndication.

Laurel & Hardy's huge success on TV could have been a turning point for the comedians. Television was to give other teams a new lease on life: Abbott & Costello brought their familiar patter routines to TV and won enough new fans to warrant a whirlwind personal-appearance schedule. The Three Stooges had a new feature film into theaters within months of their TV revival, and rode the crest of their new popularity into the next decade. Unlike Abbott & Costello or the Stooges, however, Laurel & Hardy could not capitalize on their TV fame—again, thanks to their involvement in the ill-fated **Atoll K**.

Upon their return to America in 1951, they became aware of the Laurel & Hardy TV phenomenon. It was gratifying and frustrating. They enjoyed the renewed recognition, but they didn't receive any residuals, and they were upset that their old theatrical pictures had become vehicles for commercial advertising. Stan Laurel was particularly chagrined when he saw the reckless editing of some of the films, and often wished he could have recut them himself.

The Hollywood that Laurel & Hardy knew died while they were abroad. Government anti-trust proceedings brought an end to the studio system, where a film company owned a network of theaters and maintained a staff of several hundred actors and technicians. Laurel & Hardy returned to find a new game with new rules and new players.

Stan and Babe returned to safe ground, touring provincial theaters in Europe again for Bernard Delfont. Little did they know, the rules had changed there, too. "The first time they went there in '47," recalled Tony Hawes, "they were playing the number-one theaters: the London Palladium, the London Coliseum, and all the Moss Empire theaters, which were magnificent. When they came back in '51–'52, they were playing the second-class theaters. It was still [for] Delfont, but it was the [lesser] Butterworth circuit. In '52–'53, they were playing, really, the third-class type of theaters. I don't know why they went down. They were still getting very good money, but it was destroying them. The dressing rooms were filthy, they were dirty and drafty, and because you had a smaller town and a smaller theater, you got a smaller hotel. So they were terribly uncomfortable in those days. It was absolutely dreadful." Was the decline due to the team's bad health? "I think it brought on the bad health," said Hawes.

Stan Laurel rewrote one of the old Laurel & Hardy shorts for live performance. **Night Owls**, with the boys as inept burglars, was played before theater audiences in 1952. In some halls the skit was called *A Spot Of Bother*; in others *A Spot Of Trouble*. "At two theaters they didn't do it at all," amended Hawes, "because they couldn't get the props on the stage. So they did a stand-up routine and Babe sang a couple of extra songs." This emergency version of the act came in handy on November 9, 1953, when Laurel became ill at Finsbury Park and was hospitalized in London. "A double act in England, Jimmy Jewell and Ben Warris, went on in their place," remembered Hawes. "But just to keep the audience who had paid to see Laurel & Hardy, Babe came on and sang 'Lazy Moon' and 'Shine On, Harvest Moon.'"

At age 61, Babe Hardy was no longer up to the strenuous demands of physical comedy—at least, not for two performances nightly. To accommodate his partner, Stan Laurel adapted the 1932 short **County Hospital** into a sketch called *Birds Of A Feather*. Babe played a bedridden patient, which allowed him to perform without pratfalls.

Birds Of A Feather toured the more obscure outposts of the British Isles in 1953. Laurel & Hardy's old routines were becoming increasingly familiar to audiences, and the team's standbys offered more nostalgia than novelty. Stan Laurel was determined to freshen up the act.

While *Birds Of A Feather* was touring, Michael North of the British Broadcasting Company approached the team about starring in a comedy series for radio. Laurel & Hardy didn't commit themselves, but they were receptive. Encouraged, BBC Radio hired scriptwriters Tony Hawes and Denis Gifford to prepare a pilot, with more episodes to follow. The radio show was designed as a situation comedy; instead of being a variety program with music and humor, each episode would contain one long sketch.

The show had an amusing premise, evident from the series title: *Laurel & Hardy Go To The Moon*. "We originally did something about a spaceship or a rocket," Hawes related, "and then Stan said, 'Let's *get* to the moon.' They get into an elevator at Fortnum and Mason's [department store] at Piccadilly, and something happens whereby they take off. I distinctly remember them going to the moon—in the elevator!"

Hawes and Gifford's script was enthusiastically received by the comedians, who staged a read-through in their dressing room. (The session, unfortunately, was not recorded.)

Two weeks later, on November 16, 1953, Laurel & Hardy were appearing at Brixton's Empress Theatre. The writers delivered the rough draft of the first show. Tony Hawes poignantly remembered the occasion: "We sat in the dressing room with Stan, who was very quiet and very subdued. He said, 'This may not happen. We may not get around to doing this. Just a minute, and I'll show you why.'

"He slowly went to the other door. 'You've just got to look at Babe. I'm not going to say anything. I'm just going to show you the condition he's in.' Stan opened the door, and Babe was fast asleep in the dressing-room chair, and he looked terrible," said Hawes, still saddened by the recollection. "And we both looked at Babe. And realized that there was not going to be a radio show."

The collapse of this project was especially disappointing, in that it would have given new spark and direction to Laurel & Hardy's career. While their bag of tricks in the '40s was considered old-hat, their ideas for the early '50s were novel and up-to-the-minute (as illustrated by **Atoll K** and *Laurel & Hardy Go To The Moon*).

Laurel & Hardy continued playing the old hospital sketch. The venues were getting smaller, but the public remained warm and appreciative. One of the most memorable highlights of the team's long partnership occurred during this period. Laurel & Hardy had just arrived by boat at Cobh, Ireland, where the docks were swarming with admirers. Amazed by the reception, the comedians were overcome when the church bells of Cobh began ringing out Laurel & Hardy's theme song.

Time was running out for *Birds Of A Feather*. Oliver Hardy's declining health did not allow him to complete the full season, and the last several playdates in 1954 were cancelled. Laurel & Hardy returned to America and retired their act. Their last personal appearance, in November of 1954, was for the press; Stan and Babe were among the invited guests of a new western-wear shop in Culver City, California, and they dressed as cowboys for the occasion.

Late in November, producer Bernard Delfont arrived in California to discuss yet another European engagement—or so Laurel & Hardy thought. He was actually helping to arrange an elaborate ambush.

This Is Your Life was a top-rated NBC television show, hosted by its producer, Ralph Edwards. Each week Edwards would surprise an unsuspecting guest—sometimes an ordinary citizen, sometimes a distinguished individual, but usually a show-business celebrity—and reunite the guest with former friends and associates. The show was broadcast live, before a theater audience, so there was always great excitement in each installment.

On December 1, 1954, the surprise guests were to be Stan Laurel and Oliver Hardy. It was a "where-are-they-now" episode, since they were keeping a low professional profile in America while their old films were sweeping the nation. Lois Laurel Hawes recalls that her father "was going to the Knickerbocker Hotel for a business conference with his attorney, Mr. Shipman, and Mr. Delfont was there to discuss a tour. I did not know, until that morning, of this. Lucille [Mrs. Hardy] knew about it quite a way in advance, and then she, under pretense, got pictures from Ida [Mrs. Laurel]. *Ida* didn't even know until the last, because they were afraid she would slip. I got a phone call that said, 'Be at this beauty shop in Beverly Hills at such-and-such a time.' Someone was doing a surprise for my father. I had no idea it was televised. I thought it was just a party or something."

The "party" began at 6:30 p.m., Pacific time, when NBC cameras burst into Suite 205 at the Knickerbocker. Edwards's disembodied voice thundered through a loudspeaker: "Mr. Stan Laurel? Mr. Oliver Hardy!" as the studio audience gasped in recognition. For a moment the boys looked like frightened deer caught in someone's headlights, as the technicians' bright spotlights shone upon them. The comedians were totally dumbstruck by the intrusion, although Hardy was quick enough to "go into the act" and do a sheepish tie-twiddle for the camera.

This was the first time Edwards's production staff had attempted to cover two biographies on the same program, and it was essential that things move like clockwork to cram everything in to a half-hour. Unfortunately, just like in a Laurel & Hardy movie, good intentions turned into another nice mess. The Knickerbocker was conveniently located behind Edwards's theater, the El Capitan, and it should have taken just a couple of minutes to escort Laurel & Hardy from the hotel to the stage.

They didn't show up. Poor Mr. Edwards, alone on stage before millions of viewers, had no idea of what had gone wrong, and had no way of finding out without abandoning the live cameras. He nervously began ad-libbing, waiting for the guests of honor to arrive.

Various explanations have been published about what caused the delay. One version has Stan Laurel refusing to go on. Another has their taxi getting caught in traffic. Ralph Edwards recalled in 1990 that a door was stuck in the hotel room. "He must have just completely forgotten," says Lois. "The taxi had a flat tire! My dad said it was so funny because Babe got in and sat down, and when they started off the tire went flat! Somebody took them down a little alley way which was quicker. They should have thought of that in the first place, because it would have taken longer for the cab to go around the block. They could have just gone out the back door of the hotel and down through the alley to the theater on Vine Street."

Meanwhile, back at the El Capitan, Stan and Babe still hadn't shown up, and Ralph Edwards was desperately trying to remain poised and jovial without betraying his nervous tension. As the camera mercilessly held its position for an agonizingly long take, Edwards died a slow death in front of the entire country. The few minutes of awkward ad-libs seemed like hours, but finally the guests arrived and Edwards miraculously regained his composure. (When Edwards prepared a new edition of this episode for syndication, he wisely deleted all of the "awkward" footage, but it still exists in the kinescope versions, which are sometimes offered on the film and video markets.)

Once the tribute got under way, Edwards was under extreme pressure to make up for lost time. Because there were two lives to chronicle, with twice as many guests to introduce, he was forced to usher the participants on and off stage as rapidly as possible. His job was inadvertently made easier by the guests of honor, who didn't use up valuable time talking. Laurel & Hardy said very little during the broadcast. Babe Hardy seemed pleasantly surprised by seeing boyhood friends, volunteering a few kind words about them in their presence, and he good-naturedly endured Edwards's crude jokes about his weight. He also earned laughs from the studio audience with his facial reactions to the various surprises. Stan Laurel was not as animated; he was so taken aback by the whole experience that he barely spoke at all.

Backstage, in the "green room" waiting area, Laurel & Hardy's former director Leo McCarey was ill at ease about appearing on live television. He had been drinking heavily to steady his nerves, and his hands were visibly shaking. Fortunately, when he walked on stage he beamed broadly at his old friends, and smoothly related a story about the silent-movie days.

In 1978 Lucille Hardy remembered planning the show. She had suggested that someone should hand Laurel & Hardy the wrong derbies, which would prompt them to automatically do their "mixed-up hats." It was always good for a laugh, she told the producers, and would help to fill time. On the air, Leo McCarey started to hand them their own hats, and then realizing what business they were going to do, he swapped them. Laurel & Hardy were so unprepared that they forgot the routine! They meekly handed each other their correct hats. "And they were the wrong size!" laughs Lois Laurel Hawes. "Both of them! Nobody knew."

Vivian Blaine, then enjoying great musical-comedy success in *Guys And Dolls*, told the audience about the warm reception the boys received in Cobh. Finally, Hal Roach, Jr. came on to represent his father's studio, Roach senior having declined. Laurel & Hardy appeared glad to see him, but according to Lois, "my dad did not have any time for Roach junior." As the program drew to a close, and family members joined Stan and Babe on stage, Lois glamorously smiled and briskly approached her father. ("My Loretta Young entrance," she chuckles. "They told me to hurry!") The live-TV nightmare finally ended as Edwards delivered rapid-fire promotional acknowledgements. *This Is Your Life* never tackled a dual biography again.

Did Stan Laurel consider *This Is Your Life* a big career boost? "No," says Lois flatly. "He was still upset over it, for *quite* a few years. He did feel that Ralph Edwards had a good thing going, getting top talent and paying them nothing. He got a projector and a copy of the film, and Ida got a charm bracelet.

"My dad being such a perfectionist, he felt that they weren't prepared. He mellowed in later years, because so many people would say, 'Oh, I really loved that,' because they didn't know too much about the backgrounds of either one of them."

Once again, Laurel & Hardy could not capitalize on their TV exposure. Lois explains it was "because Babe wasn't well. This was in December of '54 and he just wasn't all that well."

Someone did cash in on that particular *This Is Your Life* show. The surprise appearance of Laurel & Hardy on December 1 generated a great deal of public interest. This was very good news for a Philadelphia-based salesman named Jack H. Harris; he had secured **Robinson Crusoeland,** the 82-minute version of **Atoll K,** just a few weeks before. His aptly-named Exploitation Productions, Inc. struck while the iron was hot, rush-releasing the "new" Laurel & Hardy comedy. The film was retitled **Utopia.**

Harris did a magnificent job of selling **Utopia.** He arranged a first-run opening on Broadway just before Christmas—an amazing feat on such short notice. He assembled a terrific coming-attractions trailer, which downplayed Stan Laurel's illness-ravaged physical condition and pointed up the frantic, helter-skelter nature of the comedy. He even set up a promotional tie-in for additional revenue: during a scene in the film where the comedians pour a drink, he spliced in an insert of a Welch's grape juice bottle! Finally, and perhaps most incredibly, he kept **Utopia** in circulation for at least three years.

Utopia did not receive a national release, nor was it advertised (or even mentioned) in the motion-picture trade periodicals. Exploitation Productions' Jack Harris may have tainted his firm with an unfortunate business name; in 1954 and 1955 the entire "exploitation" field of fast-buck promotions was under fire, with numerous "buyer beware" warnings issuing from the trade press.

Harris, avoiding print ads, apparently spent his entire advertising budget on theater accessories. He created an imaginative pressbook containing press releases, contest ideas, and newspaper ads. He also commissioned several attractive posters and lobby cards, featuring original artwork of Laurel & Hardy (instead of photographic likenesses from the film, which would not have been appetizing at all).

The confident Mr. Harris appears to have generated interest in **Utopia** strictly by telephone, and his sales calls were persuasive. As **Utopia** played its first bookings, the prosperous Harris hired an assistant and moved into newer, larger offices in Philadelphia. He later moved to California, where he continued to acquire second-run independent features. In the 1960s Harris became a science-fiction specialist, shuttling chillers like **The Blob** and **Dinosaurus** from theaters to drive-ins to TV stations. In an odd reprise of his **Utopia** tactics, Harris took an old, obscure, foreign-made slapstick comedy (**Mother Riley Meets The Vampire**, 1952) and modernized it by hiring humorist Allan Sherman to perform a new title song: **My Son, The Vampire**. Harris began the 1970s importing sexploitation features. If there was money to be made from a movie, Jack H. Harris knew how to get it.

Harris did not ask an exorbitant fee for **Utopia**. Financially, the New York premiere of the Laurel & Hardy feature was a Christmas present for the theater manager, who spent very little on film rentals for this show. **Utopia** was booked with **This Is Your Army**, a 54-minute Technicolor salute to the military which was offered practically gratis as a public service. **Utopia** was the *second* half of the double feature, perhaps the only time an eight-reel comedy with "name" stars was subordinated by a five-reel documentary.

Utopia got by on its novelty and curiosity value, but was a definite disappointment to Laurel & Hardy's new TV fans. They had no way of knowing that Stan Laurel was no longer as dissipated as he looked in **Utopia**. Nor did they know that Laurel & Hardy's "first new comedy feature in years" was itself several years old.

At any rate, Laurel & Hardy were back in the spotlight, and Hal Roach, Jr. tried to sign them for a television series. The Roach studio was a major manufacturer of broadcast fare, filming such series as *My Little Margie* and *Amos 'n' Andy,* and Roach junior envisioned a weekly situation comedy starring Laurel & Hardy. He proposed that 39 half-hour episodes be filmed in nine months, as was then customary. Stan Laurel, horrified by the rushed schedule and the staggering amount of work involved, held out for occasional comedy specials. Roach junior agreed to four installments, to be filmed in color. These really *were* supposed to be special: they were one-hour programs, scheduled for NBC's powerhouse Tuesday-night lineup. In 1955 color was reserved for variety "spectaculars" and a handful of adventure series, and was never used for comedies.

Stan Laurel was very excited about the TV deal, because he was given complete creative freedom to make the films. He devised a storybook format, which would allow the team to re-create classic children's literature. The new series would be called *Laurel & Hardy's Fabulous Fables.*

Production was scheduled to begin in May, 1955. Laurel completed the script for the first episode and had prepared material for the others. His work was interrupted in late April by a medical setback—a minor stroke which injured his leg. The shooting schedule was postponed, but Laurel was anxious to keep the series going, busying himself with scripts during his recovery. NBC announced *Fabulous Fables* as part of the network's Fall 1956 schedule.

Oliver Hardy, meanwhile, had been ordered by doctors to lose weight, in hopes that it would improve his heart condition. He achieved drastic results, going from 350 pounds to 210. In 1956 he and his partner posed for new professional photographs, which revealed the former "fat-and-skinny" team as two moderately built seniors.

But they would never work in television. Hardy was victimized by a paralytic stroke, which robbed him of several functions. His mobility was reduced to almost nothing, and his speech was slurred. Lois Laurel recalls that Stan would visit Babe "on his good days" during this period, and that Babe would greet his partner by twiddling an imaginary necktie.

Hardy lost an additional sixty pounds as his condition deteriorated. Although his faculties were severely hampered, he bravely tried to maintain an interest in life. In the summer of 1957 he suffered two additional strokes, from which he did not recover. He died on August 7, at the age of 65.

Oliver Hardy's passing seemed to herald the end of Laurel & Hardy, but the team was resurrected less than a year later. Laurel & Hardy came back to the silver screen to win new acclaim, thanks to a man named Robert Youngson.

Robert Youngson

Laurel & Hardy hit like a bombshell in 1958, through the most unlikely of circumstances. Their old silent comedies, unseen for thirty years, were fashioned into a full-length feature by writer-producer Robert Youngson. Nobody could have predicted such an overwhelming reception—to a commodity that had long been written off as worthless.

The motion-picture industry abandoned silent films in 1931. The obsolete reels were put into vaults and forgotten, or even destroyed for more valuable storage space. When an occasional silent film did return to general release, it was strictly as a novelty. Old dramatic films would be gagged up with satirical narration and exaggerated sound effects. Slapstick comedies would be torn apart and lumped together into two-reel nostalgia festivals. The primitive techniques of the silent era were displayed not for serious study, but for the amusement of a more sophisticated public.

By the 1940s the studios' interest in silent footage was marginal. Antique film was always repackaged in disposable short-subject form. Only one feature film showcasing silent comedies had ever been attempted. **Down Memory Lane** was co-produced by pioneer filmmaker Mack Sennett in 1949. Sennett selected film highlights from his personal library, and director Phil Karlson and writer-comedian Steve Allen resourcefully filmed new connecting footage in just two days. But even Sennett knew that an entire feature of silent Keystone comedy was risky business, so he included a good deal of talkie footage to insure audience satisfaction.

Silent movies were not fashionable in the 1950s. They were literally museum pieces, to be examined and dissected only by moviegoers with very specialized tastes. Their passion for these archaic exhibits bordered on the eccentric. "I was working at the Museum of Modern Art," recalls Jeanne Youngson, "and all these kinda weird guys came in to see the movies, because in the fifties the Museum was just about the only place where you could see **Nosferatu** and **The Unholy Three** and the early silents. These were not your usual, run-of-the-mill people, these were all very strange individuals."

A few diehard film buffs tried to spark serious interest in Hollywood's silent era, organizing unofficial screenings in New York. The cause was championed by Robert Youngson.

Robert G. Youngson was born on November 27, 1917, in Brooklyn, New York, and like many of his contemporaries he soon became an avid movie fan. Graduating from the prestigious Harvard University with a master's degree in business administration, Youngson entered the movie business in 1941, writing scripts for Pathé's weekly newsreels. During World War II he honed his screenwriting talents, doing training films for the U. S. Navy.

After the war, Pathé News was absorbed by Warner Brothers. Youngson was intrigued by the wealth of historic newsreel footage that Warners now owned but wasn't using. The studio allowed him to go through the old reels and make new one-reel shorts out of them. Warners gave Youngson complete charge of this project, not expecting anything more than a saleable novelty. The series earned critical praise, box-office success, and Academy Award recognition (two awards and six nominations).

For the first time in decades, silent movies were being treated with a measure of respect. The Youngson shorts looked back at "the era of wonderful nonsense," focusing on bygone celebrities, headline news events, sports heroes, politicians, daredevils, crackpot inventors, and everyday people. "That trilogy on World War I—**This Was Yesterday, It Happened To You** and **Those Exciting Days**—is a wonderful group of films, and a wonderful piece of historical reconstruction, rescuing a lot of the very, very best Pathé newsreel footage at a time when nobody else was paying any attention to it," said William K. Everson, author and silent-film expert who attended many of Youngson's pre-production screenings. "Not just the historical subjects, but the political reels like **I Never Forget A Face**. Even when he was dealing with sports or motor racing, it was always put into a kind of context. He didn't really give a damn about sports, but he always tried to give it a sick sense of humor.

His films on auto racing and skiing are full of the most horrendous spills and thrills!" One particularly hair-raising reel, appropriately titled **Spills and Chills**, never pauses for breath as it unspools ten daring minutes of stunts, crisply narrated by sportscaster Dan Donaldson.

One of Youngson's more ambitious goals was a capsule history of the twentieth century. This was a worthy idea, but too much for a ten- or twenty-minute short. Warner Brothers agreed to an extension of the project, which was released as a full-length feature in 1951. **Fifty Years Before Your Eyes**, narrated by folksy radio personality Arthur Godfrey, offered the usual review of historical footage, but a section centering around comedy films was singled out as the film's highlight. Youngson would not forget.

In addition to his theatrical films, Youngson launched a companion series especially for schools, called *The News Magazine Of The Screen*. He prepared a two-reel picture every month for six years. The films were seen by over twenty million students. For the sake of convenience Youngson drew upon his theatrical shorts for material, but he would also personally cover special events and ceremonies, specifically for the educational reels. Those new episodes that worked well would be incorporated into his theatrical releases.

Youngson soon extended his searches through the Warner vaults, awakening the management's phobia about silent pictures. "He was looking at a lot of negatives at Warner Brothers, and he would often run off silent features that he thought might make interesting one-reel condensations," recalled Bill Everson. "I think he arrived in that field [of silent-film revivals] just a little bit too early, when it was not yet fully accepted. I know his bosses at Warners didn't like it too much when he did one-reel cutdowns from silent films. They felt 'one out of every ten is all we can allow you to do.' He had a free hand in what he did, but if he tried to do more of the one-reel cutdowns of silents, they would have probably stopped him."

Youngson's preoccupation with silent Hollywood films was his undoing, at least temporarily. In 1957 he completed a feature-length revision of Warners' 1929 epic **Noah's Ark**. Warner Brothers didn't want it. Youngson distributed it independently through the Continental organization.

Noah's Ark gave Robert Youngson the opportunity to embellish seven reels of mute picture with a soundtrack. He went all-out, adding a musical score, sound effects, and his own distinctive brand of florid narration. "He loved his own words on screen, and would *never* cut them," said Bill Everson. "Even when both friends *and* preview cards complained about unnecessary narration, he took no notice—and it got worse. The nadir was his version of **Noah's Ark**, where he even gave God new dialogue and rewrote the Bible.

"But at least you could kid Bob about all that and make your feelings plain. He didn't mind the criticism. He always had an answer, and was always sure he was right. He just smiled and did it his own way."

Youngson had been toying with the idea of expanding the most successful episode of **Fifty Years Before Your Eyes**. He wanted to devote an entire feature to the slapstick greats of yesteryear. Again, Warner Brothers was not interested; the studio had released its own two-reel comedy compilations years before, and they were nothing outstanding. Youngson approached Herbert Gelbspan, Hal Roach's representative in New York, to arrange access to Roach's collection of silent classics. Gelbspan conferred with Roach, and they extended full co-operation. Roach even offered his own ideas and input, in addition to his exclusive library.

The next step was to preserve the old films, which had been unused for three decades. Some of the footage was literally crumbling into dust, as nitrate decomposition began to wither the image away. Other films were still fresh, and retained their original sparkle and definition.

Some film buffs have questioned Robert Youngson's archival methods, claiming that he copied only those scenes he intended to use, allowing the rest of the original negative to degenerate. This may have been true when Youngson was extracting one brief clip out of a six-reel feature, but not when he worked with a Hal Roach two-reeler. "In most cases he'd preserve the whole thing, because he was never sure when he might want to come back to it later and handle it differently," according to Bill Everson. "He would sometimes screen negative, just to see what he had, and then make workprints of that material." Nor was it a case of Youngson only being able to afford a certain amount of lab work. "He'd invested in one of the labs, and he had a lot of regular income coming in from labs," said Everson. "He was an extremely good businessman."

Youngson screened dozens of two-reel comedies from the Hal Roach studio. Most of his favorite scenes involved Stan Laurel and Oliver

Hardy. He carefully extracted the major sequences from seven of their better silents: **The Second Hundred Years, The Battle Of The Century, Two Tars, You're Darn Tootin', Habeas Corpus, We Faw Down** (identified in the finished compilation under its British title, **We Slip Up**), and **Double Whoopee**. He combined two Will Rogers comedies, **Uncensored Movies** and **Big Moments From Little Pictures**, into one continuous scene spoofing Hollywood. He indulged his fondness for comedian Charley Chase by including scenes from **Limousine Love** and **The Sting Of Stings**.

Youngson augmented the Hal Roach reels with vintage Mack Sennett films starring Harry Langdon, Ben Turpin, Billy Bevan, and Andy Clyde. (One juicy clip had a knee-slapping poker game played by Cameo, an incredibly intelligent dog.) Between the Roach and the Sennett material, Youngson had the makings of a comedy blockbuster.

For the finishing touches, Youngson rounded up his crew from the Warner shorts—editors Albert Helmes and Al Dahlem, and narrators Dwight Weist and Ward Wilson. Helmes and Dahlem were veterans of the Youngson cutting room, and they knew what the boss wanted. Weist and Wilson were television and radio performers who divided Youngson's script between them. Wilson handled the lighter, wiseguy commentary; his brisk tenor was familiar from the *Can You Top This?* joke-telling panel show. The straight historical narration fell to Weist; his dignified baritone gave him a versatile range, from the title role of *Mr. District Attorney* to Adolf Hitler on *The March Of Time*, to the announcer who introduced various patent medicines on *The Ted Mack Original Amateur Hour*. In addition to his Warner standbys, Youngson hired composer-conductor George Steiner to provide the music and technician George Graham to record the soundtrack. The team came through with flying colors.

Yet the film still had some bugs in it. Youngson and Everson looked forward to screening a short called **The Battle Of The Century**, because it was a rare Laurel & Hardy film directed by Clyde Bruckman, a "name" comedy writer and director. Their high anticipation soon faded. "It was a *terribly* disappointing short," remembered Everson ruefully. "The first part was actually quite dull. [Youngson] had actually almost written it off when the pie fight came on. And even the pie fight wasn't terribly well organized. In his final version, he recut it and gave it much more punch." It was one of the few times Youngson would rearrange the sequence of shots in a film. The original film was showing signs of decay, and Youngson decided to streamline the sequence, removing damaged or redundant footage and tightening the action to three riotous minutes. George Steiner's inspired musical setting, an orchestration of "Pop Goes The Weasel," was a stroke of genius.

Youngson's emergency surgery of **The Battle Of The Century** paid off. The pie fight has gone down in history as one of the great comedy clips, but it survives today only as Youngson rebuilt it. While purists argue that Youngson's tampering has prevented them from ever seeing the complete film, they might not have seen any of it, had it not been for Robert Youngson.

A rough cut of the new comedy compilation, titled **The Golden Age Of Comedy**, was assembled for a preview. Youngson was anxious to note the spectators' reactions. The audience enjoyed the slapstick sequences immensely, but didn't warm up to the situational humor of Charley Chase. Youngson grudgingly removed the **Limousine Love** sequence entirely and whittled **The Sting Of Stings** down to one brief gag—but Charley Chase was going to be in Youngson's picture, no matter what. The advance crowd also objected to the copious narration—could some of it be removed? This was one concession the proud producer refused to make, and the narration stayed in.

Youngson created his own logo, customized from a vintage Buster Keaton comedy: a 1920s movie audience watches the producer's name flash on the screen. Chopin's "Etude In C Major, Opus 10, No. 3" was orchestrated for the **Golden Age** main titles, and Youngson would adopt this classical piece as his theme music. The final cut ran 85 minutes, trim but respectable, and the film now had wall-to-wall laughs.

After years of preparation, **The Golden Age Of Comedy** was ready for release in 1958—and no major studio would touch it. Silent movies were still too much of a gamble for the big companies, so Youngson released his feature through Distributors Corporation of America (DCA). DCA was a subsidiary of The Walter Reade Organisation, a British-based distributor of art-house and classic films. DCA aimed much lower than Reade for success, specializing in cheap quickies for drive-ins (like **Monster From Green Hell** and the notorious Grade-Z epic **Plan 9 From Outer Space**). The company, unsure of how to sell Robert Youngson's "unusual" picture, planted a publicity item about comedian Andy Clyde *in the present tense!* Frame enlargements from the film were passed off as current human-interest photos, showing suburbanite "Mr. Andrew Clyde" playing checkers with a cat. Youngson's novelty feature would be just another exploitation item from DCA.

The material was so old that it was new to most people. **The Golden Age Of Comedy** opened in New York and was more than a hit—it was a sensation. The film opened simultaneously in two theaters, the Radio City Music Hall and the Embassy on Broadway. The New York media loved the film and gave it numerous plugs in national newspaper columns and television programs. Steve Allen and Jack Paar, New York-based talkmasters with network affiliations, showed Laurel & Hardy clips on their respective programs to very favorable response. Paar was so taken with the feature that he sang its praises for five consecutive nights. **Golden Age** even turned up on a network game show, *The $64,000 Challenge*, as celebrity contestants answered questions about the film clips. *Life* magazine gave Youngson's film a two-page, ten-photo spread captioned "Sight Gag Revival."

DCA shrewdly cashed in on the media attention, scrapping their original ad campaign and printing an entirely new presskit, with all of the critical raves included (three dozen from only four engagements!). The company even printed up a demonstration reel of the Laurel & Hardy pie fight, offering it to TV stations for additional ballyhoo. Audiences flocked to see what all the shouting was about, and **The Golden Age Of Comedy** was the biggest success DCA ever had.

Stan Laurel and Oliver Hardy were billed without emphasis as "Laurel & Hardy," just one of the acts. They monopolized the action and stole the film. Suddenly they were movie stars again—less than a year after Oliver Hardy's death.

Bill Everson pointed to **Golden Age** as being "tremendously important, because it brought back all the Sennett and Roach material which nobody had seen. It literally revitalized Laurel & Hardy, and led to a tremendous new interest in silent films, silent comedy in particular."

Robert Youngson was justifiably elated with his first independent production. "He always had a fond feeling for the first one," says his wife. "Just looking at his face, when the movie was on and people would laugh, was well worth the price of admission."

Now, even though he had won Academy Awards with his short subjects, Robert Youngson was finally recognized as an established filmmaker. The new box-office value of Youngson and Laurel & Hardy was too tempting for the major studios to ignore any longer. He was invited to release his films through 20th Century-Fox and Metro-Goldwyn-Mayer—where Laurel & Hardy had been good drawing cards in the 1940s. Youngson shipped off five features to Fox, with M-G-M asking for two (a third project was never completed). Although he was a big-name, big-studio producer, Robert Youngson had no ambitions to direct his own movies or TV shows. He was completely happy making new pictures out of old pictures.

Youngson continued to enjoy silent films socially, in private screenings with fellow enthusiasts. Jeanne Keyes, from New York's Museum of Modern Art, also went to these shows. She met Robert Youngson in 1959. "One night I saw this very handsome fellow in there, but he was kind of overweight, which didn't appeal to me," she recalls. Youngson repeatedly invited her to join him for late-night coffee, but she declined. "About three weeks went by, and I went to see **The Gazebo**, starring Debbie Reynolds, at one of my local theaters up on 68th Street. I saw him sitting all by himself about four rows ahead of me, so I tapped him on the shoulder and he said 'Oh! Come up and sit next to me.' So I did, and he never looked at the movie once. He kept his eye on me through the whole thing." Before long, they were married.

Mrs. Youngson remembers her husband as "a lovely man, really a lovely person. He was a real old-world, courtly fellow." She was slightly taken aback by his businesslike demeanor. "He smiled easily and did have a good sense of humor, but I thought he should have been funnier. I remember once telling him, 'You know, your movies are really so humorous, I see them and I laugh. But why aren't you funny in person?' And I think I hurt his feelings, poor guy."

The Youngsons took an apartment, which became Robert's professional headquarters. "He was *always* here in New York," commented Bill Everson. "He had a very big apartment at 1 Fifth Avenue, and he and Jeanne lived just across the square in a penthouse. But almost all the work was done at 1 Fifth Avenue. I sat in on a lot of the screenings there, and Al Dahlem, his cutter, would work out of there."

Jeanne Youngson adds, "Later on, when he started working at M-G-M and Fox, he was going out to the west coast quite frequently. He took me out there a few times to sightsee a few thousand times," she laughs.

Her husband agreed to visit Hollywood by himself, encouraging her to travel on her own while he was away.

The first of the 20th Century-Fox films, released in 1960, was **When Comedy Was King**. (Youngson had used the same phraseology for a Warner short, **When Sports Were King**.) Determined to outdo his **Golden Age** success, Youngson wanted to do with comedy what **Fifty Years Before Your Eyes** did with history. He would thoroughly cover a specific period of time, documenting the changing tastes in popular culture.

To trace the development of movie comedy from 1914's improvised roughhouse to 1929's choreographed slapstick, Youngson used a wider variety of clips and comedians. Still drawing from the Mack Sennett and Hal Roach studios, Youngson studded the new film with major achievements from major stars: Laurel & Hardy (saved for the end, using most of their 1929 classic **Big Business**), Charlie Chaplin, Buster Keaton, Harry Langdon, Ben Turpin, Fatty Arbuckle, Gloria Swanson, Mabel Normand, and Wallace Beery. To this impressive list Youngson added the two-reeler perennials: Snub Pollard, Edgar Kennedy, Billy Bevan, Andy Clyde, Charley Chase, Al St. John, and The Keystone Cops.

Youngson had chanced upon a Broadway performance of the jazz-age musical *The Boy Friend*, and was enthralled with its peppy musical numbers. He asked the arranger, the prolific Ted Royal, to compose the music for **When Comedy Was King**. It was a difficult assignment; on Broadway, Royal could concentrate mainly on the highlights of a show, but here was a film that was *all* highlights. Youngson visited another Broadway play, *My Fair Lady*, and engaged its roadshow conductor, Sylvan Levin. The maestros came up with a truly superior, full-orchestra score, the best of any Youngson feature.

Youngson and his usual gang put everything together. His right-hand man, cutter Al Dahlem, was now being billed as "assistant producer," along with lab supervisor-film dealer John E. Allen.

Youngson's script was dangerously ripe. He wanted to include background information about the various film clips, but his phrases were alternately sentimental, reverent, and cute. This time narrator Dwight Weist would be working alone, and would have to read both the sober and the silly passages. (And Youngson's silly passages could be *very* silly.)

Weist overcame the pomp and circumstance of the script and turned in a fine job.

The finished product was an 81-minute comedy cavalcade that played to an even wider audience than did **Golden Age**. The clips may have seemed familiar to the arts community, but they were completely un-known to the general public. Judicious editing captured the cream of the silent era, with remarkable balance and variety. This was one case where bigger was better, as Youngson exceeded his own standard. "He felt that **When Comedy Was King** was the best," recalled Bill Everson. "He felt it was the most polished, and was introducing people like Kea-ton and the best of Laurel & Hardy to an audience that otherwise wouldn't have seen them. So he was very satisfied with that one." Fox's extensive theatrical (and later, television) distribution kept **When Com-edy Was King** in the spotlight.

It is worth noting that Youngson was now the industry leader for this sort of film, and often the only theatrical source. When Buster Keaton toured Canada in 1964, a local province wanted to have a Keaton film shown in his honor. Thanks to the legal machinations of his own busi-ness manager, none of Keaton's famous silents could be acquired easily. The only Keaton on the market was **When Comedy Was King**.

Robert Youngson was rapidly using up the choice silent-comedy ma-terial available to him in New York. A rival producer, Paul Killiam, was reviving silent films on a weekly television program, so Youngson was under pressure to use certain films theatrically before their value was diminished by TV exposure.

For his next feature he decided to broaden his scope, and mix adven-ture serials and melodramas into the usual slapstick recipe. The project was called **Days Of Thrills And Laughter** (1961). Youngson may have hoped that this new combination would popularize silent-screen adven-ture, as his other features had revived silent comedy. It didn't work out that way. The film was less accessible to the 1961 public; the comic parts were timeless but the straight footage dated badly.

The "thrill" clips weren't the greatest, either. "In **Days Of Thrills And Laughter**, what he used was public-domain stuff that he could find, like the Houdini, Douglas Fairbanks and serial material, most of which he found here in New York," noted Bill Everson. "It certainly wasn't the Grade-A stuff that he really wanted."

The laughter in **Days Of Thrills And Laughter** is provided mostly by Charlie Chaplin, in scenes from his early shorts. Stan Laurel and Oliver Hardy are included solely for name value; they appear but briefly, and not as a team. The film's bumpy continuity lacks the unity and momentum of the all-comedy shows.

Jack Shaindlin's musical score, amplifying the many moods of the film, is serviceable silent-movie accompaniment. A recording of Shaindlin's work was actually issued separately for that purpose.

The producer indulged himself more freely for this effort. During the credits sequence, when "Robert Youngson" appears on the screen, the name spins and pirouettes all over the place as the narrator grumbles, "What a showoff."

Bill Everson confirmed Youngson's one-man-bandwagon style. "He loved the sense of being a total producer with all the power it brought, and he had a tremendous ego. [He supervised] absolutely *everything*, and designed all the ads and the copy for the pressbooks. He was very proud of the fact that he was an Academy Award winner and nominee for other films, and always made sure that that byline was in all the ads."

Youngson was sorely tempted to narrate his own scripts, but he wisely engaged a broadcasting veteran, Jay Jackson, to handle the microphone. Jackson is the series's most familiar voice; he narrated five of Youngson's eight features, as well as most of the preview trailers.

Dissuaded from reading his own narration, Youngson tried composing his own music. "He was very talented," comments Jeanne Youngson. "I wouldn't say that he was a frustrated full-time composer, but he could do all these things." For his fourth anthology, Youngson wrote a special song, "Bring Back The Laughter." It was a slow, slushy hymn to days of yore, and he was determined to feature it in his new movie. He prevailed upon musical conductor Bernie Green to sing it under a pseudonym. The ballad of Robert Youngson didn't help the picture.

30 Years Of Fun (1963) is Youngson's most disappointing effort. It is an unsuccessful compromise between **Fifty Years Before Your Eyes** and **When Comedy Was King**. Once more, Youngson devotes himself to a fixed span of time: from "the gay nineties" to "the roaring twenties." This time the comedy footage is watered down with newsreel clips, which set the time frame admirably but lessen the film's overall impact.

Charlie Chaplin again comes off best; he is represented by long excerpts from four of his best shorts. Buster Keaton ranks a close second with two clips. Laurel & Hardy, billed third, are scarcely *in* the film, their appearance confined to a too-brief flash of their first appearance together, in the comedy **Lucky Dog**. (This long-lost short was a major find, and Youngson trumpeted his discovery for publicity purposes.) The other comedians in **30 Years Of Fun**—Syd Chaplin, Harry Langdon, Billy Bevan, Charley Chase, Snub Pollard, and Carter DeHaven—make no more than fleeting appearances.

Youngson's narration is often overdone. He wrote much of it for his own amusement, adapting nonsense words from family nicknames. Thus Billy Bevan is renamed "Givney Gleeps, The Sheep Dip King." Many characters in Youngson movies would be assigned such colorful but pointless names. To Youngson's credit, his narration never made fun of the old films, and his respect for motion-picture history always came through.

Youngson's sincere concern for film preservation earned him an invitation from Metro-Goldwyn-Mayer. M-G-M had a vault full of old films but didn't know quite what was in it, so the studio asked Youngson to investigate.

It was a gold mine. The M-G-M collection, featuring the brightest stars and the landmark titles from Hollywood's heyday, was entirely at Youngson's disposal. The possibilities for a megawatt comedy cast were very promising indeed. M-G-M meticulously kept its films in pristine condition, so there would be no film-lab headaches.

Youngson mapped out an all-star collection, **M-G-M's Big Parade Of Comedy** (1964). A movie studio had never sponsored its own retrospective; ten years later M-G-M would enjoy tremendous success with its **That's Entertainment** compilation, but in 1964 the "sampler" format was still a novelty to movie audiences.

Youngson dived into the vaults and came up with dozens of films, both famous (Greta Garbo in **Ninotchka**; William Powell and Myrna Loy in **The Thin Man**; Cary Grant and Katharine Hepburn in **The Philadelphia Story**) and forgotten (Carole Lombard in **The Gay Bride**; Clark Gable in **Too Hot To Handle**; Red Skelton in **A Southern Yankee**).

Buster Keaton in **The Cameraman** was the plum. This rare 1928 comedy got extended screen time in the feature, another example of Robert Youngson preserving a legendary silent comedy for posterity. For almost three decades the Youngson adaptation of **The Cameraman** was the only available footage of the subject. M-G-M no longer had a reference copy of the film (having worn it out from repeated projection-room screenings), so the studio made a fine-grain print and gave it to Youngson. According to Richard May of Turner Entertainment, owner of the M-G-M backlog, M-G-M subsequently lost or destroyed the original negative of **The Cameraman**; many years later, Turner Entertainment referred to the Youngson collection, then in private hands after the producer's death, to restore this elusive Keaton film. Turner's current prints of **The Cameraman** are based on Youngson's personal copy.

Buster Keaton was still working in pictures when **Big Parade Of Comedy** was released. Some of the other stars in **Big Parade Of Comedy** were current favorites in 1964: Cary Grant, Katharine Hepburn, Red Skelton, Joan Crawford, Lucille Ball, Groucho Marx. Jean Harlow, the subject of two movie biographies at the time, was another newsworthy celebrity.

Youngson reserved the first third of **Big Parade Of Comedy** for his traditional roundup of silent clips and behind-the-scenes footage. The major sequence here was taken from **The Cameraman**. Then, for the only time in the Youngson features, "talkie" scenes are introduced.

For the next hour the viewer is bombarded by a dizzying blitz of comedy clips. Unfortunately, most of them are too short; Youngson, insistent on finding a place for his pet scenes, shoehorned them uncomfortably into the feature. Famous comedians like Abbott & Costello, W. C. Fields, The Three Stooges, and Jimmy Durante are on screen for only a few moments. Other stars, like Lionel Barrymore, Robert Taylor, and Bert Lahr, barely register.

Laurel & Hardy have almost a full reel to themselves, in an egg-breaking episode from **Hollywood Party** (1934) and a dance routine from **Bonnie Scotland** (1935). Youngson actually *improved* the dance by erasing the repetitive band music and recording a jaunty medley of Scottish airs instead.

Film editor Al Dahlem, now an associate producer, deserves a medal for crowding everything into 91 minutes. The frenzied cutting varies from excellent (four "Thin Man" features are woven into one seamless scene) to awful (instead of building up to a big finish, the film just stops on a mild blackout gag). The film would have been improved with fewer and longer clips. "Great as those sound comedies were, they didn't lend themselves to excerpting," observed Bill Everson. "A lot of that material just didn't cut down out of context. [Youngson] was an absolute genius at getting the real nuggets out of the silent stuff, but I think the sound stuff tended to drag."

M-G-M's Big Parade Of Comedy was narrated by Les Tremayne, the finest of the Youngson commentators. Not merely an announcer, Tremayne was a professional actor in radio and pictures. Youngson handed him another one of his challenging scripts, filled with equal doses of saccharine sentiment and hokey humor. Tremayne's sensitive delivery made the overwritten parts bearable and the tongue-in-cheek parts amusing. (During a train chase, Tremayne dramatically informs us that speed is vital, as The Marx Brothers are "bucking for the chicken-liver-sandwich concession.")

Youngson exercised his musical inclinations again with *four* original tunes. Together with Bernie Green, he composed "theme songs" for Marie Dressler, Jean Harlow, and even Robert Benchley, in addition to the rather stilted "Big Parade Of Comedy March." The results proved that Green and Youngson weren't exactly Rodgers and Hart. There were to be no further vocals in Robert Youngson movies, one of Youngson's few defeats.

"He loved to get opinions, but he would never really accept them if they disagreed with his own," Everson remarked. "If he thought something was great and it *was* great, everybody else agreed and he was delighted to have it confirmed. But if other people disagreed with him, he felt they were wrong, and he would just go his own way. Which was his privilege."

Undaunted, Youngson threw himself into the film's promotional campaign. The star-packed trailer and the glittering ad copy and posters guaranteed audience interest, and Youngson's cheerleading worked. Critics and moviegoers were dazzled by Youngson's newest creation. The Hollywood trade papers and the metropolitan magazines and newspapers responded charitably. *Variety* liked the Laurel & Hardy sequence best, and predicted that the new film would do as well as Youngson's previous hits. The reviewer gave special credit to Jeanne Keyes "as research supervisor, a mammoth undertaking well executed."

Mrs. Youngson modestly downplays her research duties: "I used to go to the New York public library and check out copyrights." The producer billed his wife under her maiden name, she explains, because "he was also billing his father [as production manager], and he didn't want to have too many Youngsons. He thought it was tacky."

Robert Youngson always made a point of including Laurel & Hardy in his anthologies, however briefly. Stan Laurel didn't care for the compilation format, preferring the original, unedited films, but he was pleased by the public's reaction. Now happily retired, Stan seldom went out to movies, but friends and fans kept him current on the Laurel & Hardy scene. "He was very happy, and such a modest man," recalls his friend Bob Burns. "He could not understand why Laurel & Hardy were so popular. The resurgence amazed him. 'We haven't done anything new,' he'd say."

On February 23, 1965, Stan Laurel died at age 74. Tributes poured in from editors and columnists, friends and colleagues around the world. A network television special and a major Hollywood feature (**The Great Race**) were dedicated to Laurel & Hardy. Robert Youngson offered his own tribute with a 90-minute feature devoted to the team.

Laurel & Hardy's Laughing '20s (1965) was another ambitious first for Youngson: a comedy collection with a single star attraction. The narrower focus allowed the producer to be more generous with film highlights; several of the Laurel & Hardy scenes are extended, each running six to sixteen minutes rather than two to four minutes. Some of the most famous Laurel & Hardy silents, like **From Soup To Nuts**, **The Finishing Touch**, and **Liberty**, are shown virtually complete. Except for a brief clip at the very beginning, Youngson drew from the Hal Roach library for the entire film, finding room for Roach's other comedy stars, Charley Chase and Max Davidson.

Around this time, the production values of the Robert Youngson pictures began to slip. The films remained entirely presentable, but the producer's economizing became noticeable. The last reel of **Laughing '20s** borrows scenes from **The Golden Age Of Comedy**, partly for the chance to show off the famous clips to new audiences, and partly for convenience since they were already preserved and assembled. The reprise includes the punchline gags from **Two Tars**, **The Second Hundred Years**, **Habeas Corpus**, **You're Darn Tootin'**, and **We Faw Down**, plus yet another re-edited version of the pie fight from **The Battle Of The Century**.

Laughing '20s also dispenses with the lush orchestra scores and uses a smaller, cheaper jazz combo instead, but the music does lend a roaring-twenties flavor to the film. Skeets Alquist furnished the score, which was conducted by John Parker (better known in recording circles as ragtime pianist Knocky Parker).

Youngson was ever resourceful when it came to publicizing his films. For the newspapers, Youngson supplied an original promotional sketch of Laurel & Hardy, drawn by respected caricaturist Al Hirschfeld. This would offer a "fresh art angle for the Sunday page." Youngson failed to mention that the "fresh art" was borrowed from M-G-M's pressbook for **Nothing But Trouble**—published a full twenty years before!

A last-minute survey by a research company revealed that **Laughing '20s** "holds the record for laugh content of any comedy we have measured in our 30 years of experience." Youngson jumped on this tidbit, prominently featuring it in all the newspaper ads and splicing a congratulatory announcement onto the trailer. He even commissioned special decals of the survey results, which exhibitors could affix to their window posters.

M-G-M and Youngson proudly called **Laurel & Hardy's Laughing '20s** the "sleeper of the year." Reviews were up to Youngson's usual standard. During a time when mature themes were overtaking Hollywood films, family-fun escapism prompted a positive response. Elinor Hughes of the *Boston Herald* strongly recommended Youngson's film as "something to see if you just want to relax and laugh and not worry about a thing." With the two-picture M-G-M deal concluded, the producer took his business back to 20th Century-Fox.

Robert Youngson usually plunged into his next venture as his current one was being released. Each project was time-consuming. "I'm sure it was a couple of years for each one, because it was blood, sweat, and tears," says Jeanne Youngson. "Nothing was easy, it seemed. He was so painstaking when he made his movies, [but] he seemed to be perpetually on a cloud while he was working."

It was tough to think of new approaches to old material. Each idea had to be completely new and untried. "He got a little nervous in between, before he started another project," Mrs. Youngson admits. "His thing was biting handkerchiefs while he worked—and boy, we had a lot of shredded handkerchiefs around our house!"

Each of Robert Youngson's films had contained a different combination of ingredients, and if the results were variable, at least they were unique. However, when it became apparent that Laurel & Hardy were the main selling point of Youngson's films, the producer forsook his ambitious historical mosaics. His next feature for Fox would be a strictly commercial venture.

The Further Perils Of Laurel & Hardy (1967) is only a slight variation of **Laurel & Hardy's Laughing '20s**. It's another L & H marathon (clocking in at 98 minutes, the longest of Youngson's films), and again the highlights are plentiful. **Laughing '20s** had "the great pie fight," so Youngson touted his new assortment as "the great mud fight" (**Should Married Men Go Home?**), "the great water fight" (**Angora Love**), "the great soup fight" (**That's My Wife**), and "the great furniture fight" (**Early To Bed**). **Further Perils** also includes more of Stan and Ollie's solo work, pre-dating their teaming, as well as a number of Charley Chase and Snub Pollard clips from the Hal Roach vaults.

Knocky Parker was retained to assemble another "chamber" orchestra. Parker added several offbeat instruments to the usual ragtime-band lineup; there was even an electric guitar, as a concession to 1960s pop music. Parker's group did an outstanding job synchronizing the music, particularly in a band-concert vignette from the film **You're Darn Tootin'**. (*Variety* thought the score was "inclined to be over-loud at times.")

The name "Youngson" had become synonymous with a certain type of picture. All *Variety* needed to say was "another Youngson compilation" to tell exhibitors what to expect. "Nostalgic in appeal and a gasser for those who like this sort of stuff."

Fox's publicity department was cutting back on advertising accessories. The pressbook for **Further Perils** contains only one feature story, a mere six-sentence squib about the film. None of Youngson's enthusiastic ballyhoo ideas and traditional promotions are included, although a new book by William K. Everson about Laurel & Hardy is mentioned as a possible tie-in.

The lack of attention was deliberate. Fox's 1967 marketing approach was focused on the lucrative "youth" market, with films intended to appeal to stylish young adults. Robert Youngson's nostalgic silent-movie collection didn't fit into Fox's trendy advertising scheme at all, and was discreetly omitted from all ads listing the studio's exciting new releases.

Unlike Youngson's other films, **The Further Perils Of Laurel & Hardy** was not given regular "program" playdates in theaters. Fox tossed it to the kiddie-matinee trade instead, planting promotional copy in juvenile publications instead of popular magazines. **Further Perils** stayed in circulation as a mere filler, and neighborhood theaters didn't waste advertising space on the lengthy title; weekend matinees were some-times advertised as "Sat.-Sun. Laurel & Hardy."

Robert Youngson had been issuing new features about every eighteen months. After the indifferent release of **Further Perils**, Youngson took more time off before tackling his next project. "He was constantly busy on *something*," said Bill Everson, who remained a close associate. "He was always acquiring film. I remember there was one Fatty Arbuckle film which was never released called **Leap Year**, which I had access to, and which he fell in love with when he saw it. He wanted very much to use it, and spent a lot of time and money making a new negative and prints from it. I don't think he ever used a foot of it in any of his films. I know he was always very disappointed at audience reaction to what he thought was very funny Arbuckle footage. So an awful lot of time went into screening and preparing between releases." Everson also recalled Youngson's periodic involvement in television; the producer helped to prepare history programs incorporating archival film footage, but the pilot films were never sold.

Youngson made another theatrical feature, which was released by Fox in 1970. He devoted his latest effort to his favorite comedians: Stan Laurel, Oliver Hardy, Charley Chase, and Buster Keaton. He titled the film **4 Clowns** (a mild pun on the popular play and film **A Thousand Clowns**).

4 Clowns contains elements of the best and worst of Robert Young-son. By this time, fresh Laurel & Hardy highlights were scarce— Youngson had virtually depleted the library of L & H silents in his previous films. He was forced to use secondary scenes that he had for-merly cast aside. (He had to settle for the lesser half of **Two Tars** because he had used the better half on two other occasions.) The only untouched two-reeler in the Roach collection was **Their Purple Moment**, which Youngson used almost in its entirety. Otherwise, **4 Clowns** is a banquet made of leftovers.

To compensate for the humdrum nature of the "team" clips, Young-son unearthed some surprising items from the boys' solo careers. Oliver Hardy played a grubby villain in a rare Hal Roach western, **No Man's Law** (1925); it was one of Hardy's favorite performances, and Youngson showcased it with all of the color and earthy humor intact.

Charley Chase, who had flitted in and out of Youngson's other pic-tures, was finally given a featured segment in **4 Clowns**. The Chase shorts were usually situation comedies in which the hero innocently got into embarrassing predicaments. This type of humor needed time to build, as one disaster followed another.

One of Robert Youngson's favorite Chase comedies was **Limousine Love** (1928). Charley, on his wedding day, gets mixed up with a woman who has lost her clothes. The remainder of the film has Chase trying to keep his poise without revealing his new companion. It's a hilarious situation, and Youngson thought it was a sure bet for one of his features. He tried to use it as far back as 1958, in **The Golden Age Of Comedy**, but in abbreviated form the sequence didn't work. Throughout the 1960s Youngson kept sneaking it into his pictures, but preview audiences always disappointed him. He finally was able to expand the sequence for **4 Clowns**, and it vindicated his judgment. (*Variety* noted that hard-boiled trade reviewers applauded Chase in the screening room.)

The fourth of Youngson's favorites was Buster Keaton. By 1970 Keaton's silent films were locked in a legal stranglehold, and the man claiming to own the films would allow Youngson to borrow a single title—for a price.

Raymond Rohauer was a theater operator with a consuming passion for film. A chance meeting with Buster Keaton in 1952 led Rohauer to pursue a one-man crusade to get Keaton's old silent films preserved and distributed. Rohauer used all manner of persuasions, threats, and maneuvers, legal and otherwise, to collect the entire Keaton library and control the rights himself. He jealously guarded his prize from envious peers, and even re-edited the silent films (with rewritten titles) to trademark his coveted property. Rohauer's manipulations were so successful that he extended his quest, and staked legal claim to the Mack Sennett library, which he also claimed to control exclusively.

Youngson couldn't proceed without Rohauer's dubious assistance. He was obliged to give Rohauer "associate producer" credit, but in exchange he received one of Keaton's more obscure features, **Seven Chances** (1925). Rohauer wasn't being generous; Keaton himself considered this film the weakest of his silents. Youngson extracted the best material for a half-hour Keaton sequence.

Having to buy expensive Keaton footage from Rohauer forced Youngson to cut corners elsewhere. **4 Clowns** is the thriftiest Robert Youngson feature. The sound recording is not as crisp as usual, and the music is tinny. Youngson saved on composers' fees by using public-domain classical themes, mostly by Chopin and Gilbert & Sullivan. He saved even more by re-using stock music from **When Comedy Was King** and **Days Of Thrills And Laughter.** Manny Albam's little band valiantly tried to match the sound of the old big-band tracks.

If Youngson despaired about his lower budget, he never let on. Neither his wife nor his accountant recall any discouraging words. According to Bill Everson, "He never commented about that. I don't say this critically, but he felt that everything he did was tremendous, and if he had to cut down on production values, he was adding enough in terms of new material to make up for it. I don't think he really felt that he was shortchanging the public, or cutting down in an obvious way."

Youngson remained as fussy as ever about the films' presentation. When projected on modern wide screens, the top and bottom of the picture would be cut off. Youngson anticipated this, and arranged for his films to be printed with a special optical mask. The mask shrank the image slightly, and kept it fully contained within each film frame.

4 Clowns had first-run aspirations at 97 minutes. It was the first Youngson film to be classified under Hollywood's new rating system, and it rightfully received a general-audience rating. Perhaps Youngson hoped his new picture would be widely programmed as a family entertainment, in the manner of Walt Disney's live-action, G-rated comedies.

Laurel & Hardy buffs thought **4 Clowns** could have used more of two clowns. So did *Variety*: "Laurel & Hardy for sell but Charley Chase and Buster Keaton supply the amusement. Okay release in the Youngson series from silent era."

Nick Yanni of *The Motion Picture Herald* was more encouraging, calling the film "an avalanche of belly laughs." The columnist took his hat off to the producer: "We are indeed indebted to writer-producer Youngson for putting together this marvelous film . . . **4 Clowns** should do well in commercial playoff, not only with the film buffs and oldsters, but with a whole new generation of film-conscious kids who will come to appreciate this comedy artistry for their very own. Who says there's no way to bridge the 'generation gap' today?" Yanni's prediction, unfortunately, was only half right. Youngson's film did find a kid audience— because, like **Further Perils**, it was relegated to weekend matinees in neighborhood theaters. The film was not promoted in the trade at all.

Fox aimed its advertising at the juvenile audience. The coming-attractions trailer was narrated not by the mature Jay Jackson but by a younger, more lightweight announcer. The posters were also attractive to children; the bright graphics were almost garish.

4 Clowns was the last of Robert Youngson's 20th Century-Fox releases. Raymond Rohauer saw to it that Fox didn't own the film outright; the studio controlled the picture for twenty years and then withdrew it from theatrical and television distribution.

With numerous features, shorts, and Academy Award citations to his credit, Robert Youngson could look back on a long and illustrious career. But at 53, he didn't want to look back. Bill Everson recalled Youngson's concern about advancing age: "I remember I was with him on his 35th birthday, and he suddenly said, 'My God, do you realize in fifteen years I'll be 50?' For him, that was the end of the world!"

Health considerations plagued Youngson as well. "It's really a pity that he didn't take better notice of his doctor," Everson said. "He certainly had the money to eat well and properly, and keep within a doctor's diet. He was an extremely large man, and on a number of occasions he went on crash diets to lose weight. In fact, just before he got married he went on a crash diet to lose a lot of weight. And then suddenly he'd say the hell with it, and order up about six ice-cream sodas—and polish off the lot in one fell swoop."

Robert Youngson now had more leisure time to pursue hobbies—but there weren't any. "One time he said, 'I'm not really interested in anything but film,'" recalls Jeanne Youngson. "No hobbies, except going to the movies, that's what we shared. And that was it."

Youngson couldn't stay away from film production for long, and tried to come up with yet another original premise. It was more of a challenge than ever, according to Jeanne Youngson, because prime material was hard to get. "I know there were some guys that handled their own stuff, and they wouldn't let him have it. Harold Lloyd, for example. I think Robert was very disappointed about that, even though we were great friends with Harold Lloyd. When Robert was gung-ho about moving to California, he wanted to buy Harold Lloyd's house.

"I have a feeling, way down deep, that he had come to the end of his rope, creative-wise. After the last one [**4 Clowns**], he kind of *talked* doing a movie, but he never did anything concrete about going ahead and doing it. And I wonder if maybe he didn't think that it had been done at that point. Maybe he couldn't have gone any further."

To get out of his rut, Youngson plotted a radical course of action. He abandoned Laurel & Hardy and the comedy format he had established, and returned to his newsreel roots as an archivist of thrill footage. He approached M-G-M with a proposal for a feature-length cavalcade of thrills, a dramatic companion piece to **M-G-M's Big Parade Of Comedy**.

The silent material Youngson had used in **Days Of Thrills And Laughter** was grainy and second-rate. Bill Everson saw that the flawless M-G-M prints piqued Youngson's interest. "When he had access to all the Metro material he obviously saw a chance to do something really worthwhile, because at that time none of those M-G-M silents had ever appeared on television. In the interim, the Chaneys and the Garbos and certain others have become fairly regular on television, tape and laser disc, but at the time it was completely novel."

Youngson combed the archives for exceptional silent footage. He found reels and reels of surprisingly effective action pictures and melo-dramas—**Ben-Hur, The Trail Of '98, The Fire Brigade,** and several Lon Chaney chillers like **The Penalty**, among others.

Youngson compiled the most spectacular scenes into a ten-reel work-print. The new film, not yet fitted with a soundtrack, impressed his friend Gordon Berkow as being almost identical in structure to **M-G-M's Big Parade Of Comedy**. The working title reflected Robert Young-son's lifelong affection for the motion picture: **There's Nothing Like The Movies**.

Progress was slowed by Youngson's deteriorating health, brought on by his reckless dietary habits. "He had diabetes, and wasn't too well," Jeanne Youngson discloses. "He was kind of enjoying himself, but I knew he was not feeling well."

By 1974 Youngson was in decline. He spent less time reviewing and collecting films. He also shelved **There's Nothing Like The Movies**, leaving his assistant, Al Dahlem, to catalogue films for his wife's projects. "He may have lost some interest and become a little despondent," sus-pected Bill Everson. "That may be one of the reasons why he suddenly said, 'The hell with the doctors, I'm just going to eat what I want.' He was constantly warned by his doctors that this could be fatal, and that's what finally happened. It's a pity, becase there was so much left in him." Robert Youngson died in 1974, at the age of 57, and his last contribution to cinema remains unfinished.

Laurel & Hardy fans are indebted to Robert Youngson. He rescued many of their most famous scenes, which might have been lost forever. He kept Stan Laurel and Oliver Hardy before the moviegoing public, long after their own pictures had stopped playing. He captured the essence of their comedy and presented it with taste, respect, and showmanship.

Youngson was gratified by the fans' affection for his works, an affection shared by Jeanne Youngson. "I know that Robert was very attached to his full-length films, because before he died he did see his name in the books as a pioneer of a certain kind. Some of them are a little [backhanded] about it, you know, saying that his stuff wasn't very professional and really wasn't very good.

"But we know different, don't we?"

Home Movies

For the Laurel & Hardy buff whose interest went beyond casual movie-going, there were home movies. The concept of motion-picture entertainment in the home was a high-tech marvel. Over the years, hundreds of old movie prints, discovered in abandoned theaters, film libraries or exchanges, found their way into the hands of private collectors.

As early as the 1920s, major department stores were buying worn-out theatrical release prints and cutting them into smaller lengths for toy projectors. Because the vendor acquired the junked films at random, the purchaser had little choice of material and took what he could get.

Portable projectors, geared for narrower film stock, became popular. The amateur-gauge 16mm format, introduced in 1923, became very successful in home and classroom applications, and an even more compact 8mm format was invented in 1932. Manufacturers of photographic equipment began to offer ready-made, mass-produced films for the hobbyist to enjoy. The Kodak company initiated the Kodascope Library, a selection of professionally edited abridgements of famous Hollywood features and short subjects. Local dealers rented and sold these reels to their customers.

The earliest joint appearances of Laurel & Hardy, filmed by Hal Roach in 1927 and released by Pathé, were licensed for home use in the 1930s. Many of these Kodascope releases were printed on amber-toned or yellow-colored film stock, which mellowed the harsh black-and-white image. Kodak used the added color as a precaution against unauthorized copying; the bright color was supposed to foil attempted duplications in darkrooms. Ironically, some sixty years later, these same toned prints are used as first-generation master material for copying purposes, and the colors don't matter to today's technicians at all.

The "nontheatrical" industry performed an unwitting service to future historians. The films were printed complete and unedited, and were sold direct to the consumer. These 16mm prints survived while the studios' 35mm originals were destroyed or ravaged by time. One of the early Laurel & Hardy collaborations, **Why Girls Love Sailors** (1927), was presumed lost forever, until a 16mm copy turned up six decades later.

These embryonic Laurel & Hardy comedies were reprinted more or less continuously throughout the next four decades. A typical retailer was vintage-movie enthusiast Charles Tarbox, who operated a California rental library, Film Classic Exchange. Tarbox struck new 8mm and 16mm prints of these public-domain Laurel & Hardy comedies, and sold them outright.

Most of the L & H films were still under copyright to Hal Roach, who recognized the market for home movies. In 1949 he licensed Walter O. Gutlohn, doing business as Library Films, to issue six Laurel & Hardy films in one-reel form. (The ten-minute, one-reel length was the industry standard for decades.) The Library releases, taken from Film Classics prints, were unusually well edited from twenty minutes to ten, and were sold in 16mm sound and 8mm silent versions. The films went out under their original titles: **The Hoose-Gow, Hog Wild, Brats, Come Clean, County Hospital**, and **Dirty Work**.

A rival distributor, Hollywood Film Enterprises, had only one Laurel & Hardy title to its name, the 1936 feature **Our Relations**, but still managed to compete by extracting four one-reel episodes.

Entertainment Films sold a silent edition of **Pardon Us** on five 8mm reels, although the actual footage of this version barely exceeded three. The company released **The Flying Deuces** as a full-length feature in 16mm (and as a ten-minute silent in 8mm), and condensed the feature films **Pack Up Your Troubles, The Bohemian Girl**, and **Swiss Miss** into five single-reel comedies. Over the next two decades Entertainment Films adapted two dozen Laurel & Hardy talkies into 8mm silents.

Blackhawk Films, operated by Iowa businessmen Kent Eastin and Martin Phelan, secured the license to reprint Hal Roach's productions. The Roach library, and the Laurel & Hardy comedies in particular, became a staple of the Blackhawk inventory of vintage films. Virtually all of the L & H features and shorts produced between 1927 and 1940 were issued in 8mm and 16mm, intact and unabridged, by Blackhawk.

Blackhawk worked with 35mm source material when it existed. Many of the Blackhawk releases derived from Film Classics reissue editions of the 1940s. Film Classics' own laboratory work was hit-and-miss, and Blackhawk's home-movie copies occasionally inherited technical errors from fuzzily focused masters. Kent Eastin admitted that the Laurel & Hardy films were in worn condition as early as 1969: "These subjects have been widely printed for theatrical distribution throughout the world, and some twenty-five years ago were used extensively in direct reduction printing for nontheatrical release. More recently they have been turned to extensively for television purposes. Thus, the original negatives have had far more use than would an average release, and the negatives have suffered accordingly. Further, almost all additional preprint material that exists today has been made from original negatives in relatively modern times and thus perpetuates all these deficiencies."

When the source material was good, however, Blackhawk's reprints were premium-grade. The Laurel & Hardys became a favorite target of counterfeiters, who sold unauthorized bootleg copies at cut-rate prices. To keep the pirates at bay, Blackhawk replaced the Film Classics logos and artwork with plain, block-lettered titles of their own manufacture.

Blackhawk did maintain an ongoing program of upgrading existing films, and superseded old merchandise with newer, superior material. In 1968, when Hal Roach transferred his storage facilities from the west coast to the east coast of the United States, literally thousands of reels of 35mm negatives and positive prints were shipped from California to Fort Lee, New Jersey. Kent Eastin of Blackhawk Films arranged for the films to be routed through Davenport, Iowa, so his staff could hunt for prime original footage. "That was the beautiful thing about Blackhawk Films, when Kent Eastin was at the helm," says technician-collector Jack Roth. "For years Blackhawk did not have a sound version of **Berth Marks**. The television prints that were out there had horrible soundtracks. Blackhawk's policy was to release something the way it was originally released, and it took them years before they found a good soundtrack." Blackhawk's other restorations included Laurel & Hardy's silent classics **Two Tars** and **Big Business**.

Blackhawk was the official source among collectors for Laurel & Hardy home movies, but that didn't stop a number of smaller companies which serviced the toy-projector market. Most 8mm toy machines had a capacity of 50 feet—only three minutes of silent film—while a "deluxe"

model might accommodate 200 feet, or twelve minutes. Three distributors, Atlas Films, Coast Films, and Carnival Films, specialized in inexpensive movie miniatures for these machines.

Dozens of "kiddie movies" were excerpted from Laurel & Hardy
talkies. Of the three budget brands, only Atlas bothered to edit the films
sensibly, splicing title cards into their silent versions. Coast and Carnival
merely copied 16mm sound prints without further ado. The viewing
experience was like watching half of a Laurel & Hardy talkie, with no
sound and a murky, scratchy picture running at a slower speed, but kids
savored the team's pantomime and overlooked the aesthetic flaws. "It
didn't matter to me that these prints were often of such poor quality that
nitrate decomposition seemed to be occurring right before my eyes,"
laughs author Ted Okuda. "So what if the footage was badly selected
and didn't make sense out of context? For less than a dollar, you could
have three minutes of Stan and Ollie flashing across the screen in your
own living room."

Many of the random Laurel & Hardy snippets were given pseud-
onyms, some of which made sense. **The Fisherman** was an obvious
vignette from **Flying Elephants**; **The Duel** was the basic premise of
The Fixer Uppers. But few Laurel & Hardy fans knew what a carton
labeled **What A Pal** contained (the second reel of **Helpmates**), or what
The Meeting was about (a bit from **Blotto**). Three "Laurel & Hardy"
reels, **All Glued Up**, **Too Much Baggage**, and **Black As Ink**, did not
feature Stan and Ollie at all. They were really slapstick segments from
the 1925 Oliver Hardy-Bobby Ray shorts **Stick Around** and **Hop To
It**, but the stars were fat and skinny, which was close enough.

These renegade reels might well have been deliberately vague to
avoid comparison with the authorized Blackhawk editions. "To my way
of thinking," recalls Okuda, "it was a deliberate attempt to throw me
off track, to deny me my rights as a private collector. My efforts to
decipher these 'code' titles was in no small way responsible for my mem-
orizing the plots and titles of the Laurel & Hardy films I saw on television."

Okuda, like many novice collectors, took his hobby seriously. "I had
been crazy about the film **Liberty** since I obtained the Coast Films
abridgement titled **Skywalking**, which was simply the last three minutes
of the picture. I desperately wanted a complete copy, and wrote to Kent
D. Eastin, the president of Blackhawk Films. At the time, Blackhawk

did not offer **Liberty**, and Eastin politely informed me that it wasn't on their list of future releases. Undaunted, I obtained a brochure from Atlas Films, and listed among their Laurel & Hardy titles was **Criminals At Large**. I remembered reading somewhere that this was a common alternate title for **Liberty**. It turned out to be the first reel; I reasoned if they had access to the first reel, they had access to all of it. Consulting the brochure again, I came across the title **High Jinx**. Lo and behold, it was indeed the second half. Except some footage was still missing: a key scene in which a live crab falls into Laurel's trousers. Scanning the Atlas brochure once more, I found a three-minute Laurel & Hardy short christened **Crab Bait**. Ten days and 99¢ later, I assembled a reasonably complete version of **Liberty** from these three reels.

"A few years later Blackhawk finally did release **Liberty**, which I immediately ordered. Yet I never ran off **Liberty** as much as I did **Criminals At Large**, nor did I treasure the individual print as much. After all, I merely *purchased* **Liberty**, while I *created* **Criminals At Large**."

Atlas, Coast, and Carnival films were so similar that the actual brand names soon became interchangeable. Atlas boxes contained Carnival clips; Carnival clips were reissued by Coast. The films' identities were further muddled when Coast labeled a generic carton **Best Of Laurel & Hardy** for its no-name reels.

In Canada, the toy trade offered Laurel & Hardy movies with crazier, wittier titles. Collector Chris Seguin found the rice-throwing battle from **The Hoose-Gow** in a box marked **Rice And Shine**. **County Hospital** was adapted as **Hook, Leg, And Sinker; Beau Hunks** became **Relieve It Or Not**.

In 1965 the ambitious "Americom 8mm" company, a Canadian concern with offices in New York, licensed several 20th Century-Fox feature films from a television syndicator, Seven Arts-Associated of Canada. A pair of Laurel & Hardy comedies (**A-Haunting We Will Go** and **The Big Noise**) yielded five 50-foot or 200-foot home-movie releases. Most of the Americom line consisted of cartoons and horror thrillers, but the Laurel & Hardy comedies immediately became the company's bestsellers. Within the year Americom prepared more Laurel & Hardy offerings, extracting *four* ten-minute reels from **The Dancing Masters: Dancing Masters, House Guests, The Invention,** and **The Bus**.

The Americom reels are unique among Laurel & Hardy home movies. They were accompanied by vinyl records, adding sound to silent films in the manner of the 1920s' Vitaphone system. The consumer would attempt to match the soundtrack with the movie. The films now required silent-speed projection, so the sound had to be electronically "stretched" to fit the picture.

Most viewers appreciated the challenge of synchronized sound, but they couldn't conquer it. In 1968 Jack Roth unwrapped two highlights reels (titled **The Big Noise** and **House Guests**), threaded his new projector, cued up the phonograph, and demonstrated the new process to his father. "**The Big Noise** stayed in perfect sync all the way through," he remembers. "We were thrilled: 'Hey, we finally have talkies!' We called the whole family in to watch it together, and we ran it —and it wasn't in sync. It wouldn't play the same way twice. It was always my feeling that there was some unmoving force that allowed you to synchronize the record and the film just once in a lifetime. **House Guests** floated in and out, just like Vitaphone."

Americom unsuccessfully addressed the problem by issuing sound-on-film prints for the new magnetic-sound projectors. The 8mm sound films had spoken dialogue, but they also had the superimposed subtitles of the mute prints.

The Americom film-and-disc sets stayed on mail-order shelves and in dusty camera-store showcases for five years, but the growing acceptance of home movies with built-in sound forced them off the market. Columbia Pictures' 8mm division brought the Americoms back in 1973, but their stay was short. Today the Americoms are collectors' items, a novelty souvenir of childhood.

The home-movie industry was revolutionized by a new kind of film. It was just as wide as standard 8mm film but offered a larger screen image. The "improved" film was nicknamed "Super 8." Thousands of Super 8 cameras and projectors were sold, crowding the outmoded 8mm reels off the shelves. When Super 8 sound film was introduced, it obscured the old silents even more. Laurel & Hardy movies were selling so well by 1975 that the prosperous Blackhawk Films was purchased by an ambitious conglomerate. It looked like there was no stopping Super 8.

Then it all changed. Film-stock prices soared when speculators tried to corner the silver market (silver being essential to black-and-white film processing). Home movies became too expensive a plaything to sustain, and consumers embraced the new home-video technology as film products were discontinued.

In Europe, however, Super 8 never died. New releases continued to tempt the amateur projectionist. Home movies have always been popular in continental countries, as far back as the silent era's 28mm and 9.5mm formats.

A British firm, Walton Movies, offered a selection of Laurel & Hardy features and shorts, but all of the titles were edited to a uniform length. Some titles had as much as ten minutes missing. "For years we never had the third reel of **Blotto**," muses Laurel & Hardy buff Bob Spiller. "It was always this cut-down version. Many hybrid prints circulate in this country." For the silents market, Showtime Movies offered one-reel versions of visual comedies like **Saps At Sea** and **Two Tars**.

In 1993 the Laurel & Hardy library was purchased by a video concern, which claimed exclusive European rights to the product. This took the 8mm versions out of circulation, although a few odd L & H reels continued to appear.

Most home-movie companies have vanished from the scene, although a few dedicated enthusiasts cater to serious collectors. After numerous corporate upheavals, Blackhawk dropped the "Films" from the company name and became a video retailer. Archivist David Shepard took over the film materials and has issued new, restored "Blackhawk Films" versions of old favorites. The Laurel & Hardy comedies became the "new" Blackhawk's trump card, although the high cost of film stock has limited the field, discouraging casual hobbyists. As video dominates the marketplace, home movies seem like quaint antiques.

After seventy years, home movies have come full circle. Once again they are mechanical curiosities, owned by relatively few people, but capable of transforming a tiny thread of film into a larger-than-life spectacle. Happily they still exist today, as legions of Laurel & Hardy fans are still crazy about the movies.

The Film Legacy

From the late 1950s into the 1960s, moviegoers could see Laurel & Hardy in Robert Youngson's silent-film compilations, but that was about all that was available to theaters. Laurel & Hardy's silent-era footage was novel enough to attract bookings, but there was no market for their sound films. Double and triple features had killed the theatrical short subject, and by now the Laurel & Hardy shorts were simply too old to package with first-run product. These same shorts were already very familiar from their constant showings on television. The Laurel & Hardy features met with the same fate: they were reliable TV fare, but they were too commonplace for the theatrical trade.

The Laurel & Hardy film library has passed through many hands since Hal Roach began licensing his various properties in 1943. The rights have been scattered and splintered, and the inventory has been parceled off in many different directions. A prime example is the long and checkered commercial career of **Babes In Toyland**. This property had bounced around international markets since 1948 (as **Revenge Is Sweet**). Lippert Pictures re-edited it in 1950 and successfully sold it as **March Of The Wooden Soldiers**.

In 1959 Allied Artists, the former Monogram Pictures, acquired the Lippert edition and reissued it, shortened length and all, under its *other* alternate title, **Revenge Is Sweet**. Strangely, Allied Artists didn't bother to attach new title footage to all of the prints, so some of the prints labeled **Revenge Is Sweet** still open with **March Of The Wooden Soldiers** titles. (For kiddie-matinee programs, the studio simultaneously circulated an "Our Gang" omnibus feature, **Little Rascals Varieties**.)

During the 1960s the film became a holiday perennial, not in theaters but on television. Allied Artists offered the film as a TV special, separate from its feature-film packages. **March Of The Wooden Soldiers** was telecast annually by scores of stations on Thanksgiving or Christmas Day, to the surprise of the film's original participants. "I've become a movie star in my old age!" chuckles co-star Felix Knight. "We have a very nice lady who cleans for us, and she had a young son she didn't want to leave home by himself. He came with her when she came to work. It was around Thanksgiving, and he had just seen **Babes In Toyland**. My wife was there, and he said 'Mama, don't you think Mrs. Knight's a little old for him?' 'Cause he saw me when I was nineteen in the movie!"

March Of The Wooden Soldiers soon became a staple on the non-theatrical circuit. Schools and social groups regularly booked 16mm prints for parties and assemblies. Prints originated from Post Pictures, a small-scale outfit which specialized in dual-market reissues. Since the late 1940s Post had simultaneously issued Hollywood feature films in both 35mm and 16mm formats. For the Laurel & Hardy offering, Post released 16mm and 8mm prints.

The film even came back to movie theaters in 1972, courtesy of a one-shot distributor called LBJ Films, which "saturated" regional theaters with multiple prints for weekend children's shows. The newspaper and poster art were cheaply but effectively revamped from the Lippert accessories.

During the 1970s a number of enterprising film collectors and dealers made up new prints for the home trade. Most were taken from the Lippert print. The complete, uncut version did exist (in a rare printing by Erko Films), but most copies were of substandard "bootleg" quality.

In 1983 some of the long-deleted footage was reinserted into a nationally syndicated TV version of **March Of The Wooden Soldiers**. The film wasn't entirely complete, but there was enough "new" material to satisfy curious fans. The extra footage derived from a 16mm "dupe" copy which had inferior picture and sound, but the substance of the feature was taken from a prime 35mm source print. The movie was pre-packaged on videotape for "instant" broadcast—even the commercials were conveniently included.

March Of The Wooden Soldiers was then purchased by Tribune Broadcasting, which reserved the right to show the film on its own television outlets, WPIX in New York and WGN in Chicago. Viewers in these cities were fortunate to see beautiful 35mm prints of this film (as opposed to standard 16mm TV copies), but the film remained unavailable to other markets.

This children's story does have a happy ending. A 35mm nitrate finegrain print of the original, uncut **Babes In Toyland** came to light in 1989, including a striking set of authentic title cards. This material was used by the Samuel Goldwyn company to prepare a computer-colored edition for TV syndication, which first aired in 1991. Painstaking care was lavished on the tinting process, with superior technical work by American Film Technologies, Inc. The finished product is among the very best "colorized" movies, and the quality is so good that a cable-TV network has routinely broadcast this new color-enhanced tape as the "original" version—*without* the color! (For home video, the title was changed to **March Of The Wooden Soldiers** to avoid confusion with Walt Disney's **Babes In Toyland** remake.)

Babes In Toyland demonstrated that there were many ways to package and promote Laurel & Hardy, but not so many films with which to do it. In order to find Laurel & Hardy movies that weren't owned or controlled by someone else, one had to know where to look.

In 1961 a television syndicator, National Telepix, brought a new selection of Laurel & Hardy shorts to the TV screen. These were the obscure Hal Roach-Pathé silents of 1927, no longer under any legal claim or copyright. Stan Laurel and Oliver Hardy were in the casts, but not as "Stan and Ollie"—not even as a team. The comedians had not yet become partners; they were charter members of Hal Roach's stock company at the time, and played a variety of roles in several frenetic farce comedies: **Love 'Em And Weep, With Love And Hisses, Slipping Wives**, etc.

National Telepix titled its new series *Comedy Capers*. It was a spinoff of the previous season's hit, *Mischief Makers*, which also used Roach-Pathé silents (with the "Our Gang" kids). *Comedy Capers* presented short slapstick comedies from the Hal Roach and Mack Sennett studios. Among the performers were Stan Laurel, Oliver Hardy, Charley Chase, Billy West, Larry Semon, Snub Pollard, Jimmie "Paul" (or "Poll") Parrott, Ben Turpin, Harry Langdon, Billy Bevan, Raymond McKee, and The Keystone Cops.

Comedy Capers was a fifteen-minute program, designed as a kiddie-show feature or TV-movie filler. The format called for film editor Stuart Hersh to condense each twenty-minute silent comedy to twelve min-

utes. Hersh removed all of the text and dialogue title cards, which cut
down the running time but often made the plotline a guessing game.
There was no narration, so many episodes consisted of a bunch of people
mugging and running around for vaguely apparent reasons. While the
editing hurt, the often-superlative print condition and the excellent
music by Jack Saunders helped.

Laurel & Hardy's polished pantomime carried their *Comedy Capers*
episodes. The comics received top billing as "Laurel and Hardy," but
only a handful of installments had both Laurel and Hardy in the same
film. Often the viewer saw Stan Laurel solo, as a brash slapstick star of
the early 1920s, or Oliver Hardy as a comic villain, playing second banana to Billy West or Larry Semon.

Each subject was retitled for television. **Do Detectives Think?** was
now **The Bodyguards**; **Flying Elephants** became **Cave Men**; **Sailors
Beware** turned into **Ship Ahooey**. A genuine "team" effort, **Liberty**,
was known for years as **Criminals At Large** on the collectors' market;
Criminals At Large stealthily escaped to *Comedy Capers* as **The Chase**.

There were very few "serious" silent-film programs. The well-intentioned *Hour Of Silents* offered condensations of famous features, but the
show strained under the weight of producer Paul Killiam's redundant
commentary. In the mid-1960s National Educational Television, which
later evolved into the PBS network, carried a series of 90-minute programs called *The Toy That Grew Up*. This was a sincere showcase for the
antique films, which were shown in their original form. Host Don Ferris
introduced each week's movie, which usually starred lesser-known stars
of the twenties like Rod LaRocque or Johnny Hines. The films were
supplied by private collectors, archives, and commercial firms. Blackhawk Films, a regular contributor, furnished the occasional short subject,
including Laurel & Hardy silents. The series was produced by Robert
Siepp for station WTTW in Chicago.

Television exposure was steady, but Laurel & Hardy fans wanted to
see more of their favorite comedies, particularly the talkies, in theaters.
By the mid-1960s the demand was so great that one opportunistic specu-
lator—Raymond Rohauer—prevailed upon Hal Roach to come out of
retirement to make a new Laurel & Hardy feature film.

At Rohauer's insistence, Roach met with the successful producing
team of Jay Ward and Bill Scott. Ward and Scott were genial, irreverent
businessmen who enjoyed TV success with cartoons (*Bullwinkle, Dudley*

Do-Right, George Of The Jungle, etc.) and commercials. In 1964 Rohauer sold Ward some silent footage, which Scott reworked into the nutty *Fractured Flickers* TV series. Ward and Scott's enthusiasm for a Laurel & Hardy project encouraged Hal Roach to participate himself, and he gave the producers free access to his vault of L & H films.

The Crazy World Of Laurel & Hardy, produced in 1965, was different from the concurrent Robert Youngson anthologies in that it presented Laurel & Hardy largely through talkie clips rather than silents. Only two brief examples of Stan and Ollie's silent work were used (**Bacon Grabbers,** which had never been showcased by Youngson, and **We Faw Down**). Most of the 83-minute feature was culled from eleven sound two-reelers, four featurettes, and five full-length films. The lengthiest clips were taken from **Come Clean, Helpmates, Any Old Port, Towed In A Hole, Busy Bodies, Dirty Work,** and the Oscar-winning **The Music Box.**

Bill Scott, preparing the **Crazy World** scenario, screened over fifty Laurel & Hardy pictures. He was impressed by the constant reappearance of certain props and gags. Instead of employing Robert Youngson's methods, taking complete comedy episodes and stringing them together, Scott attempted to organize the various sketches by theme. All of the Laurel & Hardy scenes involving recalcitrant doors were classified into one section. Another segment was devoted to hats. The comedians' various battles with machines were chronicled. Scott's new approach provided a worthwhile summary of Laurel & Hardy's bag of tricks, but the endless variations on the same themes proved repetitious and annoying to some critics and viewers. "Not that this is a drawback," argued *Variety,* "as with the classic vaudeville turns, the audience quickly becomes familiar with the routine and usually resents any major changes."

The producers approached Garry Moore, a popular television personality, to narrate the new Laurel & Hardy compilation. Moore's friendly tone helped the picture; his commentary was lighter and briefer than the joke-laden Youngson scripts.

Raymond Rohauer, who had wangled an "associate producer" credit, arranged a premiere of the film at the Berlin Film Festival on July 4, 1965, and took Hal Roach with him for a personal appearance. Rohauer followed up with screenings and receptions for influential critics in New York. The film played briefly in New York during the Christmas season. Newspaper critics greeted Laurel & Hardy warmly but were more guarded about the film as a whole.

The Crazy World Of Laurel & Hardy did not receive a national release until December, 1967, when it was handled by Joseph Brenner, an independent distributor in New York. Apparently Raymond Rohauer wanted more control over the film's merchandising than the major studios were willing to concede.

Rohauer did exert his all-embracing influence on the ad campaign, copyrighting the various accessories in his name. Roach, Ward and Rohauer received equal billing as producers (while the film's actual creator, Bill Scott, did not). Ward and Scott had packaged **Crazy World** with a 40-minute featurette of their animated endeavors, but just before release Rohauer substituted three of "his" Mack Sennett comedies starring W. C. Fields. Theater managers could take their choice.

Rohauer persuaded Hal Roach to promote **Crazy World** on NBC's New York-based comedy-variety program *The Tonight Show.* Roach (introduced as "Hal Roach, Sr.") chatted with host Johnny Carson and introduced a clip from the feature (Laurel & Hardy's water fight from **Towed In A Hole**). Roach's appearance was so noteworthy that the program was repeated later in the year.

Reviews for the film's official 1967 release were excellent. *Variety* called **Crazy World** "a delightful session with two of the screen's all-time great comics, and a film that should never be allowed to go out of circulation."

The film went out of circulation almost immediately. Virtually no one has seen **The Crazy World Of Laurel & Hardy** since 1967. It was nominally offered to television and film outlets by Rohauer, but his terms were apparently too prohibitive to revive the film. **Crazy World** languished in obscurity for over thirty years, but it may see the light of day as more of Raymond Rohauer's suppressed properties are released.

Laurel & Hardy's talkies stayed off the screen until 1970, when a major retrospective was mounted by The Walter Reade Organisation (whose subsidiary, DCA, had enjoyed spectacular success with **The Golden Age Of Comedy**). Laurel & Hardy's most famous features, including **Way Out West, Sons Of The Desert, Block-Heads** and **A Chump At Oxford**, were supplemented with talkie shorts and featurettes. These played as "film festivals" in art theaters and revival houses, with week-long theatrical engagements. Most of the Walter Reade prints were copied from 1940s Film Classics reissues, so films like **Pardon Us** and **Pack Up Your Troubles** had the occasional scene damaged or missing. When the Reades were released to television, Laurel & Hardy again vanished from theater marquees. Only their most famous feature, **Way Out West**, remained in circulation.

In 1980 the Reade package was taken over by a similar "classics" concern, Janus Films. Janus made new 16mm prints of the Laurel & Hardy films for television stations. For the most part, the content was identical to the Walter Reade releases. Print quality ranged from excellent to fair (the poorer ones were fourth-generation copies from *home-movie editions*). **Way Out West** derived from a nice Library of Congress print, but the last minute of the feature was missing; Janus simply spliced on a generic "The End" title and let it go!

To fill out the package of Laurel & Hardy shorts, Janus brought back those messy feature-film abridgements from the 1950s. The new Janus prints were an improvement. New titles gave credit to stars Laurel & Hardy and producer Hal Roach. The general presentation was also tidier. The awkward patches and splices were cleaned up, and the occasional line of dialogue re-recorded and re-edited for smoother transitions. (The meaningless monickers like **Where To Now** remained, unfortunately.) Janus even furnished TV programmers with two *additional* abridgements, culled from Laurel & Hardy's **The Flying Deuces.**

The Janus prints were very widely syndicated, but the rights were withdrawn a few years later. Fans who wanted to watch Laurel & Hardy could still see them on Spanish-language television. The films of "El Gordo y El Flaco" ("the fat one and the thin one") were dubbed in Spanish. Talkie two-reelers like **County Hospital** and **Brats**, or feature-film condensations like **Doughboy Daze** and **The Whacky West** were often shown. The Spanish-speaking actors tried to approximate Laurel & Hardy's vocal inflections; every time Oliver Hardy took a pratfall, his drawn-out cry of "Ohhhhh!" would be heard in Spanish as "Aiiiiiieee!" Viewers got a rare chance to see Laurel & Hardy's silent films as well: **Habeas Corpus** and **The Second Hundred Years**, among others, had their printed title cards deleted and music-and-dialogue tracks added.

The silent Laurel & Hardy library had never been released to television in America. Rights were secured by Richard Feiner, who commissioned a series of 120 five-minute *Laurel & Hardy Laughtoons*. As the title implies, these were the equivalent of live-action cartoons, with Stan and

Ollie's routines shown in bite-size miniatures. The *Laughtoons* show made a contribution to film history: it included the first reel of **The Battle Of The Century**, presumed lost for decades.

A more thorough excursion through the silents library was taken by historian Al Kilgore. Kilgore prepared a five-hour, ten-part mini-series for PBS, *The Dawn Of Laurel & Hardy*. This was an affectionate look at the team's 1920s output, with lengthy clips from archival prints. Taping was hurriedly done under "live" conditions: pianist Stuart Oderman and narrator James Dukas efficiently performed "cold" while the films were rolling. Kilgore's scholarly approach was spoiled by the way his project was ultimately handled; it was thoughtlessly promoted as a family-oriented sitcom, and only six of the ten half-hours were aired.

The home-video explosion brought about renewed interest in classic films. Producer Snuff Garrett, publishing as "The Nostalgia Merchant," secured the rights to the Laurel & Hardy library in 1981. Nine volumes of Laurel & Hardy shorts were issued, as well as a good selection of features. Garrett tried to gather the best possible material, but he was often forced to use 16mm prints from different sources. Most were the familiar Film Classics prints, some had original M-G-M titles, and a few even had Janus titles! The Laurel & Hardy videotapes were very popular and survived after The Nostalgia Merchant closed its doors. For many years the tapes were off the market until the film rights were purchased by publisher Robert Halmi. Halmi reissued the Laurel & Hardy films on his own "Video Treasures" label, using the old Nostalgia Merchant master tapes.

These videos were quite presentable, but were still several generations removed from the original negatives. These fifty-year-old elements remained untouched until 1983, when the "Hal Roach Studios" were reactivated by producer Earl Glick, in partnership with the Toronto-based Vidcolor Image, Inc. On the February 22, 1983 episode of NBC's *Today* program, Glick used Laurel & Hardy film footage to demonstrate his firm's amazing achievement, computerized "colorization" of old black-and-white movies. The system was developed by technicians Wilson Markle and Brian Holmes. The film was transferred to videotape, and each sample frame was divided into 525,000 dots, or pixels. Each pixel was assigned a color, and the computer was programmed to tint successive frames accordingly. This revolutionary technique was not developed strictly for the Laurel & Hardy films, but for the motion-picture industry in general, so that dormant movies and TV shows could be remarketed.

The Laurel & Hardy test footage was primitive (a black formal gown was tinted a bilious shade of purple), but the colors stayed in register as the scenes progressed, and Glick's demonstration was successful despite pugnacious questioning by interviewer Jane Pauley. Continued research and development perfected the tinting process, and the inventors of "colorization" trademarked their creation.

The Laurel & Hardy films were the major asset of the Roach library, and the new management relied on them to generate publicity. In July of 1983, amid much hoopla, the new Hal Roach Studios licensed Nu-Image Film, Inc. to offer six Laurel & Hardy silent shorts to theaters. The studio even hired an organist to accompany the films in person. The initial booking in Hollywood earned over $28,000 for only sixteen showings, which played to capacity crowds.

The package of 35mm two-reelers toured other cities as *The Return of Laurel & Hardy*. The six films were **Duck Soup** (1926), **You're Darn Tootin'** and **Habeas Corpus** (1928), **Double Whoopee, Big Business**, and **Liberty** (all 1929). Curiously, some of the interior title cards were crudely rephotographed—even though the original title footage was known to exist in other prints. Most of the films had rare, ornate original titles; **Liberty** had equally rare Film Classics titles. For roadshow engagements, a recording of the organ accompaniment was supplied with the films, but the canned music often failed to synchronize. The Nu-Image company had also intended to reissue the Laurel & Hardy talkies, but it was not to be. The talkies were in trouble.

The bulk of the Roach film library suffered from mishandling and neglect. The old negatives were in a precarious state, and nitrate decomposition was imminent. The new Hal Roach Studios could not afford to lose the keystone of their collection. A major preservation project was undertaken to rescue the Laurel & Hardy films from further decay. Michael Agee was the archivist commissioned to do the restoration work in 1986.

"There were scores of reels of unidentified mute picture elements in the Roach collection, which I attempted to identify," Agee later recalled. "Most was cutting picture (editor's rushes) stuff, but excellent, first-generation quality. This is what I used to restore **The Hoose-Gow** and **Unaccustomed As We Are** . . . During the 1986 restoration, I came across three reels of original camera negative from the 1926–27 era—**Battle Of The Century, Putting Pants On Philip**, etc. All was fused together in a solid rock of film, lost forever to the ravages of time." Agee immersed himself into this project and assembled new versions of several dozen films. These were sharper and clearer than any prints had ever been. (Agee later issued his own series of videotapes. His "Nostalgia Archive" tapes offered restorations of Laurel & Hardy's celebrated silent shorts and a few obscure early talkies. The producer worked with original film materials and Robert Youngson's preservation prints.)

Agee's talkie restorations were the basis of a syndicated television series, *The Laurel & Hardy Show*, which bowed in the summer of 1986. A lamentable press release suggested that Laurel & Hardy were the antecedents of such modern comedy teams as John Belushi & Dan "Ackroyd" [sic] and Cheech & Chong!

Twenty-six 90-minute episodes were produced. *The Laurel & Hardy Show* presented the team's films to good if not peak advantage. On the positive side, thanks to the new restorations, the films looked and sounded clear and sharp. The long-lost titles, with the original studio graphics and trademarks, were restored or approximated. Dialogue was preserved intact where the accompanying picture had been spliced or damaged. Each program presented a full-length Laurel & Hardy film or a collection of shorts, and a closing feature, "The Laurel & Hardy Scrapbook," offered mini-tributes to the team's supporting players and co-workers. The producers obviously put a good deal of thought (as well as technical tinsel) into these shows.

However, they gilded the lily. In an effort to improve the originals, the producers took liberties. Many features and shorts were cut (**Our Relations** by a full ten minutes) for time reasons. This was odd, since the hour-long features formerly posed no problem for a 90-minute time slot. Other films were padded with out-takes, so that a watered-down product was being passed off to viewers as the official, authentic item. New background music was added to those films which had limited or no musical scores, but the dubbed melodies were recorded at such a low volume that the viewer strained to hear them. What tunes *were* audible were often inappropriate. Perhaps most incredibly, the producers sneaked Oliver Hardy's solo starring film, **Zenobia**, into the lineup, strongly implying that it was a Laurel & Hardy comedy. Promotional clips used vague shots of co-star Harry Langdon, who like Stan Laurel was slight and innocent-looking, to further the illusion.

The series was also offered in half-hour versions, but there too, the shorts were often whittled down to make room for program credits and commercials. The TV versions were soon colorized, and were sold to cable television (for red-eye 6 a.m. time slots!) and home video.

The TV vehicle may have been a mixed blessing, but it helped to bring about a long-overdue theatrical revival in 1986. Films Incorporated (FI), a leading motion-picture distributor, arranged with Hal Roach Studios to strike new 35mm prints. The theatrical reissue was initiated by George Feltenstein, an FI staffer who went on to supervise the video activities of the MGM/UA library. Six features, two featurettes, and nine talkie shorts were reprinted. Feltenstein explained to this writer that while FI released a total of seventeen pictures, the company went further and preserved other titles that were not scheduled for revival. **They Go Boom** and **Oliver The Eighth** were in critical condition, and two negatives (**Brats** and **Their First Mistake**) were so badly damaged that the American Film Institute furnished duplicate material for restoration. **Brats** was copied from a 1937 M-G-M reissue, but the original vintage-1930 titles were salvaged. **Their First Mistake** was in a worse state of deterioration, and a Film Classics master had to suffice.

The new 35mm prints were a revelation. For the first time since the 1930s, the films included the original, handsome main-title designs. The 35mm format offered a wealth of definition, which was not as noticeable in smaller-gauge copies. The prints were so good that eagle-eyed viewers could distinguish new subtleties in the backgrounds (paintings, furniture, etc.). In **Our Relations**, for example, James Finlayson gives the boys a battered one-dollar bill to split between them. The restored print disclosed every detail of the grimy, withered note—making it plain that the actual denomination was *twenty* dollars! In at least one case (**Way Out West**), the theatrical issue was better than the restoration then playing on TV.

The market for these sparkling new prints, unfortunately, was limited to the occasional independent or art-house exhibitor, whose territory was shrinking thanks to home video. The films were first unveiled in New York for a three-week series, culminating in a four-hour marathon of shorts. The festival also played in key American cities like Boston and

San Francisco, but all of the various runs were poorly promoted and played to disappointing returns.

In 1992, after the Roach library had changed hands yet again, the entire contents of the vaults were transferred to a California film laboratory. "Film doctor" Tom Ogburn waded through thousands of feet of film on behalf of owner Robert Halmi and distributor Kit Parker. Parker orchestrated simultaneous Laurel & Hardy shows, in several California theaters, on Christmas Day, 1992. "These are all new, 35mm prints," Parker told this writer at the time. "I'm a fan, so to me this is a labor of love." Parker was especially pleased with the restoration of **Politique-rias,** the feature-length, Spanish-dialogue equivalent of Laurel & Hardy's **Chickens Come Home**. In all, twenty-five Laurel & Hardy comedies were reprinted for theaters; Parker continues to make them available at this writing.

Not only have Laurel & Hardy's Hal Roach films been shuttled back and forth over the years, but their 20th Century-Fox features have been almost as wayward. In 1959 dozens of old Fox features were syndicated for TV by National Telefilm Associates (NTA). NTA struck 16mm prints of the Laurel & Hardy films and scattered them through various packages. A TV station that wanted to air **Great Guns** and **Jitterbugs** would have to buy a package of fifty-two other films to get them.

In 1966 part of the Fox library was taken over by Seven Arts-Associated, another major supplier of TV films. Seven Arts offered three Laurel & Hardys, **A-Haunting We Will Go, The Dancing Masters,** and **The Big Noise**. Promotional copy, which hailed these films as Laurel & Hardy's all-time funniest, tried to make them relevant to contemporary youth. The Laurel & Hardy characters were compared to roles in 1960s society: blissful Stan was the original "flower child," while blustery Ollie represented "The Establishment." This trio of films saw unusually aggressive release; scores of prints were leased to television, additional copies were licensed for 16mm rental libraries, and still more were sold in 8mm home-movie-highlights form.

Fox reorganized its library in 1972 and separated all six of its Laurel & Hardy features into one specialized package. More than one station expanded its existing library of Laurel & Hardy movies by adding the Fox titles.

The package was renewed in 1979 when Fox manufactured new

prints for the last time. The quality was generally very good, but sloppy lab work resulted in a contrasty, washed-out rendition of **Jitterbugs**.

Twentieth Century-Fox also found a peculiar outlet for its Laurel & Hardy properties: they were shown as in-flight movies on airplanes. This was before the more practical method of videotape was used, so special airline versions were prepared on 16mm film. The scheme failed because the films were uniformly abridged to a half-hour length. Whoever cut the Laurel & Hardy films wasn't a fan. The editor concentrated on the plotline instead of the comedy. Airborne prints of **The Dancing Masters** and **The Big Noise** omitted most of the sight-gag material and kept the unfunny story sections intact.

Happily, Fox found more appropriate uses for its Laurel & Hardy films when home video became popular. The studio quietly released the first and last of the L & H Foxes, **Great Guns** and **The Bullfighters**. Two additional tapes, **A-Haunting We Will Go** and **The Dancing Masters**, were issued only in Europe. Several years later Fox went back to the vaults and unearthed **The Big Noise**, which became a surprise hit with widespread promotion and distribution.

The Laurel & Hardy features and compilations controlled by M-G-M have found new audiences in recent years. Four of the titles were packaged by the studio's television department; stations often programmed these Laurel & Hardy features among the prestigious M-G-M classics starring Garbo or Gable. The home video market has been so receptive that Ted Turner, owner of the M-G-M backlog, has released every Laurel & Hardy film in his possession. The M-G-M holdings offer a good cross-section of vintage Hal Roach material (**The Devil's Brother**, **Bonnie Scotland, Pick A Star**), M-G-M musicals (**The Hollywood Revue Of 1929, Hollywood Party**), obscure wartime titles (**Air Raid Wardens, Nothing But Trouble**) and comedy compilations (**M-G-M's Big Parade Of Comedy, Laurel & Hardy's Laughing '20s**).

Laurel & Hardy admirers in Europe have been more fortunate, in that most of the team's films are available on video from a single source. Vision Video (formerly Virgin Video) has maintained an ongoing series of hour-long shorts packages and feature-length tapes, under the title *Laurel & Hardy Comedy Classics*. Over three dozen installments were culled from the entire Hal Roach library, encompassing Laurel & Hardy's silent films, sound films, and cameo appearances.

The "colorized" tape of **Way Out West** was introduced in Europe in 1991. More "color" features were requested, so Vision Video acquired the broadcast master tapes from America's computer-colored *Laurel & Hardy Show.* The features were edited as often as not, but the tapes sold well as novelties—taking nothing away from the black-and-white versions, which continued to flourish.

In 1995 Vision Video remastered the black-and-white tapes, and prepared twenty new Laurel & Hardy releases with "restored sound and picture." These were sold exclusively through the W. H. Smith bookstore chain, at popular prices. A similar restoration is due in America; Hal Roach's "Our Gang" comedies were successfully issued in restored form, and Roach's Laurel & Hardy pictures may be similarly remastered when the video rights change hands again. At this writing the Hal Roach film library is shared by two major business firms. Hallmark Cards Inc. purchased Robert Halmi's RHI Entertainment, Inc., in 1994; Hallmark owns the film rights in the Western Hemisphere. Elsewhere the film rights are held by BetaFilm, a subsidiary of the Munich-based Kirch-Group.

Cable television has given Laurel & Hardy a new venue. Cable's specialized audiences pay for premium quality, and the 16mm film prints which once sufficed for local broadcasts became unacceptable for nationwide transmissions. The studios have been compelled to go back to original sources, digging up 35mm prints and negatives for the networks' use. To a Laurel & Hardy fan, their films have never looked better.

Throughout most of the 1990s Laurel & Hardy's Hal Roach comedies were telecast regularly on the "American Movie Classics" channel (AMC). The team's continued popularity prompted AMC to schedule marathon showings of Laurel & Hardy comedies, running as long as thirty hours. AMC's broadcast-master tapes, licensed by RHI Entertainment, were beautifully restored from choice archival materials, and they faithfully duplicated the films' original theatrical quality.

The 20th Century-Fox films have been shown on the studio's TV outlet. Although AMC made tentative plans to air the six films in 1997, only **Jitterbugs** was included in the rotation. The M-G-M titles have been scheduled on Ted Turner's movie networks, with special marathon screenings on Stan Laurel's birthday.

Movie fans may be thankful that virtually all of the team's work is available in one form or another. Stan and Ollie were more prolific than their comedy-team contemporaries of the 1930s and '40s: The Marx

Brothers made only thirteen starring pictures, Wheeler & Woolsey nineteen, Abbott & Costello thirty-six. Laurel & Hardy left a priceless legacy of 106 films, an impressive collection containing some of the screen's all-time funniest scenes.

As long as there are people who like to laugh, Laurel & Hardy movies will continue to delight audiences.

Sons Of The Desert

During his retirement years, Stan Laurel was intrigued by an idea propounded by biographer John McCabe. McCabe wanted to form a small group of Laurel & Hardy enthusiasts, which would take its name from the boys' filmic fraternal lodge, "Sons Of The Desert." McCabe drew up a mock-serious "constitution" which satirized the formal trappings of social organizations. Laurel was delighted with the idea, and added his own whimsical text to the document. "He had fun working with the constitution," recalls his daughter Lois with a smile.

Neither Laurel nor McCabe had any idea of what their little private club would become. From a handful of members convening in a New York lounge in 1965, the group has grown to well over a hundred regional chapters, or "tents," located throughout fifteen countries. As suggested by the constitution, each tent is named after a Laurel & Hardy film (e. g., the *Way Out West* tent in Hollywood, the *Block-Heads* tent in St. Paul, the *Live Ghost* tent in London). Members gather on a regular basis to watch Laurel & Hardy movies. Some chapters devote themselves strictly to film or video presentations; others arrange dinner parties or social meetings around the films. In 1978 the Sons began holding biennial international conventions; since then, Laurel & Hardy fans from around the world have gathered in various cities to share their affection for the comedians.

Founder John McCabe can see why Sons Of The Desert has flourished. "The first year that I met Stan and Babe, in 1954," McCabe remembers, "I told them, 'Various of your films have touched on greatness.' And they were both terribly embarrassed by that. I know they were pleased, but I don't think they believed me. The reason why all these people are [members of the Sons] in such a number, and having such a wonderful time, is because the work of these two men *did* touch on greatness, and we celebrate that."

Readers who would like to know more about Sons Of The Desert may write to the organization directly: Sons Of The Desert, P.O. Box 36, Almelund, MN 55002 USA, or Eric Woods, 102 Hough Green Road, Widnes, Cheshire WA8 9PF England.

Index

Note: In the text, some of the Laurel & Hardy films are also discussed under alternate titles. These instances are cross-referenced for the reader.

About the Author

Scott MacGillivray has been involved with Sons Of The Desert, the official Laurel & Hardy society, for over twenty years; he is the former editor of the group's international newspaper. He has reviewed Hollywood's vintage "B" pictures for *Filmfax* magazine, and he has collaborated with author Ted Okuda on several magazine articles and a book, *The Soundies Distributing Corporation of America*. He lives near Boston with his wife, Jan; both are employed as editors.